THE UNITED STATES GOVERNMENT

-THE PROMISE OF DEMOCRACY AND THE ECONOMY

25 progressive ideas whose time has arrived

THE UNITED STATES GOVERNMENT

-THE PROMISE OF DEMOCRACY AND THE ECONOMY

25 progressive ideas whose time has arrived

JOSEPH LAZZARO

The United States Government
-the promise of democracy and the economy
25 progressive ideas whose time has arrived

Printed in the United States of America.

Cover photo of Washington, D.C. by Reuters.

Cover and jacket design by Roxanne Palmer.

ISBN 978-1-7364703-0-5

In memory of Joseph S. and Gloria T. - two parents who provided more love for their daughter and son than anyone can imagine.

Table of Contents

President Abraham Lincoln's first reading of the Emancipation Proclamation, 1862. Painting by Francis Bicknell Carpenter, 1864. (Credit: U.S. National Archives.)

Preface

"No nation can afford to be on bad terms with Washington, for very long." –University of Connecticut Political Science Prof. Rudy Tokes

This book on the United States Government stems from several factors, which coalesced into an epiphany, of sorts.

The first was that ever since the graduate school years at the University of Connecticut in Storrs, Connecticut, commonly known as UConn, I wanted to write a book that summarized the U.S. Government, its many functions, policies and dedicated civil service and foreign service professionals, but I didn't want it to be an academic textbook that would be read primary by undergraduate college students. That was too narrow a focus and too technical, and would have followed the standard legislative branch description, then executive branch, then judicial branch, etc., format. Nor did I want to write an advanced placement instructional book that would be used by high school students prepping for the scholastic aptitude test (SAT) or a book for recent college graduates refreshing their knowledge before the graduate record exam (GRE), as noble as those tasks are: those markets have been written about for decades. Further, nor did I want to write a 'Government 101' or 'book for dummies' – again, those texts serve a purpose – several iterations of which have been quite successful – but they lack the richness I sought. Rather, I wanted a book with exactly that: richness – hence this book is a citizen education book that describes the United States Government in all its complexity, creativity and wonder, with a focus on the modern era. (For the purposes of this book, the modern era is defined as 1932-present.) It's designed to give the typical person a snapshot of the most important functions of the government, with an emphasis on the executive branch, including independent agencies. It enables one to turn to any chapter or section in the book and learn - in a vocabulary that's understandable and approachable - why that government department, office or agency exists. And regarding richness – if you read only one section in the book, read the Profiles. The Profiles are stories that "deserved to be told" – stories of American heroes, and other important events and places in American history and public policy/foreign policy.

The second reason the book was written was to fill a need, a book that would help find the answers to some if not many of the pressing issues and problems of our time/our era. (The book's publication is late 2020 / early 2021.) The book is overtly political, but its ideology is broader than most others that address the subject/topic I address. With that noted, the book certainly has a point of view: a progressive/Democratic point of view, and Keynesian Democrat, at that. And that point of view – which made the bigger contribution to the epiphany – was formed as a result of an ill-conceived, misguided distortion, a lie being publicized by an extremist faction in contemporary politics: the party faction ideology of no government, if not limited government - the Tea Party faction that surfaced in 2010. The Trump campaign hitched on to / grafted onto that lie, then added a faux-populist or false-populist stance, along with deeply-problematic policies and proposed programs: 1) nativism/anti-immigration, 2) isolationism and 3) protectionism. This book is designed to show the correct path the American people and the United States Government should take: it should implement progressive policies in a New Progressive Era. The book's goal is to show that, propelled by a progressive/Democratic Party-led majority, a New Progressive Era can produce a more-humane, more-just, more-egalitarian society – the more perfect union Americans seek.

In other words, essentially, the second reason for this book is to set the record straight: the Trumpian / Tea Party faction's view of the United States Government and its performance is nothing like the U.S. Government I knew and that hundreds of millions of others experience in the modern, and now postmodern era. (Really, the Republican Party's view of the U.S. Government is a caricature.) Contrary to the Republican Party's view of the role of the federal government – a stance in which Republicans at all levels, but especially at the federal level - routinely try to obstruct governance, block needed policies and shut down the government – having a progressive, activist, interventionist federal government is a good thing. (In political science terms it's called "the positive state." Much more will be said on the positive state in Chapter 18.) There's so much good your U.S. Government is doing - and it will do even more good in the future. And this book was written to tell you about it! In other words, what progressives/Democrats want is an economy and society where everyone can flourish, which is what our U.S. Constitution promises. And the federal government can play a role in achieving those noble goals. Hence, the book's title - **"The United States Government – the promise of democracy and the economy."** Within the U.S. Constitution, within our system of self-government that includes the federal government – *is the promise of democracy and the economy – the hope for / aspirations for a* *stronger democracy and a better economy, as well as the everyday practice of the two.* One could also call it "the multiple promises of X,Y and Z" because it has many benefits, including democracy, and a stronger economy, society and union, etc.

But know very clearly what this book on the U.S. Government is saying and what it clearly is not saying.

First, this book is pro-free market, but in the mixed-capitalist sense: that's capitalism with a legitimate safety net/social welfare state. It does not advocate pure capitalism, also called 100 percent capitalism, i.e., capitalism without a social safety net. Underscoring: there must be a social safety net, and it must be a full safety net, not merely a *band-aid safety net* that leaves many people vulnerable and in poverty. The free market offers many benefits: wealth building, job creation, innovation/ingenuity, a more-efficient deployment of resources, rewards for risk-taking, rewards for work and the diffusion of elites are chief among these, and there are others. But let yours truly be clear - the analysis forwarded here argues that mixed-capitalism - but one that is overwhelmingly free market - is the best economic system for the United States; what's more, additional progressive reforms are long overdue in American society – they should have been implemented decades ago. Those reforms started with the Obama Administration and should have continued had Madame Secretary Hillary Clinton entered the White House in 2017, after the 2016 U.S. presidential election. I argue that President Barack Obama's economic and social policies began the New Progressive Era, (despite Republican Party obstruction in Congress to reduce its scope and stop it, using every means possible), that Obama represented a "safety valve" for U.S. corporate capitalism, and that those reforms should have continued under Madame Secretary Clinton's presidency. [As we know, the Russian FSB/KGB intelligence's "active measures" cyber warfare operation interfered in the 2016 election, boosted support for Trump and depressed support for Clinton and/or encouraged voters to switch their vote from Clinton to Trump, and that operation influenced the election – and perhaps was the deciding factor in it. We still don't know the full impact of Russia's "active measures" campaign on the 2016 election. What we do know is that Clinton's vote total in Pennsylvania, Michigan and Wisconsin would have been at least 500,000 votes higher, had Russian intelligence not interfered.] This book's goal is to state why and how those progressive reforms should occur, and in which areas. In the process, it shows how a new progressive majority, led by the Democratic Party, can produce a more-humane, more-just society, more-egalitarian society – a more perfect union. That more-humane, more-just society is one that - at minimum - eliminates needless human suffering and pain; ideally, it is a just society that serves the common good the national interest, the public interest and also enables every person to flourish. The book is also a prism through which the reader can identify (view) and evaluate the economic and social change that is ahead, given that Democrats control both the U.S. House and Senate and the U.S. presidency in 2021. (By doing so, it will concomitantly show the reader all the good your United States Government does. In fact, as noted, *the United States Government does more for you in one day than you can imagine in a lifetime!)*

Second, the book argues the federal government must be pared-down in areas where it didn't work, must increase substantially its efficiency in activities in which it does work, *and equally significant* - it must add functions to solve social/economic problems and/or address other needs. Moreover, the Affordable Care Act (ACA)/Obamacare - the U.S.'s universal health care system – represents just the beginning of these changes in the postmodern era. Many more progressive policies should follow - and are likely to follow – now that President Joe Biden, the Democratic Party presidential nominee, won in November 2020. (The book's publication is the fall 2020, hence an Epilogue will be provided after the 2020 U.S. presidential election result is known in November 2020.) As noted, Obamacare (and by extension, the election of President Obama) represent "safety valves" that both released pressure from - and implemented much-needed reforms for - the U.S. economic/political system – pointing the nation toward that more perfect union that we all seek. President Biden's victory in November 2020 achieves the same, as does the Democratic

Party's regaining a majority in the U.S. Senate and maintaining their majority in the U.S. House.

Third, the analysis forwarded here argues that respect for U.S. freedom, and most especially for human freedom, is essential. The Republican Party, which appears to have been supplanted by Trumpism, is free to believe what it wants, and you're free to believe what you want, both restrained by the law. But one thing this book does argue is that an activist, interventionist U.S. Government can produce good things and can solve economic and social problems. (It most certainly has and will continue to do so.) What's more, when progressive ideas hit their mark, they improve the economy, reduce inequality, reduce poverty and advance human civilization. Further, nor can an extremist, right-wing faction claim it is patriotic and no one else in the nation is: nothing could be further from the truth. The analysis forwarded here argues that the people who support an activist, interventionist U.S. Government - the modern state - are strong patriots. Progressives are strong patriots because a progressive wants a decent, dignified life for *all Americans* – for all who live in these United States. That's the philosophy that is closest to the intent and law spirit of the U.S. Constitution, according to my analysis. In addition, the analysis for forwarded here argues that although the Trumpian/Tea Party /conservative faction is often loud and noisy – giving the impression more people support them than who actually do - the faction in no way represents the best government philosophy for the United States Government for the postmodern era: on the contrary, *it probably represents the worst!* It is ignorant, misguided, frequently minimalist, frequently obstructionist, sometimes nihilist and sometimes mean-spirited with a lacing that suggests spite. (Trumpism has added unilateralism and protectionism to the list of mistakes by the Republican Party, undermining U.S. national security with the former, and economic strength with the latter; Trumpism, of course, has also added nativism - which has no place in U.S. society because the United States is based on an idea, not a race or ethnicity.) To repeat: Nativism has no place in the United States because the United States is based on an idea, not a race or ethnicity. What's more, Trumpism and the conservatives who have grafted onto the extremist faction display a distain for the poor, the sick, the elderly, the marginalized and the vulnerable that goes against everything yours truly, a public policy professional, was taught by his parents - two virtuous and patriotic Americans, God rest their souls. The Trumpian Republican Party jockeys between advocating a federal government that bestows benefits only on its constituents, and advocating no federal government at all. Moreover, the Trumpian Republican Party's willingness to engage in the most destructive tactics is truly astounding: at one point during the battle to raise the U.S. debt ceiling in 2013, the faction appeared willing to let the U.S. Government default on its debt - something that would have severely damaged the U.S. economy, and lowered the U.S.'s credit rating, among other negative consequences, to the detriment of the U.S. and global economies. In other words, the Trumpian Republican Party's ideology, if deployed by the U.S. Government, can't solve the nation's economic and social problems. In short, Trumpism is irresponsible and just not sensible, at best; it is dangerous, ill-informed, cruel, and ineffectual, at worst.

Further, left to its own devices, Trumpism would reduce the United States from what I call the New Gilded Age (1981-2008) to something akin to the awful conditions present in Charles Dickens' England. The robber-baron, Gilded Age (1877-1895) was dominated by economic and social Darwinism, pervasive mass poverty, horrible work conditions and massive corruption, along with chronic social injustice, and several other social problems. If Joe Biden and the progressives/Democrats had not won in November 2020, new segments of U.S. society would likely have been immiserated, to go along with the poor, the working poor, the working class, and the elderly. Moreover, as noted, if every idea the Trumpian Republican Party advocated became law, it's not an overstatement to argue that economic and social conditions in the United States could degenerate into something approximating the economic and social conditions present in Dickens' England. What's left of the Republican Party apparently wants to return to a so-called idyllic age, pre-federal income tax. But there was very little that was "idyllic" about the Gilded Age: it was a period of massive economic and social problems, and horrific living conditions for most people. Few American citizens of the 21st century would want to return to and live under those conditions.

Hence, by extension, yours truly argues that a New Gilded Age started in 1981, the start of conservatives' massive income tax cuts for the rich/upper income groups and deregulation under President Ronald Reagan, and the New Gilded Age ended - and a New Progressive Era started - in 2008 with the election of Democratic Party nominee, President Barack Obama. Therefore, yours truly argues the New Gilded Age (1981-2008) lasted roughly 30 years. According to my analysis, the 2016 U.S. presidential election is the anomaly, and the 2020 U.S. presidential election has determined that 2008 marked the start of the New Progressive Era.] Some may disagree that a New Progressive Era started in 2008, but this is incontrovertible: something "democratic" is occurring in the nation – the Democratic Party has won the popular vote in every U.S. presidential election since 2008. (2008, 2012, 2016, 2020.)

As such, one of this book's premises is cyclical theory - the theory that U.S. ideological/political eras or ages occur in cycles: the cycles are not identical in length, but one can detect a pattern, a cycle - i.e. a conservative era, followed by a liberal reform period - going back to at least 1860, and probably for much longer than that. Underscoring, the cycles are not equal in length, but there's a pattern: i.e., the cliché has an element of truth to it: "History does not repeat itself, but it rhymes." Again, the 2020 U.S. presidential election has provided additional evidence that cyclical theory is accurate; moreover, the evidence is persuasive if not overwhelming that 2008 marked the start of a New Progressive Era.

A second premise of this book is the belief in progress - in other words, that, in general, conditions in the 20th century are better than the 19th century, and if we implement the correct public policies, conditions in the 21st century will be better than the 20th century, and so on. If the reader does not accept the assumption of progress, then perhaps it's best not to read this book: it's a basic assumption or premise that the author argues there is ample evidence to support. Progressives believe in *progress* through science, innovation, experience, creativity, learning from the past, learning from mistakes etc. - it's intrinsic/implied in the very name: PROGRESSive. Moreover, it was intrinsic in President Franklin D. Roosevelt's New Deal program started in 1933 to end the Great Depression: "But above all, try something." And, as noted, the analysis forwarded here argues progressives have a sound evidence foundation supporting this premise, which includes the accumulation of knowledge, scientific breakthroughs and advances, especially in medicine, agriculture, manufacturing and technology: conditions for most people in the 1st century during the Roman Empire and in the 19th century in the United States and other newly-industrializing nations were worse, for most people. In other words, few people would want to go back to those periods and live the life of a slave, which was a common practice in both centuries.

[Some readers may not be familiar with the Gilded Age (1877-1895): it was a period of rapid expansion of industrialization, massive increases in wealth, but also an era of abject poverty, inequality and corruption, and a failure to address worsening social conditions. Those unaddressed economic and social problems became more visible and socially-destabilizing, with the human misery sparking a massive political movement that led to the election of reform-minded progressives in the Progressive Era (1896-1916), including Presidents Teddy Roosevelt (1901-1909) and Woodrow Wilson (1909-1913). The era's main objectives were addressing the problems caused by industrialization, urbanization, increased population, and political corruption. Progressives also sought to eliminate political machines and their bosses, break up trusts (trustbusting) and corporations through antitrust laws, which were designed to promote equal competition - something that would benefit consumers and shareholders alike. Numerous new government institutions and roles were born, and regulations passed, including agencies to enforce these laws and regulations, such as the Food and Drug Administration (FDA). Women gained the right to vote, at the end of the era, with the ratification of the 19th Amendment to the U.S. Constitution in 1920. In short, the Progressive Era addressed and corrected many of the problems created by the maldistribution of income and wealth and the laissez-faire economics of the Gilded Age - a period of conservative economics similar to the post-1980 U.S. era thru 2008. Further, the eras are so similar, yours truly argues our 1981-2008 period with its conservative, supply side Republican economics was a New Gilded Age, with even worse, monstrous inequalities income and wealth, and a band-aid social safety net that was not nearly adequate to address intensifying economic and social problems. (One example: the top 10 percent possess almost all U.S. wealth, but Republicans would not increase the federal minimum wage from $7.25 per hour - a rate last raised in 2009.) As noted, in this book, the author argues the election of Democratic Party reformist President Barack Obama in 2008 and again in 2012, represented the start of a new reform period, the New Progressive Era, that provided the necessary safety valve for U.S. corporate capitalism to continue.]

Similarly, the Trumpian Republican Party's description - it is rhetoric, really, that often approximates propaganda, and all-to-often incorporates disinformation - of the United States Government bears almost no resemblance to the U.S. Government that my parents worked for, that I knew while growing up, that I studied in graduate school, or that I worked alongside in Washington, D.C. after my graduate training at the University of Connecticut. And, as this book outlines, the U.S. Government has been an incredibly constructive and beneficial component of society. No government has done more good, for more people, at home and abroad, or solved more economic and social problems, than the United States Government. Its civil service, foreign service and military service professionals are heroes who demonstrate their bravery and virtue daily, and they perform noble work.

Fourth, the book does not suggest that yours truly has all the answers. Hardly. Occasionally, what's left of the Republican Party, and selected conservatives, have a good idea or two. The analysis forwarded here is an eclectic one: it seeks a variety of institutions and actors - public, private, non-profit, public-private partnership - to solve the nation's economic and social problems and move the nation forward in the postmodern era. But know very clearly that this eclecticism does not equate to following the same path as President Ronald Reagan or the person who entered the Oval Office in January 2017. For 28 years (1981-2008) the nation had been in a conservative cycle - with a smaller role for the U.S. Government, accompanied by an enormous increase in private sector wealth - U.S. investment capital totaled more than $115 trillion in 2020, according to U.S. Federal Reserve research – with a concomitant increase in economic and social problems, the chief of which are: poverty, economic inequality, and the seemingly permanence of an underclass. (High-cost health care insurance and health care services is another problem, along with the global existential problem of climate change.)

Fifth, the book "raises performance expectations" for the U.S. Government, and by extension, for the United States and for Americans. It proceeds and offers as an inspiring virtue, from the Catholic New Testament proverb, "To whom much is given, much is expected." (Luke 12:48). The analysis forwarded here argues that the United States has received enormous blessings, or graces. Yours truly believes they are divine in origin; others may believe they just represent fate, good luck or natural processes that gave the U.S. landmass certain, highly-valued, agricultural, geological, geographical, and meteorological advantages. But the point here is that the United States has not made good on its blessings - used them to their best and fullest potential. *In the postmodern era, the U.S., led by the U.S. Government, has to be a dispenser of goodness and generosity to solve economic and social problems - both at home, and then internationally. Period.* Yours truly is firmly in that camp. Progressive policies will go a long way toward achieving that goal. The aforementioned may seem like a large/daunting tasks, and in some sense, it is. [Much more will be said about this topic, later; for now, know that the issues discussed in this book - the programs proposed to solve 25 economic and social problems, create a more democratic economy and a more perfect union - represent just the first step in a larger, overarching goal.]

Sixth, yours truly also believes in the ability of Keynesian economics to solve a multitude of social ills. There's an adage in baseball that argues, "Good starting pitching can overcome a multitude of problems." Keynesian economics is business's / commerce's / public policy's equivalent of "good starting pitching." The analysis forwarded here argues that by creating a more-just, more-humane economy with a living wage for all workers, and a full social safety net / social welfare state, that change *will melt away many U.S. social and cultural problems.* (That may appear to be myopic, but you'd be amazed at how many economic and social ills are solved by having all citizens employed fully and fairly paid, with full benefits.) Further, yours truly argues that many of the negative, counter-productive and extremist stances by Trumpist adults – racism, intolerance of different groups, opposition to equal rights, advocating illegal acts of protest (including violent acts) against the U.S. Government, and participation in extremist and/or hate groups - will melt away, once blue collar / service workers and others in comparable sectors know that they can earn a living wage, support their families, and achieve all that upper-middle-income citizens can achieve in American society. In other words, once most Tea Party / Trumpists know that they have a substantive stake in the American economic and democratic system – a stake in its success, because they know when the system succeeds, they succeed - they will support it fully, for all citizens.

(As a corollary to this, yours truly also believes that most people, the overwhelming majority of society, are good – that all they want is to live decent lives, be paid fairly for what they do, support their families, and have their children have a good life too, and to live in harmony with their neighbors, and they wish the best for them. The author is not saying that every person believes this – all yours truly is saying is that most people with a legitimate stake in the system will do the right thing and also want the best for their neighbor.)

Finally, as the above suggests, the book argues that every actor in society - individual, group, private, corporate, non-profit, public, co-op, public-private partnership etc. - must help solve the U.S.'s economic and social problems. And that includes the U.S. Government. It's not, "Oh, we could eliminate poverty, but oh, sorry, we can't pass this program, due to our limited government tenet." Or, "We could re-train tens of millions of adults with the skills they need to compete in the global economy, but sorry, the marginal income tax rate on millionaires can't be raised." Or, "We can see to it that every person who works earns a living wage, but sorry, it's best to let the free market set what the bottom/floor hourly wage should be, even if that wage violates human dignity." Every actor in society must be used to solve the nation's economic and social problems. The market/private sector will provide many answers, and thank goodness for that. But so will the federal government. Guided by progressive policies and the Democratic Party, the U.S. Government will do so much good - even more good than you can imagine - and this book was written to tell you about it! In a summary, my goal is 'modest': to change the way you view the United States Government, forever. Or for eternity. Whichever occurs first.

A Note on Profiles, Trivia Tests, Presidential Humor: Also, the book contains 24 Profiles. These are stories about American people, policies, institutions and events that deserved to be told. The book also contains a 100-question Trivia Test (in 10 parts), for those who enjoy that challenge, and 3 features on Presidential Humor. I hope you enjoy all special features.

***

Addendum: As noted, as a friend / U.S. public policy colleague pointed out, if you read only one section or one part of the book, he recommended that you, "*Read the Profiles, as they are stories worthy of being told and read - stories of American heroes – stories that deserved to be told.*"

I'll add that included in the Profiles are stories about important events and institutions in American history and in U.S. public policy/foreign policy - stories that don't get a great of attention these days, but to agree with my public policy colleague, are worthy of your consideration; and I'm grateful for my colleague's kind words.

Joseph Lazzaro

President Franklin D. Roosevelt in 1933. (Credit: U.S. National Archives.)

Introduction

"We have always held to the hope, the belief, the conviction that there is a better life, a better world, beyond the horizon." -President Franklin D. Roosevelt

After the start of the coronavirus pandemic in the United States in February 2020, which led to the shutdown of the U.S. economy, to varying degrees, by region, Philanthropist George Soros may have captured the zeitgeist of the era the best, when he said:

"The scale of this pandemic has laid bare the fault lines and injustices of our world," Soros said in a statement. "We missed the opportunity to create a more just economy after the financial crisis of 2008 and provide a social safety net for the workers who are the heart of our societies."

"Today, we must change direction and ask ourselves: What kind of world will emerge from this catastrophe, and what can we do to make it a better one?" Soros said. Soros also contributed at least $130 million for coronavirus relief.

After the 2008 financial crisis, the United States failed to bolster its social safety net. To be sure, the U.S. Congress provided economic stimulus, along with support for unemployment compensation programs, and those social programs, along with the start of Obamacare / Affordable Care Act (ACA), did decrease human suffering, household bankruptcies, business failures and pain caused by +11 percent U.S. unemployment, but the assistance was too small and too narrow in scope. That small, inadequate response, according to many economists, led to the weakest U.S. economic recovery in the post-World War II era. What's more, that elongated the period of high unemployment, kept wages stagnant in many job segments – which did little to decrease economic inequality in the nation. The inadequate Congressional response also did not strengthen the U.S.'s social safety net: it remained a fragmented, state-specific system in which benefits for those unemployed or displaced by the Great Recession varied, depending on which state you lived in. In general, blue states (led by Democrats), such as New Jersey and California, offered a substantially better social safety net than red states (led by Republicans), such as Alabama, Mississippi, and Kentucky. And more broadly, the U.S.'s social safety net remained a "band-aid" compared to those of other, developed European democracies – especially Germany, France, the United Kingdom, Sweden, Denmark, and Norway. In addition, as Philanthropist Soros noted, that adequate response left the United States – and in particular blue collar/service workers and the poor - vulnerable to another, severe recession or crisis. As it turned out, two crises – public health and economic - struck the United States in the 2020 coronavirus pandemic, which caused first a public health crisis, and then, due to months-long quarantine and shutdown of the U.S. economy, a severe recession. (By July 2020, the U.S. unemployment rate had risen to 10.2 percent, from 3.5 percent in January 2020.) The double-whammy would expose the weaknesses in the U.S.'s social safety net, in its economy more-generally, and, for that matter, many other weaknesses in the U.S. economic system – especially regarding public systems at the state and local level. In fact, at times it seemed the coronavirus, which as of January 2021 had killed more than 400,000 Americans and infected at least 25 million people, was uniquely designed to attack the United States at its weakest points – causing the most economic damage since the Great Depression: at least 35 million adults lost their jobs, as a result of the pandemic. (More will be said about the impact of job losses, later.) This is certain regarding the U.S. response to the 2008 financial crisis and ensuing Great Recession: Congress failed to strengthen the social safety, and the 2020 coronavirus pandemic exploited every systemic weakness, flaw and inadequacy, with fatal results.

With the coronavirus pandemic killing more than 1,000 people per day by mid-March 2020, the problem became what political scientists call a crisis. Now, historically Congress and the U.S. president respond to the crisis in a classic reform-within-the-system way, but it's useful and educational / illuminating to note that there are other response types, called *scenarios*. (The *five scenarios* are listed below.) Again, given the U.S economic system – U.S. corporate capitalism – scenario no. 1 is most likely and almost always occurs. Conversely, European democracies, and other nations, have implemented different scenarios. How Congress responds to the crisis will likely influence the changes that are ahead. In formulating the scenarios, I applied the thinking and lense developed by two scholars – University of Southern California Political Science Prof. James Rosenau (author of "Thinking Theory Thoroughly") and the University of Connecticut Political Science Prof. Howard Reiter (author of "Parties and Elections in Corporate America"). Later in the book, you'll see why this type of analysis - five scenarios which correspond to varying scope/strength of intervention - was deployed.

Five Scenarios:

1-Reforms within the system (Typical reforms after a crisis in U.S. corporate capitalism.)

Basically, under this scenario, the two political parties, the Democratic Party and Republican Party, identify the problem, then devise solutions within the corporate capitalist framework, usually including modest economic and social reforms, but also regulatory reforms, then U.S. corporate capitalism continues.

2-Reforms within the system with structural changes (One example: a guaranteed minimum income or Social Security.)

The pandemic's capacity to freeze large sections of the economy for a long time presents an opportunity for guaranteed minimum income (GMI) advocates to make their case. Also called the "universal basic income," GMI has increased in popularity in Europe and in other regions of the world, but has not achieved majority-support status in the United States - at least not as of late-2020. The United States, which is a mixed-capitalist system featuring large corporations, (and substantial small business and sole proprietor activity), with a modest social welfare state, has historically viewed GMI as a form of 'undeserved income.' However, in the early 21st century, particularly as the wealth of the top 10 percent increased massively, 2000-2020, creating enormous wealth and income disparities, more Americans started to support GMI. Some entrepreneurs and other decision makers even favor GMI or view it as inevitable. As of late-2020, on Capitol Hill, Democratic Party support was modest; Republican Party support was miniscule, if not zero. As of late-2020, there was no Congressional effort to pass a GMI as part of the economic stimulus response to the coronavirus pandemic; it wasn't even discussed in committees, let alone on chamber floors. Further, given the United States' private sector first/public sector second culture, and its federal system, passing a GMI would represent a major, substantive change – a change equal to or larger than President Franklin D. Roosevelt's (FDR) successful effort to start Social Security - the U.S. senior citizen pension program. [The U.S. Social Security system now includes old age, survivor and disability insurance (OASDI).]

3-New system (One example: democratic socialism, or a variant thereof.)

After roughly a century and a half of corporate capitalism, the democratic socialists still have not made their case to a majority of Americans. However, support for democratic socialism has increased in the last two decades. About 15 percent of the U.S. electorate favors democratic socialism, and about 35 percent favors some form of socialism, including: a job guarantee, Medicare for all health care insurance, free college education, student loan forgiveness, a low-cost mortgage or housing ownership plan, or fully-paid day care.

As of late-2020, due to the severity of the economic crisis caused by the coronavirus pandemic and the economic, familial and social hardship, pain and deprivation it has caused, reformers who advocate "substantive" or "big change" will likely find greater appeal among voters, and democratic socialists are in this "big change" camp. Essentially, at least a portion of the electorate will be saying, if U.S. corporate capitalism or the traditional way of doing things in the United States can't solve the problem, then we may have to consider options offered by a different economic model, and democratic socialism is one.

4-Change even beyond a new system (The slow, incremental de-activation of life/the world as we used to know it. Examples abound: a more-localized life with little international travel, the addition of dozens of new nations as nations break-up, a confederation of nations with no hegemon or binding global authority, a world dominated by 10 or 12 multinational corporations which control almost all economic activity.)

The coronavirus pandemic poses many questions and creates unknowns among areas of life that we thought were givens, if we did not take them for granted outright. (Yours truly tried to not take them for granted, but like almost everyone else living in the modern world, we all got used to certain aspects of daily life in the modern/postmodern world. The coronavirus pandemic has thrown those habits/practices into doubt.) The coronavirus and the changed public health practices it will require until perhaps as long as 2022, or at least until a nation's populace has been 90 percent vaccinated, means many practices may have to changed, and still others may have to end temporarily, if not permanently. (As of October 2020, there was no safe, effective, widely-available vaccine.) From one perspective, the coronavirus represents a critique or "a nudge." Unfortunately, as of late-2020 it is hard to discern what is being critiqued and what practices may have to end. In other words, the "change even beyond a new system" is not known. As nations continue to battle the coronavirus through 2021 and into 2022, how much of modern life – and in particular urban life - will change/end? Will globalization end? Will regionalism/mercantilism (defined as making everything in your home nation) become the new norm? How about suburb-to-urban mass transit commutes? Will home-offices become the norm, with more than 40% of full-time U.S. employees working from home? Will we still be consumer-oriented? We will be as materialistic? Will industrialization end? What about air travel? What about free markets and the norm of most economic decisions being made in the private sector? What about the globalization of labor/transfer of production to lowest-cost production areas? Will people work as long as they did, prior to the 2020 coronavirus pandemic? What about schools – will grade school education occur as it did prior to 2020? And ditto for entertainment and leisure?

5-The not likely (but still possible) scenario

This scenario, too, is possible, but not likely. (At least, yours truly, according to his graduate training and analysis, does not believe it is likely in the near future/the decade ahead – 2020-2029.) It involves an entirely new way of undertaking daily life, and will be discussed in my second book, Book 2. What's more, in Book 2, the logic and rational for using the "Five Scenarios" analysis will be demonstrated and shown. A person trained in the social sciences in graduate school – that's my approach, how I test theories:

with data, with the real, with the tangible – I rely on what can be counted, what can be seen, the known. In a summary, a social scientist focuses on the natural realm. That said, I'm open to other explanations, other reasons, other theories for things happening the way they do. And that's the reason for including scenario 5 – it is possible, I'm open to that possibility, but because I'm not trained in identifying that response type/scenario, and its impact, I'll leave it for one who is (or for people who are). At this juncture, the description of scenario 5 may sound too vague, but it will have to remain somewhat of "a tease," to borrow a television show phrase communicated to viewers, as it won't be used as a potential type of response for public officials when discussing the 25 policy areas yours truly expects Congress, the president and the states to address in the New Progressive Era. (As mentioned, in Book 2, yours truly will describe an example of Scenario 5 - that entirely new way of undertaking life.)

2020 And Beyond...

In summary, the response type/scenario President Biden, Congress and other public officials select to address a given problem/issue will go a long way to determining how each problem is resolved and in what manner, and those decisions will ultimately have an impact on what the new U.S. economy and society will look like in the decade ahead, and probably for a much longer period than that. Yours truly argues progressives/Democrats have the superior public policy response or answer – the stronger philosophical argument – for most economic and social problems facing the United States. Now, it's on to discussing them.

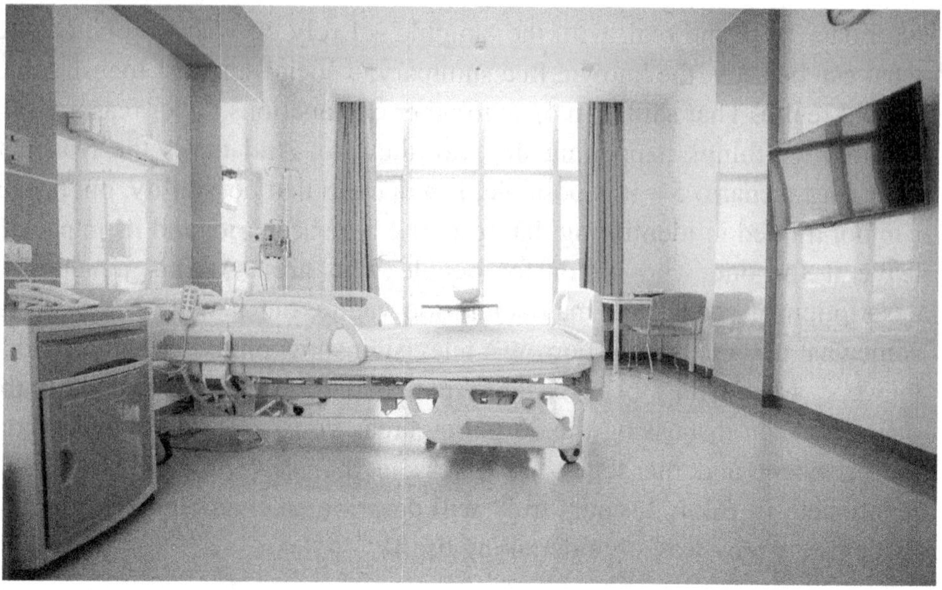

(Credit: Shutterstock.com.)

Chapter 1: Public Health Care Investment

"To know the right thing to do is easy. It's just hard to do it sometimes." -former University of Connecticut Men's Basketball Coach Donald "Dee" Rowe

One incontrovertible fact stemming from the coronavirus pandemic is that the U.S.'s private sector-dominated health care system, while possessing many virtues, did not have nearly the capacity and resources needed to quickly contain the virus outbreak. To be sure, part of the failure to contain the virus can be attributed to the Trump Administration's slow response, after it became clear that the Wuhan, China-based virus had spread to Europe, and then to the United States in January 2020. The administration failed to act for at least six weeks, basically, delaying quarantine measures, testing, contact tracing and the ramp-up of personal protection equipment (PPE). As a result, a virus which became known to local public officials after they had identified several superspreaders in New York City, triggering an outbreak in and around the nation's largest city, could have been contained, if comprehensive federal action had been taken in January. It wasn't, and as a result, the State of New York had to scramble and create an entirely new, centralized health care command headquarters to prevent the health care system from being overwhelmed. Further, through astute, effective and judicious leadership from Gov. Andrew Cuomo, D-New York, the state was able to avert a disaster, but the Trump Administration's delayed federal resource response meant that tens of thousands of New York residents were infected....before anyone in the New York area even knew what the coronavirus was – and this invariably led to tens of thousands of needless, preventable deaths nationally. As of January 2021, 41,561 people in New York had died from COVID19. It's a ghastly total - the highest death total among states - and one that medical professionals, health care researchers and scholars will study for decades to identify what the federal government should have done to avoid the calamity, with an eye toward preventing a repeat during any possible future virus outbreak / pandemic in the United States. In fact, look for the incoming Biden Administration to learn from the Trump Administration's many mistakes and correct them to decrease the size of the virus's second wave, which began in the fall 2020.

Even so, while the Trump Administration's six-week delay was inexcusable – the mistake, for all intents and purposes, meant that the coronavirus would affect most if not all states – the delay is not the sole factor in the nation's becoming the no. 1 country in the world for COVID19 deaths, which totaled more than 400,000 as of January 2021. The second, major factor was the fragmented, inadequate U.S. health care system – specifically the overburdened public health care system. The ACA has done a good job increasing total citizen coverage in the United States, as well the number of people who regularly access health care services, but the ACA did not do enough to improve public health care services. So far in the coronavirus pandemic, private hospitals have performed reasonably well to very well. Conversely, public hospitals - New York City has 11 - encountered massive shortages of PPE, ICUs, ventilators, related equipment and nurses/medical personnel. As a result, thousands of people died needlessly, as New York City's public hospitals became overwhelmed, prior to Gov. Cuomo and New York State health officials doing yeoman work to create a new, centralized health care command headquarters: that improvised, on-the-fly operation has saved thousands of lives, if not tens of thousands of lives. (To be sure, New York State's response was not perfect, but when viewed in totality, the effort to organize and manage the state's COVID-19 intervention was truly one of the modern medical marvels of the early 21st century, but that is a subject for another time.) Still, it never should have come to that: the nation should have had in-place a strong, robust public health care hospital network to ensure that every American received adequate care – including during a pandemic or another health care emergency.

With the above noted, the United States' fragmented, inadequate public/private health care system must end, in two steps/ways. First, we must establish a public option and/or universal health care insurance so that everyone who is sick will seek treatment. Second, we must invest in hospitals and supplies: these are medical assets – assets that should always be maintained at the highest level, as they are among our most vital public goods. The alternative is simply unacceptable: the coronavirus pandemic exposed the U.S. system's chronic underfunding by conservatives and Republicans – and that must end, because if we don't establish a system based on the above, the infected will not seek care – infecting hundreds, and risking another, horrific pathogen/virus outbreak. Further, it seems unconscionable that in 2020, the United States remains the only major western democracy without a robust, national health care system and universal health care insurance. (The ACA/Obamacare - including the historic, necessary Medicaid expansion that started in 2009 - came close to achieving the goal of universal health care insurance, but now progressives/Democrats must complete the mission, now that they've won the presidency and control of the U.S. House and U.S. Senate in November

2020. For example, as of September 2020, 12 states – largely red Republican states – have not expanded Medicaid: Texas, Mississippi, Alabama, Georgia, Florida, South Carolina, North Carolina, Tennessee, Kansas, Wyoming, South Dakota and Wisconsin. Moreover, Medicaid expansion – although it will not lead to 100 percent coverage - will go a long way toward achieving universal health care insurance coverage.) Other, developed economies with fewer resources (United Kingdom, Germany, France, Sweden, Denmark, Spain, Italy and Greece, to list a few) have managed to establish an adequate public health care system with universal coverage – ensuring that every citizen receives adequate health care services. And that begs the question, why can't the United States achieve the same? In many cases, it's because Republicans and conservatives in Congress from those red states do not want to see a universal health care system implemented: even more outrageously, they don't even want to expand Medicaid at the state level! What's more, the coronavirus pandemic exposed the decades of underinvestment in this public good – an underinvestment largely caused by Congressional Republicans - and that inaction has been ominous: a tragedy ensued. That underinvestment must end, and now that Democratic Party presidential nominee Joe Biden has been elected in November 2020, along with a Democratic Party-controlled Congress, he must prioritize the investment in the public good of health care, to end the nation's fragmented, inadequate, inconsistent system of health care insurance coverage among the states, once and for all. However, do not misunderstand: private health insurance plans with private sector doctors and hospitals can remain, but the nation must establish a robust public option: call it a United States Health Care Service (USHCS) to ensure that every person living in the country receives adequate care and that the nation has the equipment, personnel and hospitals to handle a virus outbreak and/or other health emergency.

Scenario: Now, what scenario from the 1-5 list will likely occur in this policy area and what form will the U.S. public health care policy take?

As my former University of Connecticut U.S. Constitutional Law Professor Jon Sandberg used to say, (when he was trying to stimulate students' critical thinking skills and/or already had an answer he wanted to mention, but was just pausing to build suspense), "That's a good question."

Answer: Probably a combination of scenario 1 (reforms within the system) and scenario 2 (reforms within the system with structural changes). Outside the U.S. Veterans Administration (VA), the United States lacks an adequate public health care system at the federal level/national level, with hospitals, clinics, test facilities and rehabilitation centers – and therein lies a very good model regarding a solution. The United States can establish a network of 200 U.S. health care hospitals – strategically located and allocated, based on population and health care service needs. Again, call it the United States Health Care Service (USHCS). Next, along with the federal government recruiting a new corps of doctors and nurses for these facilities, local doctors and nurses also can provide services at these hospitals. The goal would be to create a federal public health care system that's robust – one that can withstand the surge in patients caused by a pandemic or other national emergency – and that, at minimum, can ensure that every citizen, regardless of insurance plan, has access to adequate health care services. A good model for this proposed 200-hospital network is the Veterans Administration (VA). The VA's fiscal 2020 budget was about $200 billion: the new federal hospital network should not cost more than $50-70 billion annually. The network will also contain funds to enable patients to obtain care from their current doctor and currently-used hospital. But don't misunderstand: the new, federal hospital network is designed to provide care when it can't be provided elsewhere and to have the capacity to handle patient surges during emergencies. The 2020 coronavirus pandemic, and the U.S.'s inadequate, unacceptable, slow response to the crisis at the federal level, [no national lockdown, failure to invoke the Defense Production Act for personal protection equipment (PPE), and failure to mobilize health care personnel to outbreak zones in New York, New Jersey and Washington state], must serve as the wake-up call for a new, attentive, battle-ready federal policy. The United States must never again experience a situation in which a pandemic led to people dying because there weren't enough ICUs, doctors and nurses to treat them. And with the 200-hospital federal hospital network, it won't.

To be sure, there are other dimensions of U.S. health policy that require reform that are not directly related to progressive policy number 1, the U.S. Health Care Service and federal hospital network, but the analysis forwarded here argues it is the philosophically stronger argument than what conservatives/Republicans have proposed, and it helps the United States achieve the long-sought and long-overdue goal of universal health care insurance coverage. Moreover, the United States must improve its public health system for the reasons stated above and as a memorial to those who so tragically lost their lives during coronavirus pandemic: based on the evidence the author has reviewed so far, (as of January 2021), tens of thousands of adults and children died needlessly because the public health care system was not big enough, prepared enough, or strong enough. That is a national tragedy that will go down in history as one of the worst U.S. public policy failures of modern/postmodern era. Simply, it is a national tragedy: these citizens did not have to die! To repeat: these citizens did not have to die!! It is our fault and our failing that led to this calamity. Accordingly, progressives and Democrats must expand the public health care system to ensure that the tragedy never happens again. Then and only then will we as Americans be able to say that those who lost their lives to the coronavirus/COVID-19 will not have died in vain.

****

Before Anyone Knew About Al Qaeda, FBI's John O'Neill Knew

By Joseph Lazzaro

Few among us will ever be called to sacrifice as much as the late FBI Special Agent John O'Neill (1952-2001) sacrificed for our country.

Further, although O'Neill had a unique personality and swagger about him that was not 100 percent in-sync with the FBI's low-profile, reserved culture and posture, one could make a very strong argument that no one was better-suited to be an FBI special agent than John O'Neill.

Already an accomplished crime fighter in Chicago, in 1995 O'Neill was promoted to chief of counter-terrorism, based at the FBI's Washington, D.C. headquarters. There, working with Counter-Terrorism Security Group Chairman Richard Clarke, O'Neill gathered information and coordinated the effort that resulted in the capture of Ramzi Yousef, leader of the 1993 World Trade Center truck bombing plot.

O'Neill: Connecting The Dots

Even more significantly, O'Neill continued to gather information on the individuals behind the attack, their commonalities, sources of financing, methods, and

John O'Neill (Photo credit: FBI.)

organizational structure. As the intelligence grew, O'Neill repeatedly warned about the growing threat of a group of Islamic militants, in particular. After a January 1997 transfer to the FBI's New York office, to become Special Agent in Charge of the FBI's National Security Division, O'Neill created an office to investigate the network of terrorists that took the name of their training site, "The Base," or in Arabic, "Al Qaeda," and its leader, a person by the name of Osama bin Laden.

In other words, long before other intelligence resources had become aware of the threat Al Qaeda posed, John O'Neill was "connecting the dots" regarding the network's ability to inflict massive harm and damage on its targets.

O'Neill: A Maverick

However, due to a series of factors - including several mistakes by O'Neill - his rise through the FBI's structure – and the Bureau's making Al Qaeda its No. 1 counter-intelligence / anti-terrorism priority - slowed. O'Neill violated Bureau policy by losing a cell phone, Palm Pilot, and by losing track of a briefcase (for a short period) that contained sensitive documents. Later, a series of other counter-intelligence procedure differences and personality clashes prompted O'Neill - the person with the most knowledge about Al Qaeda and its potential for destruction - to retire from the FBI, in favor of a higher-paying job in the private sector in August 2001.

The job, which O'Neill started on August 23, 2001? Chief of security at the World Trade Center.

O'Neill was killed during the September 11, 2001 terrorist attack on the World Trade Center, and his remains were recovered on September 28, 2001.

O'Neill: A Hero

The failure of intelligence officials to give O'Neill's intelligence gathering on Al Qaeda and Osama bin Laden the highest priority - with O'Neill in charge - represents a major intelligence failure. Moreover, the 9/11 tragedy should end, once and for all, any remaining rivalry that exists among organizations in the U.S. intelligence community. It should end - in tribute to O'Neill.

John O'Neill was a maverick. He made mistakes. He is also an American hero.

TRIVIA TEST 1: U.S. PRESIDENCY

(Answers in Appendix, Page 354.)

1. President Abraham Lincoln's favorite song was?
a) "The Star-Spangled Banner" by Francis Scott Key
b) "Over There" by George M. Cohan
c) "Yankee Doodle Dandy" by George M. Cohan
d) Dixie

2. George Washington, after leading the U.S. Revolutionary Army to victory over the British, wanted to undertake which endeavor next?
a) Start a line of drug stores
b) Write a novel
c) Return to Virginia to farm
d) None of the above

3. Alexander Hamilton wanted the president of the United States to serve for how long a term?
a) 1 6-year term
b) 2 4-year terms
c) 1 10-year term
d) life

Washington Resigning His Commission 1783
(Credit: from John Trumbull painting, WikiCommons.)

4. President Calvin Coolidge was noted for which of the following?
a) Traveling to Japan every six months
b) Singing before the U.S. Congress

c) Advocating that the nation break up into 4, equal sections
d) Not talking too much

5. Among other reasons, President Franklin D. Roosevelt declared a "bank holiday" in 1933 to:
a) Restore the public's confidence in the banking system
b) To prevent Russia from taking over U.S. banks
c) To prevent Germany from taking over U.S banks
d) To help the nation recover from the Civil War

6. In his "farewell address," President Dwight D. Eisenhower warned the nation against what phenomenon?
a) The agricultural lobby
b) The Hollywood lobby
c) The Argentina Lobby
d) The U.S. military-industrial complex

7. Which of the following was true about President John F. Kennedy?
a) He did not want his brother Robert F. Kennedy to be U.S. Attorney General
b) Kennedy disliked sailing
c) JFK was a substantially more-liberal president by November 1963 than when he was inaugurated in 1961
d) JFK graduated from Yale

8. After being shot in 1981, President Ronald Reagan said which of the following as they told him doctors were going to perform emergency surgery?
a) Reagan said nothing
b) Reagan smiled and said, "Great."
c) Reagan gave a thumbs up
d) Reagan said, "Oh, I hope the doctors are all Republicans."

President Reagan and First Lady Nancy Reagan, 1981 (Credit: U.S. National Archives.)

9. The only U.S. president with known, public CIA service has been:
a) Theodore Roosevelt
b) James Polk
c) George H.W. "Poppy" Bush
d) Bill Clinton

10) President Barack Obama is not one of the following:
a) He was schooled in Canada first, then later in France
b) He's a Columbia University graduate
c) He has a law degree
d) He was born in Hawaii

[President Lyndon B. Johnson signs the Medicare Act of 1965. Former President Harry Truman (seated, right) and former First Lady Bess Truman (standing to his right) became the first Medicare program recipients. Credit: U.S. National Archives.]

Chapter 2: Medicare Expansion To Age 55

"I will finish what President Harry Truman started and sought to achieve – health care insurance for all senior citizens." -President Lyndon B. Johnson

A second issue where progressives and Democrats have the philosophically stronger argument and a better solution is Medicare – and it also constitutes the second part of the U.S. public health care policy solution. The analysis forwarded here argues that Medicare, which currently covers adults, regardless of income or medical history, beginning at age 65, unless you qualify by disability, should be expanded to include all adults beginning at age 55. Further, U.S. Sen. Bernie Sanders, I-Vermont, is perhaps the strongest proponent of Medicare expansion, having advocated "Medicare For All" during both his 2016 and 2020 campaigns to secure the Democratic Party's presidential nomination. (Sanders has also advocated some form of universal health insurance since entering public policy more than 40 years ago; he is, arguably, "Mr. Universal Health Insurance.") U.S. Sen. Elizabeth Warren, D-Massachusetts, is also a strong advocate for Medicare expansion, having also made that a major theme of her 2020 campaign for the same nomination. And President Biden, D-Delaware, in April 2020 said he favors lowering Medicare's eligibility age to 60. The Medicare expansion is driven by several factors. First, the dominance of employer-based health insurance plans means that when employees are laid off, they lose their existing employer-based health insurance if they cannot afford the Consolidated Omnibus Budget Reconciliation Act of 1985 (COBRA) extension. Many adults losing their job at 60 cannot afford COBRA, and they also often have longer job search times finding subsequent employment, which can create a longer period without health insurance coverage. Second, as a result of the 2008-2009 Great Recession and the 2020 coronavirus pandemic, an usually large number of plus-60 employees lost their job: the United States has now experienced two recessions (2008-2009, 2020-undetermined) where a disproportionate number of this demographic segment sustained a job loss: the larger bloc of older, unemployed adults speaks to the need for Medicare expansion. Third, many service sector, retail and related blue-collar jobs either offer no group health insurance benefit, or offer pay/compensation that's too low for the employee to purchase a group health care insurance on the ACA exchange. The prevalence of service sector jobs is another clarion call to expand Medicare to age 55, in order to ensure that these adults retain adequate health care services. To be sure, the above do not address all of the United

States' health care access problems, but they do a great deal to address the problems of a particularly vulnerable group: those age 55 and older, and especially those who have lost their job at this life stage. Further, globalization (assuming it continues after the coronavirus/COVID-19 has been contained) and the likely, decreased job replacements driven by reduced company revenue in the new post-pandemic U.S. economy, will undoubtedly lead to a large number of new, age 55-and-older, displaced workers – and that likely scenario all the more underscores the need for Medicare expansion to age 55.

Also, Medicare is not, as some critics, including many conservatives/Republicans argue, an 'unearned entitlement' or 'unearned benefit' for senior citizens. It's paid in the only way possible: by all employees (and employers) during their work years: by the Medicare tax. A system that taxed only senior citizens upon retirement would be untenable: premiums would be too high for retirees, due to their higher medical care usage rate. The only feasible plan for a senior citizen health care insurance was to spread that cost over the largest pool of recipients possible (all employees/employers), in the format of an insurance policy, and "pay for service in advance." As with any insurance, some people pay more than they receive back and others receive more than they paid, but that is the social price to be paid to obtain the goal of having every senior citizen insured and cared for: it is a humane policy.

Recent critics, including many conservative and Tea Party faction members, have advocated a "voucher" system to make Medicare 'more-efficient.' Their argument asserts that a voucher plan will take advantage of market forces, and turn senior citizens into price-comparison shoppers, who will then (presumably) force health insurers and health care providers to contain costs or even cut costs. The problem is that vouchers, where the federal government gives each senior citizen a set dollar amount per year – for example $4,000 or $5,000 – and then says, "Here – now go pay for your health insurance," – come up substantially short regarding the true cost of senior citizen health care insurance premium costs. In 2014, that cost was roughly $11,000 to $14,000 per year – which means a voucher system would leave senior citizens up to $10,000 short annually. And as one might sense, many senior citizens do not have that much in savings/investment capital. Wealthy senior citizens presumably would fund their gap; those who could not, would go without insurance...and probably without health care services – an intolerable situation for the nation. Hence the need for the Medicare insurance system.

Further, one must always be suspicious and careful regarding vital services and allowing a pure-free market, pure private sector, or "pure capitalist" system to provide that service. Free markets create winners and losers. Pure-free market systems result in the loser receiving nothing. If a pure-free market system is applied to a vital service or program, such as senior citizen health insurance, the losing senior citizens will receive nothing – in other words, go without health care services, to their detriment. That is *economic and social Darwinism* – a barbaric system that no enlightened, developed democracy, civilization and economy should ever tolerate. It's also why free market systems, in general - for education, jobs, housing, as well as health care - should always have a humane floor, or a humane minimum standard, that ensures that every person lives a dignified, humane life. (More on that topic, later.)

To be sure, Medicare supporters', including those in Congress, are always open to ideas, innovations and other ways to increase Medicare's efficiency. One way would be to let Medicare take advantage of its size/scale is to let it negotiate what it pays for prescription drugs from U.S. pharmaceutical companies – something it cannot legally do now. Congress, under pressure from a powerful pharmaceutical lobby, prevented Medicare from using its size to bargain. And the lawmakers who are blocking this change? Conservatives / Republicans, but also some Democrats. If that law is repealed, the cost of Medicare's Part D program will fall substantially.

Progressives/Democrats must push to finally obtain for Medicare what it and senior citizens deserve: the ability to negotiate with pharmaceutical companies and lower prescription drug prices, across the board: it is a long-overdue policy change. In addition, Congress also passes an annual "Doc fix" that maintains what physicians receive per Medicare patient treated: while supporters argue the Doc fix encourages doctors to accept Medicare patients, an adjustment in the formula would save Medicare tens of billions of dollars annually.

Medicare, the second largest social welfare program in the United States, is an American success story. Since Medicare's creation, life expectancy has increased, and science and medical research have advanced. It has taken the nation from one where more than a third of its senior citizens received little or no medical treatment, to one where every senior citizen receives medical treatment. Medicare has made the United States a more-humane country, and for this reason it's another example of your federal government at work - another example of the good your United States Government does.

Another U.S. public health care issue concerns the ACA/Obamacare. Simply, progressives/Democrats have better ideas and ideas that insure more people than conservatives and Republicans. (This is not to say that conservatives / Republicans do not have any good, new ideas regarding health care – they do – but they are not as comprehensive, and generally require beneficiaries to pay more out of pocket. Much more will be said about conservative ideas on a number of topics, in Chapter 24.) For now, know that progressives and Democrats have the better ideas on many issues, particularly regarding how to improve the ACA. Further, in 2020 and in the immediate years ahead, progressives/Democrats, along with moderates, must combine political capital and resources to improve the ACA, which was a very good first-step toward universal health insurance. The ACA is the United States's largest social advance since the establishment of Medicare in 1965. U.S. Sen. Sanders has often noted that roughly 87 million Americans are either underinsured or uninsured: expanding Medicare to age

55 will help eliminate that problem. In addition, creating a public option as a side car to the ACA involving the largest pool(s) possible of adults will further reduce the uninsured/underinsured category, and possibly eliminate it entirely. Here, the United States Government should seriously consider a federally-paid public option, due to the likely high monthly premiums these citizens would face, if private insurers were allowed to offer a massive group policy for the currently underinsured/uninsured in the United States. It's always possible that the group could achieve an "economies of scale / critical mass" to keep rates low, however historically, that has not been the case with this group. Hence, progressives/Democrats, united with moderates, should propose a program similar to Medicare for this group. To be sure, this will not be an easy task, nor cheap, but the alternative is far, far worse. The nation cannot sit by while the ranks of the uninsured/underinsured continues to grow: the spillover rate to high-cost emergency rooms, alone, is enough to justify the federal effort. (One example: In New York City, if you require an emergency room visit, expect a minimum $1,000 bill, with costs quickly exceeding $3,000 if you need just modest care, and vectoring toward $10,000, depending on the complexity of care provided.) Finally, leaving this issue to the states will yield more policy stagnation and a continued, fragmented health care insurance system: blue states will likely pass policies to solve the problem, red states won't, leaving a large bloc of uninsured/underinsured. It, like Medicare expansion to age 55, must be tackled at the federal level.

Scenario: This policy change, Medicare expansion to age 55, would draw from scenarios 1 and 2 – and perhaps scenario 3. Both Medicare and the ACA/Obamacare can be modified in order to achieve their stated goals. ACA improvements that lower premiums and broaden coverage will address two coverage issues for all citizens under age 55; Medicare expansion will address them for citizens age 55 and older. For progressives and Democrats, the foremost goal must be inclusion – we want every person in the United States to have health care insurance, with no monthly coverage gaps. All developed, western democracies provide this; it is long overdue – a century overdue – for the United States to do so, as well.

Harry Truman - Personifying All That Is Good About The U.S.

By Joseph Lazzaro

It is hard to envision a better civil servant and a better example of all that is good in these United States in the modern era, than President Harry S. Truman.

However, readers should know that the initial reviews of Truman's presidency when he left office in January 1953 contained average grades. With the Korean War in a stalemate, with an end to it not in sight, Truman chose to not run in 1952 against the popular Republican Party nominee, former Gen. Dwight D. Eisenhower. But now, Truman is consistently ranked among the Top 10 presidents by historians and political scientists - often 7th or 8th!

Why the high rank? Take your pick: The Truman Doctrine and U.S. containment policy (which checked the spread of Soviet Communism). The Marshall Plan to rebuild Europe after World War II and revitalize Western Europe's free market economies. The Berlin Airlift that saved Germany's greatest city. Truman's pivotal support for the creation of the state of Israel. And NATO. Also: his decision to desegregate the U.S. Army. And Truman's appeal to the public to vote out a "Do-Nothing Congress" in 1948, dominated by conservatives from the South U.S., to win the 1948 presidential election as an underdog. His support for organized labor and the working man/woman. Truman's efforts to pass a universal health insurance plan for senior citizens. (In 1965, President Lyndon B. Johnson finished what Truman started with the passage of Medicare.)

'Give 'Em Hell, Harry!'

In other words, Truman was a populist – someone who did his best to put the interest of the typical person on a par with corporate or other institutional interests. The public rewarded Truman for his effort with a victory in the 1948 presidential election – a campaign boosted by Truman's historic "Whistlestop Tour" via train across the country.

One popular refrain on the tour was this: someone would say, "President Truman, what are you going to do with that Congress when you get back to Washington?"

President Harry S. Truman (Credit: U.S. National Archives.)

"I'll tell you what I'm going to do," Truman said. *"I'm gonna give 'em hell! That's what I'm going to do."* And the slogan, "Give 'Em Hell Harry!" was born.

'The Buck Stops Here'

The phrase 'The Buck Stops Here' also was popularized by Truman, who kept a sign bearing the motto on his Oval Office desk. It references presidential budget responsibility, but its symbolism is a more-theoretical generalization: it is the president who has to make the decision and who is ultimately responsible for the United States Government.

Truman: Decent, Honest, Modest

After he left the presidency, Truman and First Lady Bess Truman returned to their home in Independence, Missouri. Further, this will stun many readers: his only income was his U.S. Army pension at $112.56 per month ($1,090.89 per month in 2020 dollars). He had not amassed any wealth, and not wanting to take a corporate board position because he believed it would diminish the integrity of the nation's highest office, he faced financial challenges. A book deal - the first of what are now regular memoirs by post-presidents – and Congress' 1958 passage of the Former Presidents Act, which established a yearly pension for former presidents, created a normal retirement for the Trumans.

Harry and Bess deserved much more, because the nation never had a more decent, honest, and modest civil servant than Harry Truman.

(Warehouse workers. Credit: Shutterstock.com.)

Chapter 3: $15 Per Hour Minimum Wage / Living Wage

"I want an America where every individual has a decent job, that pays a living wage, and has health care insurance." -President Lyndon B. Johnson

Perhaps no issue, no factor can lead to a more perfect union in these United States sooner than creating a better stake for labor in the U.S. economy. An economics colleague of yours truly said it best, years back, during the 2008 financial crisis: "Unless labor secures a more equitable stake of the excess profits from labor, the nation will remain under stress, and drift toward crisis."

That colleague is correct. But what does a more equitable stake include? What does it mean, in terms of U.S. public policy? It involves policy measures both short-term and long-term, both small and big. Here, we'll focus on four: 1) the minimum wage, 2) support for unions and collective bargaining, 3) education and vocation skills training/job training, and 4) a job bank.

The minimum wage: Simply, most red/Republican states have not increased the minimum wage since 2009, and that is scandalous. Most blue/Democratic states have increased the minimum and that has helped reduce labor's losses during the globalization era – but it has not been nearly enough to counteract the powerful macro forces depressing wages and incomes. In addition, as noted, at the federal level the federal minimum wage has been stalled at $7.25 per hour since 2009 because conservatives / Republicans oppose increasing it, and the Republican Party has controlled at least one chamber of Congress and/or the presidency, since Jan. 2009. [Note: A clarification - in this book, references will be made to conservatives and Republicans, and their policy mistakes: that said, know that some Democrats are conservatives, but nearly all Republicans are conservatives, and the author just wanted to define that shorthand, for the references ahead, so that it is clear to the reader that the author is aware that not all conservatives are Republicans.] Moreover, it is absolutely scandalous – it reflects retrograde policy of the worst sort - that conservatives/Republicans have blocked every minimum wage increase at the federal level since 2009: since that period, had the $7.25 per hour amount merely kept pace with inflation, it would be $8.65 per hour in July 2020, according to the U.S Consumer Price Index, as tabulated by the U.S. Bureau of Labor Statistics. (Side note: the federal minimum wage was $1.60 per hour in February 1971: had it just kept pace with inflation since then, it would have been$10.35 per hour in June 2020 - a much higher real wage than $8.65 per hour, but that is a subject for another time.) In general, and pulling the lens back for a long-term view, blue collar/working class earning power has been under pressure, arguably, since the early 1970s, and the deterioration really accelerated at the dawn of the globalization era in 1991. Accordingly, the analysis forwarded here argues red/Republican states must substantially increase the minimum wage to at least $12 per hour, and some higher-cost red states should go directly to $15 per hour. Ideally, the U.S. Congress, led by progressives/Democrats in 2021, will pass legislation requiring a $15 per hour federal minimum wage, with some float down/up for lower/higher cost regions. (For example, the cost of living in rural Idaho is substantially lower than in the metropolitan Phoenix, Arizona area.) One cannot underscore enough the importance of increasing the minimum wage:; it will 1) more-equitably distribute corporate/business revenue, 2) encourage firms that typically pay at the new minimum wage to increase their wages paid – further increasing labor's share of the revenue pie - and 3) it's also likely to improve employee productivity, attendance and loyalty to a company's operation; 4) and equally important, it will enable more citizens / families to amass savings – capital, the lifeblood of the American economic system – creating more Americans with a stake in the U.S.'s economic system: corporate capitalism. (That last factor, a stake in the economic system, says a lot about public support for a particular economic system: the more people who have a stake/a vested capital interest in the economic system, the higher the percentage of people supporting that system.)

Collective bargaining/support for unions: Simply, progressives and Democrats must lobby and legislate at the state level and federal level for laws that strengthen unions, encourage union formation and that strengthen collective bargaining rights and powers. Ideally, every union should be as strong as the Longshoremen unions: ILWU (International Longshore and Warehouse Union) on the west coast, and ILA (International Longshoremen's Association) on the east coast; or as strong as the SEIU (Service Employees International Union) or the Teamsters: you get the idea. A United States with a high percentage of its workforce organized and belonging to a union, is a strong United States! And: What's good for the AFL-CIO is good for America! The goal should be to create a U.S. workforce that is dominated by unions – a workforce where 95 percent of employees belong to a union, not the current 10 percent or 12 percent. All 'right-to-work' laws must be defeated. A 'right-to-work' state is a 'right-to-drive-wages-down and immiserate another job classification or another sector' state. For more than 40 years, conservatives/Republicans at the state and federal level have sought to break-up unions and make it harder for employees to form them at companies large and small. The results have been disastrous for U.S. society: income and wealth inequality has increased - to near-monstrous levels in 2020 - and there are fewer American adults with an economic stake in the system than ever in the modern era. That 'beating labor into the ground' economically has also led to increased individual indebtedness. Further, the analysis forwarded here argues that has also led to an increase in radical-group and extremist-group activity, on both the ideological left and right. Hence, a good way to reduce radicalization is to encourage and support union formation and increase union membership. It's also one of the best ways to sustainably reduce poverty – all the more reason progressives/Democrats must lobby and legislate to strengthen collective bargaining and union formation, especially now that President Biden has won the 2020 presidential election, and the Democratic Party controls both chambers of the U.S. Congress.

Education and job training: Third, progressives/Democrats must re-commit themselves to a massive increase in education funding and job training, and there's no more urgent time than the current decade, 2020-2029. The coronavirus pandemic may alter and/or slow down globalization, and increase regionalization of economic activity, but the analysis forwarded here argues that the leverage that business operations have over labor and job/production location is not likely to change that much. Net result: in the decade ahead, tens of millions of employees will likely lose their job to offshoring/automation/acquisitions/downsizings and they will need to be retrained. Further, we know that there have been disparities in elementary and secondary education in the United States based on income/race and to a lesser extent, gender, and that these disparities are a factor in long-term income disparities: that's all the more reason a Biden Administration should re-commit to a new Great Society. Yours truly would like to see it called the "New Society." (It would combine terms from the U.S.'s two major reform periods: President Franklin D. Roosevelt's New Deal and President Lyndon B. Johnson's Great Society.) Like the New Deal, that New Society would offer to pay tuition, fees and board for an adult to retrain to learn a new vocational skill – such as auto repair, plumbing, electrical work, solar panel installation, roofing, bricklaying, exterior landscaping, masonry or carpentry, among other trades/fields. And like the Great Society, that New Society would seek to cut public school class sizes in half, establish a $60,000 minimum salary for teachers and make sure every school has world-class supplies, computers, and broadband access/connectivity. Further, like the FDR and LBJ periods of reform, progressives / Democrats must re-commit themselves to higher education: simply, the decline in aid to colleges, especially public colleges and community colleges, must end. In sum, globalization may slow down, but it's not going to disappear, as a result of the coronavirus pandemic, hence job dislocation will continue to occur at a high rate. Therefore, the United States must recommit itself at the federal level to supporting skills retraining/higher education in order to help citizens obtain the skills they need to earn, to support their families, to thrive.

Job bank: More controversial than the others, this program, arguably, is no less essential. Given the large amount of job dislocation that's likely to continue to occur due to globalization, the United States must move toward some form of federal job bank. The job bank would feature up to 5 million jobs, and operate as follows: If an adult could not find a suitable, formal training-related position, and if retraining under federal/state job re-training programs was not possible, that person would be awarded a job by the United States Government for up to 3 years. While a federal employee, that person would still apply for suitable jobs outside the job bank, and to standard federal job vacancies. The program's goal is to lessen the impact of globalization-driven job losses; it won't entirely solve that program, but a 5-million-position job bank is a good start. What would be a good model or case study for the federal job bank? The U.S. auto sector's job bank that the United Auto Workers (UAW) negotiated with General Motors, Ford and Chrysler decades ago would be a good model to follow, as a starting point. To be sure, the federal job bank may not be as generous as the UAW's in terms of the types of compensation/benefits offered, but it would likely be larger – as it would cover all sectors in all states. (However, let's be clear about what the job bank would not do: it would not fill 5 million jobs, if they weren't needed, and if enough jobs existed in the private sector. These are "job positions" or "job slots' that only come into play/are activated, if the private sector cannot provide enough jobs for those dislocated/downsized.) Finally, this is a policy area in which progressives / Democrats and other attentive lawmakers should not, "Make the perfect the enemy of the good." The important point is to establish another process to re-assimilate adults who have lost their job - through no fault of their own - back into the workforce.

Scenario: Now, what scenario from scenarios 1-5 is likely to achieve the goals of a $15 per hour minimum wage / living wage? A combination of 1, 2 and 3. New regulations will obviously be required for the $15 per hour minimum wage, but structural changes also will be required for a new, progressive commitment to education at every level and job training; in addition, a new institution will need to be created for the federal job bank – call it a U.S. Job Bank. That's a lot for a Biden Administration to implement in its initial years, but these are pro-labor, progressive, public interest/national interest changes - changes whose goal is the common good – changes that will help the United States create an economy where everyone can flourish - and they are long overdue. Labor has sacrificed far too much since globalization started in the early 1970s: it is time for labor to obtain a more-equitable share of the revenue pie. These changes will also lead to a sustainable, equitable U.S. economic expansion; further, the aforementioned reforms, with adequate resources deployed and the long-term commitment that the federal government can make, will bring the United States considerably closer to that cherished, progressive, egalitarian goal of an economy that benefits all workers.

Some Americans might see that as a threat to capitalism, but in reality, it's just the opposite: it strengthens capitalism. As anthropologist Wade David argues, social democracies, such as those in Scandinavian countries and comparable economies in the region, with legitimate social welfare states and retraining programs, create dynamic capitalist economic societies, where all members/employees/citizens have a substantial stake in the economic system, and, equally significant, where all vulnerable groups are protected.

Financial Crisis: Fed Did What Was Needed To Save Markets

As of late 2020, was it possible to grade former Federal Reserve Chairman Ben Bernanke's performance, and the Fed's performance, during the financial crisis? Well, consider this:

In the summer 2008 Bear Stearns failed, followed by the failure of the colossal Lehman Brothers on Sept. 15, 2008 – the largest bankruptcy filing in U.S. history. Credit markets froze. Almost all banker-to-banker trust evaporated. That meant giant transnational companies like General Electric (GE) – which had nothing to do with the financial crisis - could not float commercial paper for daily needs. That's the equivalent of someone with $400,000 in their checking account not being able to withdraw $60. U.S./global stock markets plunged, as did bond markets, between Sept. 15 and 19, 2008.

Bernanke, along with U.S. Treasury Secretary Henry Paulson and N.Y. Fed President Timothy Geithner, convinced Congress to pass an unprecedented - but vital - $700 billion liquidity package to stabilize the financial system. Later, the three would create an $85 billion credit facility to prevent American International Group (AIG) from filing for bankruptcy. AIG was Citigroup-size: ostensibly an insurance company, as a result of poor decisions, AIG, in reality, was *the world's largest undeclared 'hedge fund.'* An AIG collapse would have been Lehman-like in destructive impact on the credit markets. A roughly $51 billion bailout of auto sector giant General Motors (GM) followed.

(New York Stock Exchange. Credit: WikiCommons.)

Unconventional, But Necessary

The Fed's and U.S. Treasury's unprecedented moves sparked an outcry by those who felt they rewarded bad banking / corporate errors; and to a certain extent, the criticism is valid. Moreover, the liquidity measures and bailouts helped spawn the Tea Party faction - the political faction adamantly opposed them.

But did the Fed and the U.S. Treasury have any other choice? The argument forwarded here is no, they did not. The alternative would have been another Lehman-sized failure in AIG – perhaps worse – with an even more destructive impact on credit markets, the economy and jobs. This is a fact the Tea Party faction does not appear to understand – or if it does comprehend it – it just doesn't care about the consequences. The U.S. economy would have been plunged into an even deeper recession than the Great Recession. I.E., 11 percent unemployment may have risen to 20 percent or even 25 percent. That didn't seem to register with the Tea Party, which appeared to be mainly concerned with limiting government spending. The Teas' said the market would be the solution – the sovereign; and if the market said unemployment should rise to 30 percent, then so be it. Thankfully, Bernanke, Paulson, Geithner et al argued otherwise and markets were stabilized: the bleeding was stopped. Credit markets normalized. Tens of millions of jobs were saved.

Tea Party Backs Austerity Too Soon

To be sure, the U.S. economic recovery, which lasted more than 10 years until the 2020 coronavirus pandemic ended it, replaced all jobs lost during the Great Recession, although wage growth lagged throughout the expansion. The view from here argues, don't fault the Fed for that, fault the Tea Party. In a repeat of misguided conservative policies of the late 1930s, the Tea Party lobbied for and won approval of federal spending cuts, called austerity. As a result, the U.S. is still short hundreds of thousands of public sector jobs. Add those back, and the recovery would be much stronger. In sum, the Fed's action, along with action by other central banks, saved the global financial system. The policies were not perfect, but they sure beat a return to the barter system.

John Maynard Keynes - One Of Three Exemplar Economists

In the pantheon of modern economic thought, there are three giants: John Maynard Keynes, Milton Friedman and Karl Marx. At universities, when your research achieves a breakthrough, you're called an exemplar. Keynes, like the other two economists, was an exemplar. And how. His work was so influential, economists/analysts used the shorthand, "I'm a Keynesian" to describe their macroeconomic view of the world.

In a nutshell, Keynesian economics argues aggregate demand – buying by consumers and businesses – is influenced by many factors, and in a free market it sometimes behaves erratically, affecting production, employment and inflation; demand can be low, or fall, leading to a recession. Keynes brilliantly argued these recessions can be offset by economic policy – especially fiscal stimulus by governments and by monetary policy actions by the nation's central bank. Those actions - an active role for government - can help stabilize the business cycle, and in the process reduce, even end, recessions. But do not misunderstand: Keynes favored a predominantly free market economy – he believed in the private sector and its many benefits – but also called for an active role for government, especially during recessions and depressions.

(Keynes, right. Credit: USNA.)

Although Keynesian thought did not inspire President Franklin D. Roosevelt's "New Deal" in 1933 to end the Great Depression, his "The Means to Prosperity" article/research was sent to FDR and was taken seriously by both the United States and United Kingdom governments. Initially, the U.S. Government did not borrow enough during the Depression to substantially reduce unemployment, but after World War II's outbreak, it did. Economist John Kenneth Galbraith, then a U.S. Government employee focusing on controlling inflation, said the U.S. defense fiscal stimulus-driven economic rebound was "a classic example" of Keynesian ideas. The stimulus worked: it was intrinsic in both the Allies' victory in WWII, and in reducing U.S. unemployment. As a result, from the Depression's end to the 1970s, Keynesian economics was the framework for U.S./Europe policy makers.

The 1970s Critique, 2008 Resurgence

In the 1970s, Keynesian economics came under criticism after both the United States and European economies underperformed, with rising inflation and rising unemployment, i.e., stagflation. Conservative economist Milton Friedman argued Keynesian policies could lead to both unemployment and rising inflation. While stagflation is complex, a key commodity supply shock, such as the 1973-74 OPEC oil shock, likely accounted for most U.S. inflation then. Government policies that hurt sectors and increase the money supply too quickly also can lead to higher unemployment and higher inflation. After stagflation disappeared as the oil shock ended, developed nations seemed to strike the correct free market/social program balance, with the U.S. more-free market and EU nations featuring generous social welfare states. And with the Cold War's end in 1989, free markets dominated, globally, and lifted 1 billion people out of poverty by 2006. At that stage, Keynesianism appeared to be a tad outmoded. However, the 2008-2009 global financial crisis/Great Recession led many to question conservative economists' triumphalism: free markets were still subject to crises, every 25-40 years, it seemed. Galbraith and economists Paul Krugman and Joseph Stiglitz - all Keynesians - called for robust fiscal stimulus, along with central bank interventions to maintain the financial system. Their Keynesian advocacy paid off: the Great Recession was checked, unemployment fell consistently, and free markets were maintained. Keynes was correct, again.

And that is the genius of Keynes' illuminations: he made capitalism more humane. Where his theories are applied, there is a social safety net to maintain human dignity, while capitalism retains its best features. In a sense, Keynes gave us a "capitalism with a human face." His influence remains significant: progressives/Democrats use his foundation to formulate public sector policies/programs to reduce needless human suffering and pain. Indeed, we are all Keynesians now.

TRIVIA TEST 2: U.S. POLITICAL CULTURE

(Answers in Appendix, Page 354.)

1. Which of the following nations had no national health insurance policy before 2009:
a) United States
b) Germany
c) France
d) United Kingdom

2. Which nation has the largest military in the world?
a) Germany
b) China
c) Russia
d) United States

3. The South opposed the economic and social reforms of which U.S. president?
a) Lincoln
b) JFK
c) LBJ
d) All of the above

4. Composer George M. Cohan wrote which of the following patriotic U.S. songs?
a) "Yankee Doodle Dandy"
b) "Over There"
c) "You're A Grand Old Flag"
d) All of the above

Actor James Cagney as Cohan
In the film "Yankee Doodle Dandy"
(1942). (Credit: Warner Bros.)

5. Which president is responsible for the "Open Door" policy with Communist China?
a) Jefferson b) Madison c) Lincoln d) Nixon

6. The only person who sat on the Warren Commission investigating the assassination of President John F. Kennedy, who later became president was?
a) Ford b) Eisenhower c) Nixon d) Truman

7. Which nation does not have a major, organized labor party?
a) United Kingdom
b) Spain
c) United States
d) France

U.S. Senate. (Credit: U.S. National Archive.)

8. The United States has two legislative chambers, a House and Senate, primarily because:
a) The Framers / Founding Fathers wanted the House to repeat the actions of the Senate
b) The Framers / Founding Fathers wanted to create as many jobs in Washington, D.C. as possible
c) The Framers / Founding wanted to follow the legislative pattern of Hungary
d) It was a compromise between populous states and small states

9. Which of the following Americans is most responsible for the advance of the science of criminal investigations?
a) Danny Thomas
b) Danny Kaye
c) Henry Winkler
d) J. Edgar Hoover

10) Which president enjoyed brisk walks daily?
a) Wilson b) Lincoln c) LBJ d) Truman

Advice For Companies: Smart Bet - Hire A U.S. Vet

At the time of this book's publication, fall 2020, the U.S. economy was in the coronavirus-caused recession, with U.S. unemployment over 10 percent. Further, the nation will need to add at least 15 million jobs to return to pre-virus employment levels, probably more.

Further, historically, high unemployment rates have made it even harder for U.S. Veterans to find employment, after they leave military service. Since the pandemic's start in the United States in January 2020, U.S. unemployment rates have roughly doubled - in some cases risen even more - in almost all job classes – white collar, blue collar, professionals, salespeople, construction, manufacturing, restaurant workers, bartenders, theatre/museum workers, custodians, and so one. Equally significant, the rate of long-term unemployment - those who have been without a job for more than six months - also has risen substantially, to 16.5 percent in July 2020. By yours truly's analysis, as of October 2020 the nation was still short a minimum of 16 million full-time jobs!

Further, the unemployment rate among U.S. Veterans has been high as well, hence the request here for all employers - small business, merchants, large corporations, millennial / new-generation / hip tech firms - to redouble their efforts and increase hiring, and especially reach out to U.S. Veterans.

U.S. Veterans: Value-Adders

All adults seeking employment deserve to find meaningful, living wage, full-time work, but this is especially true for U.S. Veterans. They've sacrificed for our country - put their lives on the line to defend the Bill of Rights, our freedom and our democratic way of life. Therefore, the least we can do is to help them as they seek employment back in civilian life. You'll be glad you did. Here's why:

First, U.S. Veterans are proven value-adders. All veterans have skills honed during military service that can be immediately applied in the private sector / civilian life. What's more, chances are that veteran has worked with tools in ways you haven't, or has undertaken procedures that you did not try that they did out of necessity...and those tacks may very well improve your sales or earnings. You never know: it may even transform your business.

U.S. Veterans: A World Of Experience

Second, veterans have amassed a world of experiences from their service - they have the maturity and poise most companies look for in employees, and chances are they'll be your best performers under pressure or "when the going gets tough." Again - and this author has seen it firsthand - U.S. Armed Force members keep their cool during difficult situations. If they did so in the military, they will do so in your operation - and that's no small plus in a business world that has its share of problems, frustrations, and complications.

Attendees at the Aiken Veteran Fair, 2015. (Credit: U.S. Department of Energy.)

Hiring A U.S. Veteran: A Good Choice

Skills, experience, grace under pressure, an ability to improvise to solve problems, an ability to find creative solutions - these are just a few of the competencies and strengths U.S. Veterans offer.

Contact your state Department of Labor for lists of qualified U.S. Veterans seeking employment in jobs vacant in your company. If not, then contact the local U.S. Department of Labor office in your state / jurisdiction. You'll be making a safe bet, when you hire a vet.

(An example of a U.S. Social Security card. Credit: U.S. Social Security Administration via WikCommons.)

Chapter 4: Improve Social Security / The Super Pension

"The only thing we have to fear is…fear itself." –President Franklin D. Roosevelt

A fourth issue where progressives and Democrats have the philosophically stronger argument and a better solution is Social Security. Simply, the United States must improve its primary pension plan for retirees such that: 1) no individual is living in poverty, 2) more individuals are leading dignified, middle-income lives, and 3) the disabled/vulnerable are adequately cared for.

Established by President Franklin D. Roosevelt (FDR) and the U.S. Congress as part of the New Deal's reforms in 1935, Social Security, as many readers know, is the U.S.'s public pension system. Originally designed to supplement private pensions, Social Security has become the primary pension system for most American retirees. Some Americans have defined-benefit plans for their private pension, but those have been phased out by the private sector, replaced with defined-contribution plans, which often take the form of 401K plans. Here is the most-important and telling statistic/fact regarding U.S. pensions: unfortunately, many Americans have not saved enough in their defined-contribution plans. The reasons are manifold, but a major reason is stagnant wages/incomes in many job segments since the 1970s – and the result is sobering: many Americans retire with too little money in their defined-contribution plans. As a result, that makes Social Security their primary pension – and it is often the household's main income source. And it is this primary reliance on Social Security as the source for retirement income that requires - indeed justifies - modifying Social Security. Simply, Social Security has to be improved so that it pays a substantially higher monthly pension, to all poor/middle-income citizens, and the disabled.

First, a little background regarding Social Security's genesis:

It 1935, the U.S.'s economic system of pure capitalism, modified by President Theodore Roosevelt's Progressive Era reforms - but not to be confused with FDR's reforms three decades later - changed to a mixed-capitalism system with the passage of the Social Security Act of 1935.

President Franklin D. Roosevelt signed the act on August 14, 1935 – the largest and most significant legislation in his New Deal reforms designed to end the ravages of the Great Depression that had impoverished tens of millions. Social Security is primarily an old age and survivors' pension, and a disability insurance plan.

Social Security is the largest social welfare program in the United States. In 2019, Social Security accounted for 23 percent of federal spending and 4.9 percent of U.S. GDP.

Over the years, Social Security has been amended and expanded to encompass more social insurance programs, as noted above, for survivors and children of deceased parents. In 2019, more than 54 million Americans received more than $892 billion in Social Security benefits.

In addition, the Social Security Administration manages the Supplemental Security Income program (SSI), which provides need-based income for the aged, blind or disabled who would otherwise be destitute. Today, 7 million people are covered by SSI.

As of 2019, the Social Security tax, commonly referred to as the payroll tax, was 12.4 percent (6.2 percent for the employee, 6.2 percent for the employer) for wages up to $137,700. A separate 2.9 percent tax (1.45 percent employee, 1.45 percent employer) covers Medicare; there's no limit on the amount of wages subject to the Medicare tax. Also, above $200,000 for an individual, $250,000 for a married couple filing jointly, there is an additional 2.90 percent tax for Hospital Insurance/Medicare Part A (1.45 percent employee, 1.45 percent employer).

FDR's Goal - end Social Darwinism: FDR entered the White House with a U.S. economy reeling from the Great Depression. The pure capitalist model, and its boom-and-bust cycle, without a social safety net, left tens of millions of workers and children destitute, with the aged and vulnerable faring even worse. Republicans, conservatives and others on the ideological right said there was nothing that could be done to reduce human suffering, put people to work or eliminate poverty among senior citizens. Conservatives said the nation had to *"Let the markets run their course,"* and if that meant 40 million or 50 million unemployed, all of whom would be impoverished, then so be it. Clearly, for conservatives, and for most Republicans of the 1930s – "the market" was the answer to society's ills, the sovereign judge, the creator of both wealth and suffering. This view, incidentally, is nearly identical to conservatives'/Republicans' view today, in 2020: it certainly represents the view of most Tea Party faction members.

In 1933, FDR begged to differ. His New Deal program of economic and social reforms represented the start of the social safety net in the United States. As noted earlier, the free market offers many benefits: wealth building, job creation, incentives for innovation/ingenuity, a more-efficient deployment of resources, rewards for risk-taking, rewards for work and the diffusion of elites, are chief among these, and there are others. (Underscoring, the analysis forwarded here argues that mixed-capitalism, but one that is overwhelmingly free market, is the best economic system for the United States.) However, the free market, and in particular the U.S.'s economic system prior to 1933, contained many liabilities: one major drawback was that it left the lesser-skilled/low-skilled and other less-productive members of society, including the elderly, vulnerable to any downturn of the economy or market, or adverse life circumstance, that resulted in an income loss/personal business failure. Literally, the U.S. economy prior to 1933 was a "survival of the fittest" form of capitalism – rugged individualism in all its harshness. FDR changed that. Many scholars argue, as this author does, that FDR saved corporate capitalism in the United States; some even argue that he saved capitalism/the free enterprise system itself. Whether FDR saved U.S. corporate capitalism or capitalism itself is a subject for another time. But this is clear: FDR's reforms, of which Social Security is the crown jewel, certainly made U.S. corporate capitalism less-harsh. The U.S. went from conditions of "Social Darwinism," to a more-humane economic and social system that protected those who were not "the big winners" in the U.S.'s performance-based economic system.

In Social Security's case, simply, it lifted and continues to lift tens of millions of retirees out of poverty each year. It is redistributive: it takes excess income from those with higher incomes and redistributes it back to those with lower incomes. Social Security is progressive: it demands that the well-off senior citizens take care of less-well senior citizens. Social Security guarantees that those who paid into the system for 10 years will receive a minimum benefit that should prevent poverty. One example: a person who earned $25,000 per year would receive about $950 per month; a person with a $70,000 income, $1,450 per month. On a percentage basis, the higher income senior citizen is getting less, but the gain for society is enormous: those redistributed funds help lift tens of millions of fellow senior citizens out of poverty each year. That achievement in an of itself justifies Social Security, but the added economic stimulus that the poverty-reducing aspect produces for the U.S. economy is another benefit for society, and frankly, for private company shareholders, as well: those dollars among lower-income senior citizens are spent for housing, utilities, insurance and food, among other items – and that's good news for business / commercial activity / GDP.

What's more, Social Security offers other economy boosts / economic pluses: the positive impact of Social Security is not fully-realized by many Americans…and by those readers outside the United States. But consider the following:

-Those cities/areas of the United States that have a disproportionately higher percentage of senior citizens tend to have more-stable economies – they're less-subject to the boom-and-bust cycle of the economy. One reason? Some would cite the natural tendency of older Americans to save more, or consume big-ticket items/goods more consistently, or be less risky, but a major factor is the constancy of Social Security benefit payments. Social Security payments remain the same whether the U.S. economy is growing at 5 percent or in a recession. Logically then, if a local economy has a lot of senior citizens, the pool of dollars to that regional economy is going to be more-stable. And as the late great New York Yankee Manager Casey Stengel would say, "You can look it up."

-Rather than hurting the U.S. stock market, the presence of Social Security payments may actually benefit the stock market, and to a lesser extent, the bond market. Here's why: while not every retiree/retiree couple has enough private savings to invest in stocks, those that do, can do so knowing that: 1) they're guaranteed to have at least some income via a Social Security benefit payment, 2) no amount of stock market gyration will affect their benefit. As a result, that may encourage some of these better-off retirees to invest in risk instruments, like stocks and bonds. And in general, as the number of people investing in stocks increases, the stock market tends to benefit.

-Social Security is solvent, and in good shape. Over the decades, many groups have tried to use "scare tactics" to achieve a craven, narrow political goal: undermine the Social Security system. And, sadly, many Republicans, conservative groups, and the Tea Party faction have been among them. Do not listen to them. *Repeat: do not listen to them.* Social Security is doing fine. Each year, the administration calculates the Old-Age Survivor and Disability Insurance (OASDI) benefit payout to evaluate the plan's health. As of 2020, the Old-Age and Survivors trust fund was funded through 2035; the Disability trust fund, through 2052, according to the Congressional Budget Office (CBO). Underscoring, your earned Social Security benefit will be there for you when you retire: don't let anyone tell you otherwise. Some Social Security plan critics, including some conservatives, are forwarding half-truths and distortions because they want to dismantle Social Security because they are ideologically/philosophically opposed to a public pension system, the redistribution of benefits from the fortunate to the less-fortunate, and/or (incredibly) oppose most modern functions of the United States Government in general. But see their criticism for what it is: a smear, a scare tactic and a distortion of reality.

Further, assuming the 2035 fully-funded date is not pushed back - if the U.S. economy resumes growing in 2021, the date will be pushed back – but for the sake of argument, let's say the 2035 date does not change. What then? Well, prior to that date lawmakers on Capitol Hill have many options to further-strengthen the Social Security system.

These include:

-Raise the payroll ceiling. The payroll ceiling is now adjusted for inflation. Economist Robert Reich, former U.S. Secretary of Labor, Clinton Administration, suggests lifting the ceiling on income subject to Social Security taxes, which is now $177,700. The Reuters news service reported that removing, not raising the cap according to plan forwarded by former U.S. Sen. Tom Harkin, D-Iowa, and for U.S. Sen. Mark Begich, D-Alaska, would extend Social Security's fully-funded date to 2050. Their plan would also increase annual cost-of-living adjustment (COLA) and change benefit formulas to increase benefits for all seniors by about $70 per month.

-Increase Social Security taxes. If workers and employers each paid 7.6 percent (up from today's 6.2 percent) into the system, the financing gap would be reduced to zero. This 1.4 percent increase (2.8 percent for self-employed) has better than majority-support of the American public, in surveys conducted by the National Academy of Social Insurance (NASI).

-Hike the retirement age(s). Raise the early retirement option from age 62 to 64 would help reduce Social Security benefit payouts.

-Means-test benefits. The phasing-out of Social Security benefits for those who already have an income over $48,000/year ($4,000/month) would eliminate more than 20 percent of the funding gap. Upper-income groups almost certainly would oppose it – arguing they paid into the system like everyone else, and are entitled to their benefit. That said, if the choice is between providing a benefit for those with incomes over $48,000 and those with little or no income, the analysis forwarded here argues the progressive, egalitarian and humane choice would be to means-test. But understand that any Congress would likely consider other ways to improve the system first, before this politically-volatile one.

-Reduce benefits for new retirees. If Social Security benefits were reduced by 3 percent to 5 percent for new retirees, about 18 percent to 30 percent of the funding gap would be eliminated.

-Tighten Disability rules. The Senate Permanent Subcommittee on Investigations' 2-year inquiry found extensive fraud in the Social Security Administration's Disability Program. Tightening Disability rules, as well as adding personnel to rigorously evaluate and investigate Disability applications and cases would lower unwarranted and illegal payouts under this system.

-Average-in more working years. Social Security benefits are now based on an average of a worker's 35 highest paid salaries with zeros averaged in if there are less than 35 years of covered wages. The averaging period could be increased to 38 or 40 years, extending the fully-funded date.

-Require all newly-hired people to join Social Security. Almost all new workers are covered by Social Security and are expected to pay the

Federal Insurance Contributions Act (FICA) tax or the Self-Employed Contributions Act (SECA) tax, so there is not much to gain by this change.

The New Deal – new life for the American people: "The only thing we have to fear is, fear itself," President Franklin D. Roosevelt said. FDR's quote was the perfect axiom, and he was the perfect person for his era and role. President Franklin D. Roosevelt, like President Abraham Lincoln and President Theodore Roosevelt before him, and - the analysis forwarded here argues, like President Obama - represented a safety valve for the U.S economic system. FDR's reforms saved corporate capitalism in the United States: there were other, radical voices in the body politic in the 1930s seeking to replace capitalism with socialism, but FDR's belief that the current system merely needed to be reformed - to be made more-humane, more-just - deflated any potential groundswell of support for socialism. It is indeed ironic that Republicans in the 1930s – not unlike conservatives/Republicans today in 2020 – saw President Roosevelt as 'the devil incarnate.' In truth, FDR was their greatest friend. And one of FDR's hallmarks is Social Security.

Social Security is the largest and most important social program in the United States. As mentioned, the monthly Social Security benefit lifts tens of millions of retirees out of poverty each year. That one fact alone justifies its existence. It is redistributive: it takes excess income from those with higher incomes and redistributes it back to those with lower incomes. Social Security is progressive and humanitarian: it demands that well-off senior citizens take care of less-fortunate senior citizens.

What's more, one could make an argument that Social Security was the first step in creating in the United States a "Capitalism with a human face."

Moreover, there's a reason why on Capitol Hill Social Security is considered to be one of those issues that represent "the third rail" of American politics. As anyone familiar with New York City's subway system knows, the third rail on the track is electrified: you touch it, you die. The same can be said of Social Security: if a member of Congress touches it

– i.e., seeks to undermine its benefit and program, he/she will die politically. In other words - be voted out of office. *Senior citizens remember and they vote:* they will vote you out of office, pronto. That's the same way as saying, senior citizens in the United States understand the role, importance and goodness Social Security: it's another example of your federal government at work – another example of the good your United States Government does.

Social Security's formula: Social Security's formula is complex – the full benefit is allocated for those who work at least 30 years and retire at age 67. (Different qualifications apply for those who are legally defined as disabled.) Do not misunderstand: Social Security was and remains a major civilizational and social advance in the United States: over the past 85 years, it has lifted hundreds of millions of beneficiaries out of poverty, and enabled the bulk of these adults to lead dignified lives. However, once again, globalization, which has led to stagnant incomes in many job segments, and the fragmentation of the workforce (including the increase in 'gig workers'), has led to too-small Social Security pensions for tens of millions of Americans. Two examples: 1) the gig worker, who worked in insurance for 10 years as a full-time employee, then as a for-contract gig worker for 25 years, who was unable to amass significant private savings, and as a result has a low Social Security monthly benefit, about $1,050; 2) the for-contact maid who worked 30 years in housekeeping/domestic service, and has never had an employer pay into Social Security, even though she's paid into the Social Security her entire work life; her Social Security monthly benefit is also low: $645 per month.

The solution to the above is obvious enough: establish a higher monthly minimum benefit. And two other changes should also be implemented: an earlier retirement age and a higher disability benefit.

Higher minimum monthly benefit: What should be the new, higher monthly benefit? That's a good question. The U.S. cost of living varies substantially by region. In late-2020, the cost of living in New York City, New York was more than double that of Kansas City, Missouri. To date, the

Social Security system does not adjust for a regional cost-of-living factor, and as the above case study demonstrates, those regional costs can differ by a tremendous amount. The revised Social Security system should take that regional cost of living into account. The minimum benefit should be $1,750 per month; ideally the minimum benefit should be $2,000 per month, but that may not be possible in the 2020-2029 decade. In addition, a cost-of-living adjuster should be added to Social Security that boosts the pension by up to 25 percent, depending on a cost-of-living calculation by the U.S. Bureau of Labor Statistics (BLS). To be sure, that regional benefit adjustment will not eliminate a 100 percent increase in fixed costs - in our example, from Kansas City to New York City - but it's a start. (Perhaps Congress can move to a regional benefit adjustment in stages: the first in the 2020-2029 decade; the second in the 2030-2039 decade, etc.)

Higher disability benefit: Second, progressives/Democrats should work to increase the disability benefit. Currently, it pays $800 to $1,800 per month. The minimum benefit should be raised to $1,200 per month. At the same time, progressives/Democrats should advocate for a minimum $1,000 monthly benefit for those who do not qualify for a Social Security benefit by other methods and who do not have a private pension. (Note: For the aforementioned, a modest amount of assets also should be allowed, with the person still qualifying.) These two changes may seem unwarranted to some, but they are what a decent, humane civilization does. *A society is not judged by how it treats the wealthy; it's judged by how it treats the poor, the most vulnerable and the elderly.* In other words, no decent, humane civilization lets anyone remain destitute. Progressive, enlightened societies also seek to reduce - with the ultimate goal of eliminating - needless human suffering and pain.

To be sure, neither change described will be cost-free. But the alternative is far costlier – a society in which potentially tens of millions of Americans enter their retirement years with a very low income and/or in and impoverished state. That can only lead to a host of higher costs and unfavorable outcomes for society and the civilization at large. The more-enlightened tack, the one that leads to a more perfect union, is one that builds on FDR's starting point for Social Security and increases the benefits so that every retiree in the United States is living a dignified, fulfilling retirement period.

Earlier Social Security benefit age: Third, progressives/Democrats should seek a gradual lowering of the Social Security benefit eligibility age. If the coronavirus-caused U.S. recession lasts longer than March 2021, progressives and Democrats should lobby for an even quicker start to this entitlement modification. As noted, there's going to be a large segment of the U.S. population who will reach the classic retirement age or close to it, with little or no defined-contribution plan funds. Others will have some funds but be physically unable to work, or otherwise not suitable for most jobs. This proposed reform would help both groups. Currently, the full retirement age is 67 if you were born in 1960 or later; the minimum retirement age is 62, with a 30 percent benefit reduction. Progressives/Democrats should lobby for a full retirement age change to 65 in 2024, and then to 62 in 2028; and lobby for an early retirement age change to 60 in 2024 and 57 in 2028. These changes will increase program costs, but their benefit is more than worth it: millions of Americans will be retiring sooner, with a pension, freeing up jobs for younger generations in the workforce. In many cases, the change will also lift these senior citizens out of poverty. No one is saying the U.S. has to adopt the equivalent of a United Kingdom public pension system, to say nothing of the more-generous systems offered by Germany and France, but the U.S. Social Security system should provide a full benefit sooner to help reduce income inequality, and frankly, to provide a pension to an at-risk group: those with inadequate private savings. It's another change that a humane, enlightened society implements and it's a long overdue reform for the United States.

The Super Pension: This is another, potential, major reform. However, the modifier "potential" has been added because the United States may not be ready for it. Politically, conservatives/Republicans will undoubtedly oppose it. The reform? In the event that an adult does not earn enough credits to quality for Social Security and does not qualify for a Disability benefit, a $1,000 per month pension is awarded. This Super Pension would be funded by a 1 percent wealth tax - a one-time tax that will serve as an endowment for the program. Again, the goal is to prevent any adult from entering their senior citizen years, without a pension. (This benefit would obviously be means-tested: individuals with substantial assets or a monthly income of more than $750 per month from other sources, would lose 40 cents in benefits for every $1 in income from other sources above $750.)

Scenario: Excluding the Super Pension, these policy changes would draw from scenarios 1 and 2 – and perhaps scenario 3, if one considers a disability benefit to be "change outside the system." Again, these are not minor changes – but the analysis forwarded here argues they are vital for the United States to transition to a robust, egalitarian, sustainable public pension system.

(Freeway/Interstate 405 in Los Angeles, California. Photo credit: Shutterstock.com.)

Chapter 5: Rebuild U.S. Infrastructure

"Millions are unemployed and our roads and bridges are falling apart....We can spend $1 trillion to put Americans to work fixing our nation's crumbling infrastructure. Let's rebuild America and create jobs." -U.S. Sen. Bernie Sanders, I-Vermont

Another issue where progressives and Democrats have the philosophically stronger argument – and it's a policy area that's guaranteed to substantially increase U.S. GDP and good-paying jobs – is infrastructure. Infrastructure – elected officials have talked about it continually, for the past decade, and certainly the U.S. Congress, in fits and starts, has allocated funds to various projects, but the bottom line as of late-2020 is this: in general, the United States' infrastructure is dilapidated, inadequate, outmoded, and obsolete. To be sure, there are some "bright stars" and green shoots across the country, but overall, the grade for the nation's infrastructure is: abysmal! According to the American Society of Civil

Engineers (ASCE), the organization's 2017 grade for the U.S. infrastructure is: D+. That is an awful grade and is a poor statement on our infrastructure - a report card grade that also reflects the nation's nearly 40-year underinvestment in physical assets, in general. What physical assets need to be upgraded/modernized? You name it. (Perhaps a better question is – what physical assets near you do not need to upgraded/modernized?) Nearly everything in the U.S. needs work: schools, hospitals, highways/roads, bridges, transit systems, airports/ocean ports, railways, water systems, parks, beaches/sand dunes, broadband/internet systems, college facilities/community colleges, rail stations/Amtrak facilities, recreation areas, electric grid/smart grid, energy systems, sewage treatment plants, dams, levees, flood control projects, hospitals/care facilities, and freshwater aqueducts, among other assets. One could spend a week with a seminar full of civil engineers from the best U.S. engineering schools and not exhaust the number of assets that need upgrading/rebuilding. Hence, the nation better start soon, because, as Sen. Sanders noted, the nation's infrastructure is crumbling.

Without question, it is a daunting task, but the nation has to start somewhere. Further, as in several, other policy areas, the United States appears to be a cycle (20 years) behind Europe, Asia and other developed regions of the world concerning infrastructure modernization. Some would argue that a comparison with Europe's and Asia's infrastructure is irrelevant or unfair because: 1) Americans might merely have a different way of maintaining public goods/public assets, or 2) Asia, and in particular China, has developed its economy in a wholesale way only since globalization began (Asia: 1960s/1970s, China: 1980s/1990s), hence they obviously would have more, modernized assets. Concerning the former, Americans might merely have a different way of maintaining public goods, but in an economy that's likely to - despite the 2020 coronavirus pandemic - feature global competitors, America needs world-class, state-of-the-art public assets to remain a contender for international business and investment. Second, Asia/China does have the "newly-developed" advantage, but their modernized status is paramount: it matters not when Asia/China became global competitors, the important fact is they *are competitors* and the United States must have a modern economy to compete. And that requires a modern infrastructure.

How big is the United States' infrastructure task? To cite a phrase made popular by actor William Shatner, "Really big." Every region, and nearly every major city, has an infrastructure/public asset deficiency. One example: In New York and New Jersey, a new railroad tunnel under the Hudson River is needed to accommodate increased train traffic by Amtrak and commuter railroads/trains. Called the Hudson Project, it will build a new tunnel, rehabilitate an existing tunnel, and cost at least $9 billion. Another: Literally thousands of bridges, small and large, are substandard and need to be strengthened or replaced. Ditto for interstate highways, secondary roads (sometimes called secondary highways), and other streets. A third example: schools, universities and related education facilities need modernization throughout the United States, but particularly in lower-income towns and counties; better-equipped schools, laboratories and schools with fast, reliable broadband, (discussed later in the book, in Chapter 7), are essential to train the 21st century's workforce. Also: water systems and sewage treatment facilities need upgrades in many cities/regions; in some cases, water systems/reservoirs will have to be enlarged to account for global warming; and modernized/upgraded waste treatment facilities will lead to a cleaner environment. Similarly, many of the nation's dams are in need of repair / maintenance. Also, the ASCE said in 2017 that 2,000 of 15,000 of the nation's dams with high-hazard potential are considered deficient, due to a lack of maintenance or investment. Concerning leisure assets, thousands of parks (national, state, local) are in need of landscaping, improved maintenance and renovation. What's more – the electric grid is in need of a major overhaul to both help meet the likely increased energy needs of the 21st century, and to create a more-efficient, more-resilient smartgrid. To be sure, the smartgrid will require the use of both private and public funds, but the important point is that it's hard to see private sector utilities funding the grid alone: the grid has to be made smart, more-resilient and capable of thwarting cyber attacks from bad actors (including certain nations) on the international stage. In addition, a number of U.S. container shipping/commercial shipping ports will need to be dredged and improved; even if cross-hemisphere international trade in goods does not grow as strongly as it did prior to the coronavirus pandemic, it's hard to envision a scenario in which export/import trade ends. What's more, regionalization may lead to increased container ship traffic at U.S. ports from markets in South America and Central America – and that points to the need to modernize ocean ports.

Another very good reason for the United States to undertake infrastructure programs now is that interest rates are very low – in some cases they are as low as they've been in 40 years. Hence, the U.S. Government can borrow at very low rates – substantially reducing the interest payment/debt service cost for capital improvement bonds. (That assumes the United States chooses to borrow for a capital expense, which is the norm.) In January 2021, the interest rate for the 10-year U.S. Treasury Note was 1.12 percent (!) Rates for other, industrialized economies were: Germany, -0.49 percent; Japan, 0.03 percent; U.K., 0.33 percent; Spain, 0.13 percent; and Italy, 0.69 percent.

In sum, the list of U.S. infrastructure items/public assets that need to be maintained and/or modernized is long – very long. It will likely take more than two decades to complete the work. And the cost estimate? Yours truly will leave that to the ASCE, but suffice it to say, it is in the tens of trillions of dollars. But the work has to begin – the nation's grade is already at a very poor D+. That very poor grade reflects roughly 40 years of conservative/ Republican Party-caused underinvestment and outright neglect of our infrastructure. Delaying needed work any longer will jeopardize the United States' global competitor status. Further, as noted, investing in infrastructure will create millions of good-paying jobs and substantially boost U.S. GDP growth: those are welcome benefits, in any era, but they are especially welcome, given that the coronavirus pandemic tipped the U.S. economy into a major recession, with at least 35 million layoffs, as of July 2020. I.E., in the words of the late, great New York City Mayor Fiorello La Guardia,

"There's much work to be done, and millions of decent, virtuous, hard-working Americans who are willing to do it." Hence, there's no time like the present to start rebuilding the nation's infrastructure.

Scenario: This policy change would likely draw from scenarios 1 thru 4. Given the size of the infrastructure rebuilding tasks, a variety of funding mechanisms is needed: public, private-public, public with a private lease, co-operative, worker-owned, naming-rights funded, and more. Further, the nation's federal system and diverse states almost require the flexible, adaptable funding format, given the number and assortment of projects involved. Still, the multitude of ingredients will lead to "a great celebratory cake," if the United States fully commits itself to undertaking these much-needed projects.

****

US Gov Employee Lenny Skutnik Took Matters Into His Own (Swimming) Hands

On a cold, snowy January day, Americans who had switched cable channels after learning about a terrible aviation accident, saw once again what U.S. civil servants are made of.

The tragedy's details are well known, almost 40 years later. On January 13, 1982 at 4 p.m. EST, a now defunct airline, Air Florida's Flight 90 from Washington, D.C. to Fort Lauderdale, Fla., attempting to take off in a heavy snowstorm, and with ice/slush on its wings, stalled on takeoff and struck the 14th Street Bridge, killing 70 of 74 passengers, 5 crew members and 4 motorists on the bridge. Four passengers and one flight attendant survived the crash. The plane wreckage sunk into the ice-laden, 24F / -4C degree Potomac River.

Within 30 minutes of the crash, a U.S. Park Police helicopter, with Pilot Donald Usher and Paramedic Melvin Windsor aboard, arrived and began attempting to airlift plane crash survivors from the Potomac River, at great risk to themselves. After pulling one man to the shore and safety via rope dropped from the helicopter, other rescue personnel had arrived at the Potomac shore. Soon three more passengers were pulled to shore, as a fourth, Priscilla Tirado, blinded by jet fuel, could not grasp the rope, as a sixth, the severely-injured Arland D. Williams Jr., unable to strap himself to the rope, repeatedly passed the rope to other survivors on the Potomac.

Lenny Skutnik Dove Into The Water

Tirado, weakened and blinded by the jet fuel, failed several times to locate the rope with a life ring attached to it, groping for it. Tirado's plight was exasperating to watch on live t.v.: blinded, she had trouble finding the rope, and when she did grasp it, she was not strong enough to maintain her grip, and the rope slipped from her hand. It was gut-wrench to watch – a person's life was within a football pass of being saved; it was all so cruel. It was at that point that a bystander, Congressional Budget Office (CBO) employee Lenny Skutnik, who traveled to the site after learning of the crash, saw the situation and took matters into his own hands.

At enormous risk to himself, Skutnik stripped off his coat and boots, and in shirtsleeves, dove into the icy water, swam out 30 feet to Tirado, and successfully pulled her to shore.

The helicopter crew then retrieved the fourth and fifth passengers with

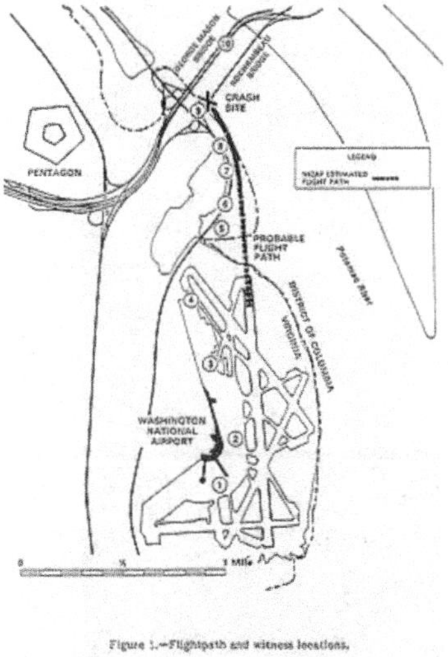

Path of Air Florida Flight 90. (Credit: NTSB.)

the descended rope, but could not retrieve Williams, who had submerged.

Lenny Skutnik dove into the water became the refrain of the popular culture on Main Streets across America. As in, *"Did you see it?? Lenny Skutnik dove into the water and saved a person after the Washington airplane crash!"*

The name *"Lenny Skutnik"* also became synonymous with a heroic act in everyday life in the United States that is recognized by a U.S. president and/or the U.S. Congress; (but it started with U.S. presidential recognition). Skutnik was honored for his heroism and selflessness with many awards, including an introduction and recognition by President Ronald Reagan at his state of the union address before a joint session of Congress in late January 1982. (Skutnik, Pilot Usher, civilian Roger Olian and Paramedic Windsor also received the Carnegie Hero Fund Medal. Skutnik, Olian and Williams (posthumously), also received the U.S. Coast Guard's Lifesaving Medal. The 14th Street Bridge also was renamed in memory of Williams, as was an elementary school in his hometown of Mattoon, Illinois.)

At the 1982 state of the union address, President Reagan said, *"Just two weeks ago, in the midst of a terrible tragedy on the Potomac, we saw again the spirit of American heroism at its finest the heroism of dedicated rescue workers saving crash victims from icy waters."*

President Reagan continued: *"And we saw the heroism of one of our young government employees, Lenny Skutnik, who, when he saw a woman lose her grip on the helicopter line, dived into the water and dragged her to safety."*

Lenny Skutnik – just your typical federal employee. Just your typical American. Lenny Skutnik – a role model for all: he represents the best of these United States.

(The University of Connecticut, Storrs. Connecticut. Photo credit: UConn.)

Chapter 6: Higher Education / Vocational School Investment

"Poverty must not be a bar to learning, and learning must offer an escape from poverty." –President Lyndon B. Johnson

A sixth issue where progressives and Democrats have the philosophically stronger argument is higher education and vocational training. Historically, higher education and vocational training have been win-win-win for the United States. The individual wins via increased earning power, the local economy wins by having a person who will likely pay more in local income, sales and property taxes, and the nation wins because GDP, median income, and, most likely, corporate profits or a small business's earnings will rise, too. To be sure, conservatives/Republicans occasionally forward a good idea regarding higher ed and vocational training, but on most occasions their proposals are modest and/or easily outdone by those proposed by progressives/Democrats. Moreover, the 2020 coronavirus pandemic and the more than 35 million Americans who lost their jobs, due to the virus and the lockdowns to contain it, present not merely an appropriate time to increase education funding, *but an urgent time to increase funding*. The Biden Administration in 2021, aided by the Democratic Party-led Congress, will do that, on many levels and with several programs.

Simply, the U.S. must create a new "GI Bill for displaced workers." In late-2020, the United States was still early in this crisis, but it looks like millions of employees – possibly more than 10 million adults, if one can comprehend that, will permanently lose their jobs due to the coronavirus pandemic. (One example of the severity of the layoffs caused by the pandemic: in May 2020, roughly 40 percent of restaurant employees in New York state had been laid off, due to lack of work.) It's not hard to see how that many jobs could be permanently eliminated if the habits of millions of consumers/businesses/non-profits permanently change. Here are a few examples: 1) concern about gathering in large groups permanently reducing movie theatre attendance, hotel stays, and air/train travel; 2) concern about optional/discretionary indoor gatherings reducing restaurant and fitness center patronage; 3) concern about being in large groups for a long time, in a confined, restricted space reducing trips in the vacation cruise industry; and there are many, other, affected sectors. One net result is obvious: the pandemic eliminated millions of jobs, and many are not coming back. Moreover, this job reduction does not include the jobs that will be lost due to the ongoing secular trend of automation, offshoring and robotics/drone technology; those factors have been eliminating U.S. jobs for at least three decades. Regarding the post-pandemic economy, this is clear: millions of Americans will need to be retrained for new jobs, and that trend points to the importance of increased funding for higher education/vocational training.

Hence, we need to support college education, vocational training and vocational retraining through a massive, federal re-commitment to U.S. higher education/vocational schools and Congress's GI Bill is a good template / example to follow. It will substantially reduce unemployment, increase required skills, and boost U.S. GDP. And, as in other policy areas, states must increase funding for higher ed/vocational training, as well, but the major push must come from the federal government. Listed below are the progressive/Democrat initiatives in education:

-Higher education: The U.S. Congress should establish a fund that pays for public college tuition, for all students, including community colleges and vocational schools. Income or wealth should not be a barrier to a college education. Special, new, modest grants should also be made available to students attending private colleges. Congress should also establish a new fund to pay for 90 percent of selected college building upgrades and expansions. Program cost: $750 billion.

Vocational schools capital plant: Simply, a $100 billion public sovereign wealth fund must be established to pay for vocational school improvements / expansions. The interest from this fund pays for the work.

-**Displaced workers:** Congress should establish a $100 billion program that provides special grants to adults displaced by sectors/industries that disappear (due to globalization or other reasons) and/or that do not yield strong prospects of a new job.

-21st century sovereign wealth fund for innovative/strategic sectors: $100 billion.

-21st century social/culture sovereign wealth fund: A special fund should be established to identify those new, innovative sectors that are likely to yield significant social / cultural benefits for the United States. Program cost: $50 billion.

-Student loan forgiveness: Another special fund should be established to pay outstanding student loans. On a sliding-scale, means-tested basis, low-income students would have their loans repaid first, then moderate-income students. Program cost: about $500 billion.

Total cost of education programs: $1.6 trillion.

Now is not the time to dither regarding increased support for higher education and vocational training. Conservatives/Republicans emphasize the wonders of and competition-based improvements in companies, products and services. Well, if they still believe that is the case, then they, like progressives / Democrats already, must get 100 percent behind increased public support for higher ed/vocational training, because the tech and related factors in globalization that are displacing millions of jobs are only likely to accelerate in the decade ahead. (This, despite the 2020 coronavirus pandemic that has tipped the global economy into a recession and that bodes several changes to global supply chains and the global economy.) Think job dislocation will decline in 2020-2029? Fat chance. Artificial intelligence, machine learning, cloud-based systems, robotics, drones, self-driving trucks, self-driving cars, fully-automated factories and assembly lines, and automated sales personnel, among other technological innovations, will eliminate tens of millions of U.S.-based jobs. Hence, most adults in these categories will have to be retrained: there are no two ways around it. The alternative is long-term unemployment for many, and that will only increase public social service costs, and these costs will be much larger than the $1.6 trillion investment recommended here. Or, as teachers/educators frequently note, *"If you think the cost of education is high, try ignorance."* On to that add: the cost of undertraining/inadequate skills. The smart tack is to prepare all Americans for the 21st century economy via a reinvigorated, progressive public higher education/vocational training program: like the other policies mentioned, that's the public policy that will lead to a more perfect union.

Scenario: The higher education/vocational training policy change would likely draw from scenarios 1 and 2, and the reason is obvious enough: the United States has the most extensive network of universities, colleges, community colleges and vocational training schools in the world. And that suggests funding through existing institutions makes the most sense. That said, the vocational skills sector has been underfunded in the last 30 years even more than four-year colleges, hence there is room here for new, federal vocational training schools to play a role. The larger point is the key: as long as a massive amount of federal dollars are allocated to education and training, the United States' workforce will be better-prepared for the 21st century economy, be it one that's largely a global economy or a regional economy.

U.S. Universities And Colleges – Still World-Class

Back when the author of this book was in graduate school at the University of Connecticut in Storrs, Connecticut, Political Science Professor (emeritus) Henry Krisch, director of Soviet Studies (now Russian Studies), would cite a quip when he had to break off a conversation to attend to lecture duties:

"Quick, let me go give my lecture...before everything changes," Krisch would say.

In 2020, the United States and world are implementing a myriad of changes, as well as coping with the coronavirus pandemic and a global recession that could amount to the worst economic downturn since the Great Depression of the 1930s. However, one thing that has not changed is the important role U.S. colleges and universities play in training adults young and young at heart, and in training many of the world's future leaders in public policy, business, and the non-profit sector. Now, one would think this would not need underscoring in 2020, but given the damage that has been done to the nation, public policy, society, and the culture from 2016 to mid-2020, apparently it must be reiterated.

1-Skills Acquisition

One individual said colleges should focus on teaching "relevant job skills," especially for his sector. [The other sectors would argue, "Well, what about our sectors? Why is your field so special?"] We'll save that discussion for another time. For now, know that universities want to teach marketable job skills to every student, of course – whether they are studying mechanical engineering, accounting, physics, agricultural economics, or puppetry. Every university wants all its graduates to get good-paying, satisfying and rewarding jobs in the field(s) of their choosing.

Harvard Yard, 2005. (Credit: WikiCommons, public domain.)

2-Research / New Knowledge

However, some colleges and many large universities also have another role: research, new knowledge, innovation, intellectual generation, and breakthroughs. Some of the world's biggest and best ideas have originated at universities. The list of accomplishments is voluminous. Think:

Einstein – theory of relativity. John Maynard Keynes. Steven Jay Gould. Aaron Wildavsky – public budgeting. Carol Gilligan. If you don't know who the above people are, they are worth learning about.

3-Democracy, Self-Government

Also, in the United States, colleges and universities have a third role: teach students about democracy, the U.S. Bill of Rights, equal treatment under the law, the separation of powers, and the independent judiciary. Universities in the United States try to instill in students – young and young at heart – that, despite how hard it is to achieve and govern under it, democracy is worth it.

And, to quote the late, great Author / Researcher Harold Weisberg, the United States admits BOTH foreign and domestic students to undergraduate programs and graduate programs because – we believe – that despite our problems and flaws, these students – no matter where they come from, and no matter what field they study – will take back to their home country (and in the case of a U.S. student, to their new career in the states) a little sample of what democracy in the United States of America is like.

Yes – that's right, the United States believes that by admitting students – no matter what they believed before entering college in the United States – they are going to learn something about American values and American interests...learn about the American system. And....they may like it.

4-Talent Acquisition

Finally, universities in the United States are a bountiful source of intelligent, versatile, capable, hard-working, cultured, persevering, poised and ambitious people – from diverse backgrounds. Can you think of any organizations that might be interested in the above, specifically any organizations and agencies within the United States Government that might be?

Analysis: In sum, as you can see, colleges and universities in the United States perform several roles, and these places of higher education and advanced training are still, on the whole, the envy of the world

(A broadband cable modem in the New York, United States. Photo credit: Joseph Lazzaro.)

Chapter 7: Universal Broadband (including wifi)

"Cyberspace, the internet is both the new frontier and the new Main Street." -Luca Ciarrocca, CEO, business news editor, author, publisher, and executive, based in Italy

Another issue where progressives and Democrats have the philosophically stronger argument concerns technology – and broadband, in specific. Simply, progressives/Democrats must pass legislation creating a universal, national broadband internet network. It should cost subscribers no more than $10 per month, with low-income homes/customers receiving the service at no cost.

Why the push for universal broadband? Simply, in the early 21st century, broadband is as vital as electricity. The 2020 coronavirus pandemic in the United States made clear that universal broadband is not merely a luxury, it is a necessity: It is vital. The second office/home-office/remote office featured during the pandemic played a major role in maintaining a functioning U.S. economy during the pandemic's quarantine – a quarantine implemented by all states, in stages, with varying time lengths. (As a side note, one should add that the United States economy and society would have been much better off had a national quarantine and lockdown occurred in February 2020 or March 2020, but the Trump Administration chose to not implement one - but that is a discussion for another time.) Further, because broadband is vital for both economic and health security, it is also vital to maintain national security. A word on broadband's important roles in the postmodern economy – roles revealed and magnified by the 2020 coronavirus pandemic.

Health care: Perhaps the area that broadband proved its vitalness the most was in health care services. Although citizens could certainly obtain information about the virus, its spread and government actions to contain it (including shutdowns, sheltering-in-place, and social distancing requirements) from other sources, the internet enabled folks and decision makers at home to obtain more information, quicker, with graphics, charts and lists detailing this vital information. Simply, everyone who had an internet connection received more information sooner, due to broadband, and that only underscores the disadvantage for those who did not have access. Of course, doctor appointments, prescriptions, and even some doctor exams could also be scheduled and conducted online. Further, the growing telemedicine sector is already conducting exams and patient symptom monitoring by Skype/video call; not all exams are suitable for telemedicine, but many are, and during the pandemic telemedicine proved it can go where a physical doctor or nurse cannot – such as quickly to a remote, rural area during a snowstorm. Health care providers are likely to expand their use of telemedicine and related health care services, and that's all the more reason broadband should be everywhere: broadband is vital for the dissemination of the latest shutdown/quarantine information; increasingly, it's also becoming vital for patient care.

Home-office: The pandemic's quarantine and new public health rules mandated mask wearing, social distancing, no congregating, and substantially reducing face-to-face interactions, in addition to frequent hand washing. What's more, not only office complexes, but entire cities also shut down. New York City, which became the national epicenter for the coronavirus in the winter/spring 2020, implemented a lockdown for all but essential employees. That substantially reduced GDP and led to more than 2.5 million layoffs in New York state, but in an adaptation that many cities and sectors replicated, outside of the hospitality sector, most core business operations continued, with millions of employees working from home, and schoolchildren in the K-12 grades continuing their education via remote learning/remote classes. ZOOM, Skype, Facetime, Google and comparable video call teleconference technologies enabled meetings and classroom lessons to continue, online. Ditto for U.S. colleges and universities: most colleges required students to leave campus, in order to decrease human density and interactions – two major factors in the virus's spread. Churches/worship centers did the same. In a nutshell, the bulk of the U.S. economy that continued to operate after the pandemic hit, operated remotely, and broadband made that possible. To be sure, as noted, many businesses could not operate: dine-in-only restaurants, movie theatres, bars/nightclubs, gyms, museums/art galleries and hotels, among others. But those that could offer services to homes – take-out food from restaurants, for example – at least had that as a minor revenue stream. The pandemic has caused enormous economic hardship, including failed businesses and layoffs, but the point here is that home-offices and remote classrooms kept the core of the U.S. economy functioning – and that functioning was enabled by near-universal broadband/connectivity.

Business/commerce/economy: As noted, broadband enabled a substantial portion of the U.S. economy to function. Further, sheltering-in-place / avoiding interactions would not have been as easy were it not for the ability of consumers and businesses to order online, with deliveries. Of course, ordering goods located elsewhere is not new – older readers will remember that long before Amazon.com there was the Sears Catalogue – but what was laid bare - in fact, what blossomed during the pandemic - was the vitalness of being able to order essential goods online – food, prescription drugs, other health care items – without violating the quarantine. Many eateries/restaurants also offered food delivery, and of course many local shops did the same with their offerings. The New York City metropolitan area, in particular, suffered shortages of paper goods (toilet paper, paper towels) and cleaning items (soap, hand sanitizer, and many other sterilizing products) early in the pandemic, then almost every region of the country was afflicted with the same: ordering online from drug stores such as CVS, Walgreen's, and Rite Aid, and from retail stores/grocers such as Target, or via online shopping portal Amazon.com, served as the back-up supply line, until local stores were able to re-stock items and/or increase physical store supplies during mid-2020. Again, the point here is not that online ordering and home delivery did not occur in years/decades past, but that during the pandemic, it was revealed as being vital: for a considerable portion of the quarantine, online ordering was THE source of goods for many, and these orders sometimes contained vital items. The crisis demonstrated that broadband could maintain essential goods distribution during an emergency – something that justifies broadband's maintenance and strengthening by federal funds, in the years ahead. And, it must be underscored, to the extent broadband kept vital goods following and the core of the U.S. economy and government operations functioning, broadband maintenance is a national security issue. (More will be said regarding broadband's and technology's role in national security in Chapters 10 and 14.)

In sum, universal broadband, like electricity, is vital for public health, for home-office operation, for U.S. commerce, and ultimately for the defense of the nation. Reiterating, when you combine the three roles amid an emergency, such as a pandemic, one can make a strong case that universal broadband is vital to maintain national security, and that's the argument forwarded here. Accordingly, progressives/Democrats must push for full federal funding to both strengthen broadband, make it universal, including wifi, and offer all citizens access to it for no more than $10 per month, with no fee for low-income households/citizens. Doing so will help the United States make up for lost time during the past four years (2017-2020), and strengthen one backbone of the nation's economy, and by extension, strengthen the nation.

Scenario: This policy change would likely draw from scenarios 1 thru 3. Given the scope of reforms required to achieve universal broadband, the United States Government may have to create new institutions, or at least new agencies. It is possible, there could be one, public U.S. Broadband Center. That center could create its own broadband network, or what's more likely, work with existing private-sector broadband providers, such as cable companies and regional telephone service providers, to improve/augment their systems, with the federal government paying for both the improvement cost and subsidies to keep broadband monthly subscription costs at or below $10 per month. Another plan would have the federal government establish broadband cooperatives in each state, or regionally (northeast, midwest, south, mountain, and west). The broadband network's administration could take any number of forms, but so long as a reliable, affordable, universal network is in place by 2022, with wifi, it will achieve progressives' / Democrats' objective.

****

Harold Weisberg - The Dean Of JFK Assassination Researchers

In the pantheon of great, investigative journalists, the life of Harold Weisberg (1913-2002) is front-and-center. U.S. citizens and readers may know about The Washington Post's Bob Woodward and Carl Bernstein and their investigation of Watergate, but not enough know about the work of the late, great Harold Weisberg. And his work deserves to be widely-known. Here's why:

Simply, Weisberg is the dean of investigative journalists who have investigated the assassination of President John F. Kennedy, and who have critically evaluated the Warren Report – the controversial initial investigation and official version of the assassination.

Long before any journalists and researchers were beginning to express doubt about the Warren Commission's conclusion – that accused assassin Lee Harvey Oswald fired three rifle shots, and acted alone in killing President Kennedy, while wounding Texas Gov. John Connally and bystander James Tague, and that nightclub owner Jack Ruby acted alone in killing Oswald two days later – Weisberg was asking probing questions, undertaking painstaking research and writing about the commission's conclusion.

"Whitewash" – A Landmark Work

Weisberg's first book, "Whitewash: The Report on the Warren Report" (1965), was the first, critical study of the U.S. Government's official version of what happened in Dallas on Nov. 22, 1963. "Whitewash" was originally self-published: few publishing houses would consider a book challenging the Warren Report. (Some publishers still express hesitancy today!) In 1965, the United States was still in the height of the Cold War with the Soviet Union. The electorate was decidedly less skeptical, and more trusting of their government. The majority of adults generally believed their government told them the truth about important matters - and the JFK assassination was one of the most important. And even more thought the notion that organized, coordinated, status-quo interests undertaking a political murder to change the nation's political and public policy / foreign policy trajectory was beyond the realm of the U.S. political system: it simply wasn't possible in the American system of government.

Weisberg, a painstaking and exacting researcher, begged to differ. Weisberg's perseverant and methodical research of the government's unpublished evidence played a major role in forcing disclosures of assassination records via the Freedom of Information Act. "Whitewash" became an essential read in the mid-1960s for those citizens and researchers who did not believe that the American people had the whole truth regarding the events of November 22, 1963. Moreover, "Whitewash" remains an essential

Harold Weisberg

read today, five decades later – an era in which, regrettably, thousands of JFK assassination documents remain classified.

No Theory

Further, Weisberg presented no theory regarding who was behind the JFK assassination, but rather focused on the commission's own files to refute numerous commission conclusions. In an unbiased, dispassionate way, Weisberg exposed the shortcomings of the commission's investigation – its suppression of key evidence, its violations of criminal justice protocols, and its unfounded conclusions. And Weisberg documented dozens of Warren Commission errors. Here's one:

From "Whitewash" by Weisberg: "The exact window of the building from which the shots were supposed to have been fired was immediately pointed out. Yet this building was never sealed off -- not ever -- despite the obfuscation in the Report. Belatedly, it and the entire two or three block area were ordered isolated by an official, but there was not even a gesture in this direction. Even more inexplicably, there was no organized search of the building either immediately or as an afterthought. No one was ordered to inspect and search the area from which witnesses immediately reported the shots were fired. Not one of the police, from private to inspector, undertook this obvious search on his own. The empty cases of the bullets that both the police and the Commission concluded were fired were found in plain view at precisely the spot reported by witnesses - 42 minutes after the assassination (R-79). The rifle was not found until ten minutes later than that, and it was on the same floor. An alleged eyewitness description of the man later accused of being the assassin was immediately reported to radio-equipped police who did nothing about it. With the supposed killer still in the building, its exits were not secured. His description was not even broadcast on the police radio for almost 15 minutes. These blunders, if that is what they were, did not stop once the immediate shock of the crime had passed. They were the persistent pattern of the entire police operation, and they have been dignified and perpetuated by the Commission in both its hearings and its Report. Nowhere in the Report will you find any criticism of the police, except for its "public relations." Nowhere will you find any suggestion that the police could or should have done otherwise, or that their "errors" were in any way suspicious."

Here's another:

"The superficial and immature manner in which the [Warren] Report deals with the possibility of a conspiracy or of a different assassin is only one of the ways in which the Commission may have crippled itself. Despite references in both the Report and the press to the Commission's investigators, the fact is that, in the accepted sense, the Commission had no investigators of its own. It drew upon the men available in the Executive Branch, chiefly the FBI and Secret Service, who were not employees of the Commission and whose primary responsibilities were to those who did employ them."

And a third:

"The [Warren] Commission was reconstructing the crime, ostensibly to find out what happened, not to prove that Oswald alone committed it. When the motorcade turned toward the Depository Building on Houston Street, for several hundred feet there was a completely unobstructed view of it from the sixth-floor window. The police photographs and the forgotten Secret Service reconstruction of 1963 also show this. There was not a twig between the window and the President. There were no curves in that street, no tricky shooting angles. If all the shots came from this window, and the assassin was as cool and collected as the Report represents, why did he not shoot at the easiest and by far the best target? Why did he wait until his target was so difficult that the country's best shots could not duplicate his feat?"

A Healthy Skepticism

Underscoring, Weisberg offered no conspiracy theory in "Whitewash." He simply presented the commission's own evidence and errors. His pronouncements are reserved / measured. And within that work, his conclusion is cogent and consciousness-raising: no matter what the Warren Report says, we do not have the whole truth regarding the assassination of president of the United States in Dallas.

In sum, Weisberg's work provided ample, valid data points as to why it is reasonable to not accept the Warren Commission's conclusion, and to seek the release of all classified documents on the JFK assassination.

"Whitewash" by Harold Weisberg. (Credit: Skyhorse Publishing, 1965.)

TRIVIA TEST 3: U.S. GOVERNMENT & U.S. ECONOMY

(Answers in Appendix, Page 354.)

1. Which of the following nations has no national vacation law / policy?
a) United States
b) Germany
c) France
d) United Kingdom

2. The most dynamic sector of the U.S. economy in the 2011-2020 decade was?
a) tech sector
b) steel sector
c) poultry sector
d) tomato sector

3. Which U.S. Government agency developed the technology that was the beginning of and helped create the Internet?
a) U.S. Treasury Department
b) DARPA
c) U.S. State Department
d) None of the above

Republican Party presidential candidate Richard Nixon meets with President Johnson in the White House, July 1968. (Credit: U.S. National Archives.)

4. During World War II, 1941-45, the U.S. Government controlled the economy, setting wages and prices, and implementing rationing. How did the U.S. economy perform?

a) The economy shrank
b) The economy grew at a very strong rate
c) The economy was taken over by Japan
d) The economy was taken over by the United Kingdom

5. Which president is most responsible for public funding of higher education, including loans, grants and federally-funded college expansions?
a) Jefferson
b) Washington
c) Lyndon B. Johnson
d) Taft

6. Which of the following is true about the U.S. economy, after the U.S. Government made a major investment, such as for the interstate highway system, higher education grants, and the Internet?
a) The economy collapsed
b) The economy did not fare any better than before the investment
c) The economy grew at an impressive rate
d) None of the above

President Bill Clinton. (Credit: U.S. Armed Forces, public domain.)

7. Which president created the most jobs - 22 million - in the U.S. economy during his presidency?
a) Hoover
b) Reagan

c) Bush II
d) Clinton

8. Which of the following is true about the U.S. Government and the U.S. economy?
a) The federal government seeks to operate in a sector, as soon as it has been created
b) The federal government has the power to prevent U.S. companies from exporting goods and services
c) The federal government will frequently establish a government department to compete with companies in a sector
d) None of the above

9. The most likely reason for the U.S. Government to intervene in a sector is:
a) National security
b) If the sector is unprofitable
c) If the sector is dominated by Democrats
d) If the sector is dominated by Republicans

10) As of 2014, which is true, at minimum, about the U.S. Federal Reserve's intervention in the U.S. economy after the financial crisis started in 2008?

a) The Federal Reserve's actions drove the economy into a depression
b) The Federal Reserve's actions led to a 15 percent annual inflation rate
c) The Federal Reserve's actions both stabilized financial markets and kept credit markets liquid
d) None of the above

(A house in California, United States. Photo credit: Shutterstock.com.)

Chapter 8: U.S. Housing Investment

"There is nothing like owning your own home." –Peter Bailey, George Bailey's father in the movie, "It's A Wonderful Life" (1941)

The eighth issue where progressives/Democrats have the philosophically stronger argument is housing. One of the values or staples/essential components of the "American dream" is home ownership. Ascendancy to or achievement of home ownership status produces many benefits, (however, not all benefits appear in every year, due to the cyclical U.S. housing market, among other factors): equity in your own dwelling/wealth creation, privacy, quiet enjoyment, a federal income tax deduction, and (long-term) a lower cost for housing than renting. (Note: There are some markets where owning a home results in a higher, overall housing cost per month than renting a home/apartment, but that is a discussion for another time.) Further, the analysis forwarded here argues home ownership, via equity, increases a citizen's vested-interested stake in the United States. As noted, the United States is a corporate capitalist economic system; by logical extension then, if you have capital, you're more likely (but not guaranteed) to support the system – it's in your financial interest to do so. Personal savings, stock/bond ownership, and business ownership all offer opportunities to amass capital. So does home ownership. Accordingly, progressives/Democrats *who share the perspective of this U.S. public policy professional* should encourage public policies that make home ownership (really, dwelling ownership, when one includes condominiums and co-operative apartment residences), *accessible to more people.*

In recent years, among elected officials, U.S. Sen. Bernie Sanders, D-Vermont, has offered perhaps the most encompassing, broad-based housing program. During his 2020 U.S. presidential campaign, Sanders advocated building 10 million affordable housing units. The cost? $2.5 trillion. Other Sanders measures include: establishing a standard for "just cause" eviction; making rent more-affordable by making Section 8 U.S. Department of Housing and Urban Development (HUD) available to all eligible families, without a waitlist; combat gentrification, exclusionary zoning, segregation and speculation; revitalizing public housing by investing $70 billion to repair, decarbonize and build new public housing; and end homelessness and ensure fair housing for all.

Sanders is to be commended for his comprehensive evaluation and prescription for housing. As with other issues, Sanders's focus is on achieving a just, egalitarian outcome based on democratic values. It will be interesting to see how many of Sanders' ideas will be incorporated into a Biden Administration agenda.

With the above as a backdrop, here are a few, modified Sanders ideas, progressives/Democrats would be wise to encourage the new Biden Administration to advocate:

-Savings match program: Under this federal program, the U.S. Government matches, on a dollar-for-dollar basis, money an individual or couple saves for a down payment, up to $5,000 for a first home/condo/co-op unit, etc. Funds are saved at a local bank or credit union, at no cost. Funds by the contributor(s) – but not the federal money invested – may be withdrawn for a defined emergency. Funds by contributor(s) are tax deductible, and there's no federal, state or local tax on the matching money from the U.S. Government. The program's goal is to encourage more adults to save for a down payment for their first home. After the down payment, any excess funds may be applied to the home's first/subsequent mortgage payment, home closing costs, property taxes and utilities payments (water, natural gas, electric, sewer fees etc.).

-Starter home: Taking a page from Sanders's housing playbook, the U.S. Government should hire local home builders to build starter homes – in many cases these would be Cape Cod-style or ranch-style homes, along with condominiums – in every region of the country. Regional adaptations of home building styles would be allowed, but the goal is to increase the supply of high-quality starter homes. A secondary goal would be to support local home builders, boosting the local economy. How many homes would be built? Sanders' plan called for 10 million housing units. That total probably won't be possible in the first four years of a potential Democratic presidential administration: a more-realistic goal would be 100,000 to 150,000 units per year.

-Expanded conforming loan eligibility: Freddie Mac and Fannie Mae should broaden their conforming loan standards to include lower FICO credit scores. How low a FICO score should the two allow? That's a good question. On the one hand, the Federal Housing Finance Agency (FHFA) should devise a standard that increases home purchase accessibility, while not leading to a substantial increase in defaults. Hence, "implement, monitor and revise" will likely be the modus operandi here, with FHFA adjusting the FICO floor down, if defaults do not become the norm, and up, if they do.

-Revitalize public housing: Taking another page from Sanders's playbook, the federal government should make a massive investment to repair, decarbonize and rebuild public housing. A special program would add green space and/or recreation/leisure amenities at most complexes. This program recognizes that not everyone will want to own a home; regardless, their residential complexes should be modernized and made more livable. Program cost: $50 billion.

-Rental assistance: Section 8 vouchers have played a substantial role in assisting the poor and working poor. In 2019, approximately $20 billion was allocated to the program. The program should be expanded so that more adults/families in need receive the voucher. In addition, a sidecar fund should be established to assist low-income U.S. Veterans who are not served by other federal housing programs. (U.S. Veterans would first have to apply and access U.S. Veterans Administration programs; if rejected, they could then apply for U.S. HUD programs.)

-Housing for the homeless: Finally, progressives and Democrats must pass a comprehensive, locally-based but federally-funded program to house the homeless. Simply, we must house everyone: it is a matter of basic human decency. No advanced, humanitarian civilization permits homelessness. This will not be a simple or short-term project, as transitioning the homeless to everyday life often involves many resources: physical health care/mental health care, elder care, substance abuse treatment and prevention, education/skills training, disability support, corrections and social work. Further, some individuals will not be able to care for themselves, for mental/psychological or other reasons, and will need to live in an assisted-living home, senior home or nursing home. Overall, European democracies, particularly Germany and France, have done a much better job eliminating homelessness than the United States, which has a more-harsh economic system, and a more-modest social safety net. That has to change, and it will if progressives/Democrats push for it in the new Biden Administration in 2021. However, underscoring – it will not be a simple or quick task: the United States will need to commit at least $10 billion per year for 10 years to solve this humanitarian crisis.

Scenario: This policy changes would likely draw from scenarios 1 thru 4. In other words, housing is so important and complex in the United States that it will require ideas in all shapes and sizes, and from many interest groups/stakeholders. As always, Fannie Mae and Freddie Mac will be key players – their ability to buy mortgages frees-up funds for banks, so that these banks can approve additional mortgages, and the pair also provide essential liquidity to the mortgage market. Further, the Federal Housing Finance Agency and U.S. Department of Housing and Urban Development (HUD) will also play an important role regarding the FICO floor for approved mortgages. Finally, private, non-profit associations will play a role, as will a new institution or two, in order to finally eliminate homelessness in the United States. With all contributing, we will finally arrive at Sanders's goal, and the goal of many progressives/Democrats, among others: an America where everyone has a decent, affordable place to live.

****

Hometown: New Britain, Conn. And The U.S. Government

By now, you, the reader realizes this book contains a great deal of information about all the good your United States Government does. Truly, your United States Government does more for you in one day than you could imagine in a lifetime. Moreover, as President John F. Kennedy did during his thousand days in office, yours truly makes the case that an activist, proactive United States Government can improve both the economy and society, and in doing so advance civilization.

The Life Of The Nation

But, you may reasonably ask, "Where did the author's idea to write the book come from?" Well, yours truly had planned to write some type of book or produce a t.v. documentary about the U.S. Government after finishing graduate school in 1996, but a busy start to work in Washington, D.C. delayed it. Those years, 1996-1999, were busy and eventful, to say the least. A move to New York and the "Roaring 90s" economy - which included a return to journalism, his first field - further delayed the project. The clarion call came in 2011: in order to correct the errors, ignorance and outright falsehoods expressed by the Tea Party faction. Simply, for the most part, the faction communicates propaganda that amounts to a pile of lies, half-truths, and distortions – lies that both multiplied and metastasized during the Trump Administration.

Public Investments That Paid Off

And the above is a matter of undeniable fact. The author would hear a Tea Party faction point and then try to square that with the U.S. Government reality he experienced while growing up in his hometown of New Britain, Conn., known as the "hardware city of the world."

New Britain, Connecticut. (Credit: VisitNewBritainCT.com web site.)

Simply, the U.S. Government made life in New Britain, a largely industrial and services city 11 miles southwest of the capital, Hartford, more-humane and more-just. A Tea Party faction member would tout something about the EPA, claiming it hurt businesses, and yours truly would think, "I don't recall that. The EPA's regulations led to clean air in our city, and clean water, and more-environment-friendly uses of both commercial and residential land." Or a faction member would criticize the U.S. civil rights movement or Social Security, and yours truly would think, "That was not my and my parents' experience with the U.S. Government while growing up in New Britain. The civil rights movement led to fair policies in hiring, education, housing and other aspects of life in these United States." And Social Security – because New Britain had at that time and still has today, a very large senior citizen population – lifted many senior citizens in his hometown out of poverty. Similarly, Medicare provided health care to many elderly citizens who otherwise could not afford to purchase health insurance.

A Growing City, A Growing Nation

Further, during the Great Depression, 1929-1941, the federal government provided dozens of social program supports as well as work projects. Later, the federal government helped build an infrastructure (highways, electric grid, water system, sewers) and create a regulated market that enabled New Britain to grow and thrive during the rapid-industrialization period that began in 1941 with the outbreak of World War II. What followed, from 1941 through roughly 1980, was the emergence of a sophisticated, innovative, local economy that manufactured an impressive array of tools, ball bearings, household goods, hardware, and manufacturing machines. At New Britain's peak, 35,000 people were employed in the city, mostly in manufacturing, hence the city's moniker the "hardware city of the world."

They Said It: Presidential Humor 1

The presidency, U.S. Government and the Washington community, in general, produce their share of humor. Hence, without further adieu…

President Abraham Lincoln was once alerted by his staff that his very-effective General Ulysses S. Grant drank whiskey. And not only that, he drank it regularly.

President Lincoln to his staff: “And if I found out what brand he drinks, I’d give it to my other generals.”

**

Will Rogers was a comedian, satirist, humorist and harpooner of many politicians’ egos. Rogers was sort of like Bill Maher, only with the softer, less-harsh humor.

Rogers was no fan of President Calvin Coolidge, a Republican. President Coolidge was known as “Silent Cal.”

Will Rogers: “Silent Cal, he’s a quiet man. He don’t say much. Even when he talks…he don’t say much.”

**

However, President Coolidge was not without humor; and he knew his quietness was the subject of many jokes, but he took it in stride. There’s that famous incident when a man placed a wager that he could get President Coolidge to say more than 2 words at a White House dinner hosted by the president.

Man to President Coolidge: “I just bet $50 that I could get you to say more than 2 words at tonight’s dinner.

Coolidge to man: “You lose.”

**

A reporter once asked President Harry Truman why he walked briskly, as opposed to leisurely?

President Truman: “Because when you walk, you should walk like you have some place to go.”

President Franklin D. Roosevelt meeting with British Prime Minister Winston Churchill, aboard HMS Prince of Wales, August 1941. (Credit: U.S. National Archives.)

President Franklin D. Roosevelt was a U.S. Navy Officer, and later, an Assistant Secretary of the Navy, hence he knew a thing or two about that branch of the U.S. Armed Forces.

Roosevelt had a particular view of the Navy's stance during budget negotiations. To say the least, FDR was exasperated by the U.S. Department of Defense's resistance to budget cuts, and the Navy's resistance, in particularly.

"Then there's the Na-a-a-a-a-vy," President Roosevelt would say. "Trying to cut the Navy's budget is like trying to shape an old pillow. You can kick it and punch it and move it all around, but it doesn't change at all."

**

President John F. Kennedy also appreciated when his wife, First Lady Jacqueline Kennedy accompanied him on political trips, as she was very popular, experienced, and refined in every aspect of public life, from campaigns to policy. Some notable JFK remarks on First Lady:

JFK during a 1961 France trip: "I have been called the man who accompanied Jacqueline Kennedy to Paris."

JFK at a speech in 1963: "Mrs. Kennedy will be down here to speak with you all, very soon. The First Lady is still getting herself together. It takes Mrs. Kennedy a little longer to get ready, but then again, the results are better."

(A solar/wind energy farm in Palm Springs, California. Photo credit: Shutterstock.com.)

Chapter 9: Renewable Energy Program

"The release of atomic [nuclear] power has changed everything except our way of thinking ... the solution to this problem lies in the heart of mankind. If only I had known, I should have become a watchmaker." –Albert Einstein

Yet another issue where progressives and Democrats have the philosophically stronger argument concerns renewable energy – the energy of tomorrow, and, increasingly, the energy of today. There is no denying that human activity by burning fossil fuels has been a major factor in climate change (global warming), if not the no. 1 contributor, since the mid-20th century. (However, fossil fuel burning predated that, of course.) Further, the scientific consensus is that humans must reduce, then eliminate, fossil fuel use, in order to slow, then end, global warming/climate change, and restore the Earth's atmosphere and oceans to their normal temperature ranges. And while there have been prehistoric periods of global warming, measured global temperature increases since the mid-20th century have been unprecedented in rate and scale - pointing to the incontrovertible role of fossil fuel burning by humans.

For its part, the United States, which has a high fossil fuel use per person, can contribute to the goal of cooling the climate by substantially increasing its use of renewable energy, and progressives/Democrats should prioritize that policy change in the new Biden Administration. (In recent years Republicans have shown a stronger interest in renewable energy as a replacement for fossil fuels – it seems like a natural fit, given that several red Republican states are wind and solar havens - but overall the Republican Party remains committed to the full exploitation of fossil fuels, and not fully-committed to green technologies.) With or without Republican support, let's be clear regarding the perspective argued for in this space for progressives / Democrats: the future energy policy *is a renewable energy policy,* and progressives, by prioritizing this issue in the first year of a new Democratic presidential administration, can change the nation's energy policy trajectory, producing a host of benefits, in addition to helping to solve the no. 1 global issue of our time. In fact, renewable energy can achieve a triple-policy win-win-win: 1) slowing then reversing climate change, 2) create good-paying jobs, many of which will not require a college degree, 3) reduce income inequality by creating millions of good-paying jobs to underemployed and down-sized employees/displaced workers.

However, before discussing each renewable energy form, here is a list of each form's contribution to U.S. energy production in 2016: overall, renewables accounted for 12.2 percent of U.S. energy production. Of that renewable segment, hydro accounted for 24.4 percent; other biomass, 24.4 percent; biofuel, 22.4 percent; wind, 20.8 percent; solar, 5.8 percent; and geothermal, 2.2 percent.

Hydroelectric power: The "unsung hero" or "least-sexy" member of the renewable energy category, hydro power currently is the largest producer of renewable energy in the United States. As of 2020, seven U.S hydroelectric plants are among the 50 largest in the world, with some achieving "iconic" or "landmark" status (even if they are not 'hip' among younger adults): Hoover Dam in Arizona, Grand Coulee Dam in Washington state, and the Tennessee Valley Authority are among that august list. Hydro has declined as a percentage of U.S. renewable energy since at least 2004, going from 76 percent to about 41 percent, but that does not mean hydro tech improvements and increased use cannot occur. Both can, especially if next-generation turbines, generators, transformers and energy storage/battery technology become available. Environmental concerns about the impact of large hydroelectric plants are legitimate, but the analysis forwarded here argues hydro's benefits far exceed its liabilities. As the adage goes, *"Cheap, reliable, renewable energy never goes out of style"* - and hydro power is a prime example: in the modern era, it has brought cheap power to tens of millions in the United States, and of course hundreds of millions globally. Accordingly, as the postmodern era continues, progressives/Democrats should find regions of the country where new hydro sites make sense. One classic case study from hydro's history: In the 1930s and 1940s, the U.S. Government's Tennessee Valley Authority (TVA), started by FDR during the New Deal, successfully transformed a depressed region into a successful, thriving, self-reliant economy; development skyrocketed after TVA commenced operations, and the power supply remains overwhelmingly popular in Tennessee among both conservatives and liberals. Point: Hydro can play a substantial role in renewable energy development in the next two decades, probably longer, and progressives/Democrats should look for good opportunities to add to hydro's megawatt (MW) or gigawatt (GW) generating capacity.

Wind power: As popular and as hot/trendy as many, new technologies are now – artificial intelligence (AI) and machine learning are two examples – wind power is almost as hot. Consider this: Wind power capacity *more than tripled* from 2008 to 2019 to more than 105 GW, according to windpowerenergy.com. And here's the real eye-opener: the United States has a 10,640-GW potential wind power capacity. In other words, the nation has not even tapped/utilized 1 percent of its wind power potential. (!) Not even 1 percent! As a newspaper publisher/owner used to say when learning about something phenomenal, which was then usually featured on one of the publisher's news pages: That is a "wow" story. Of course, not every region has sufficient wind to justify the capital investment, but most states do: and, when you take a systematic look at it, more areas of the United States than one would initially think have wind power potential: the Great Plains, Desert Southwest, Mountain Region, and the Pacific Coast are especially strong for wind. Counterintuitively, the wind sector appears in places one does not immediately expect: Texas, for example. Historically noted for its oil/energy and cattle sectors, Texas is the No. 1 wind power generation state in the nation, with 29.4 GW generated in 2019. Iowa (which immediately brings to mind farming, not renewable energy) and California are also major wind power generation states. Of course, the wind doesn't blow all the time, hence wind – at least as of 2020 – cannot be base-load power, given the unreliability factor, until electric storage capacity in batteries/energy cells is such that an area can store enough energy until sufficient wind resumes. But wind power's potential is enormous, largely because...*the United States is enormous*, with huge, open plains and elevated areas that are ideal for wind turbines. In particular, many vast, rural areas of the United States are ideal for wind farms. (Coastline windmills are more-controversial, but even in some of these locales, environmentally-friendly windmills are being constructed.) For all of the reasons above, and job creation, (a subject to be addressed later), progressives/Democrats should push hard for wind power expansion, aided by public funds and tax policy: it is a remarkable, renewable source of energy.

Solar energy: As bright as wind power's future is in the United States, solar power's future may be even brighter. (Pun intended.) As of March 2020, the United States had installed 81.4 GW of solar photovoltaic (PV) capacity. The top states were: 1) California, 27.8 GW; 2) North Carolina, 6.4 GW; 3) Arizona, 4.7 GW; 4) Florida, 4.7 GW; 5) Texas, 4.6 GW; 6)

Nevada, 3.6 GW; 7) New Jersey, 3.3 GW; 8) Massachusetts, 2.9 GW; 9) Georgia, 2.7 GW; and 10) New York, 2.3 GW.

What's more, the areas with the greatest solar power potential are: the Desert Southwest (Arizona, California, New Mexico, Nevada, Southern Utah, Southern Colorado, and West Texas), and Florida (especially the Gulf Coast and Southern Florida), according to the U.S. Department of Energy (DOE). The DOE also expects solar power to be the fastest growing renewable energy source thru 2050.

Solar energy's potential is even more astounding and encouraging. In 2012, the National Renewable Energy Laboratory (NREL), part of the DOE, outlined technically available (or capturable) renewable energy resources in each state. NREL estimated that urban utility-scale photovoltaics (PV) could supply 2,232 terawatt-hours (TWh) per year, rural utility scale PV 280,613 TWh per year, rooftop PV 818 TWh per year, and concentrated solar power (CSP) 116,146 TWh per year, for a total of almost 400,000 TWh per year. (!) That's almost 100 times current consumption of 3,856 TWh in 2011. (!!) In comparison, onshore wind potential is estimated at 32,784 TWh per year, and offshore wind at 16,976 TWh per year, while the total available from all renewable resources estimated at 481,963 TWh per year. In sum, the United States' solar energy potential is beyond enormous – it is gargantuan. Of course, there's a difference between "potential" and "put into use." Solar energy must not only be possible, it has to be transmitted to the areas of the nation that need it; next, like wind power, there is the issue of storage – battery/storage cell technology lags PV technology. (Elon Musk's regular battery/energy storage advances with Tesla, and tech breakthroughs from other companies, will hopefully close that gap in the decades ahead.) Finally, there is the issue of reliability – the sun doesn't always shine during the day, and it doesn't shine at night. For these reasons, solar obviously is not considered as reliable as fossil fuels, but if/when the affordable storage variable has been solved, solar energy use will increase by even larger amounts than current 30-year projections, all other factors being equal. However, even with current energy storage/battery storage technology, there are plans to build many, large solar plants in the United States. Many states have also set admirable, individual renewable energy goals, with solar power being included, in various proportions. For example, Hawaii wants 100 percent renewable-sourced electricity by 2045; California, 60 percent by 2030. Batteries/storage technology, in addition to providing power when solar is not able to generate it, also enable companies/individuals to store excess solar electricity at the site, instead of sending it back to the electric grid.

Solar energy accounted for only 1.66 percent of total U.S. electricity generated in 2018, hence it's important to keep that statistic in mind when evaluating its contribution, compared to other renewables, and to fossil fuels natural gas and oil, and of course, nuclear power. Still, solar remains legitimately exciting for two reasons. First, the United States, like almost all modern economies, wants to phase-out fossil fuel use to slow and end global warming. Hence, the nation must explore any viable, renewable energy resource, and solar is one. Second, solar energy is abundant – almost cosmically abundant, if you will. And, "pulling the lens back," as a mentor of mine frequently says, intuitively, most people know that there is this enormous, abundant, natural energy source right above us: it's literally been staring us in the face for thousands of years. Whether one believes it was created by God, or the product of evolution, or a combination – the task of for humanity now is to find ways to capture, store and transmit its abundant energy and in doing so end climate change and live more in-harmony with nature. Technological advances in PV and battery/storage technology will play a large role in how fast solar energy becomes the dominant energy source. Further, breakthroughs or advances in a room-temperature superconductor would also help, but that may be asking too much. Even so, due to its sheer abundance and ubiquitousness, look for solar energy to play a much larger role in the U.S.'s energy future.

Geothermal, biomass and tidal energy (GBT): The United States leads the world in electric power generated from geothermal energy, with about 16 TWh of electricity produced in 2018, or 0.38 percent of U.S. electricity consumed. Geothermal power is being generated in five states: Alaska, California, Hawaii, Nevada and Utah. What's more, a significant catalyst for geothermal projects is the U.S. Energy Policy Act of 2005, which made geothermal plants eligible for the full federal production tax credit; previously, it had been available only to wind power projects. Meanwhile, biomass generated 58.4 TWh of electricity in 2019, or 1.41 percent of U.S. electricity consumed. Biomass fuel is broken down into two categories: 1) wood, wood pellets, railroad ties, and utility poles, and 2) solid waste, landfill gas, sludge waste, and methane biomass gas. Also, tidal energy/wave power is under development in the United States, off the east coast and west coast and in Hawaii. Projects have progressed beyond research, with sites producing reliable energy; however, most sites have been limited to those where other energy forms are not economically viable, but major installations are planned for the decade ahead.

Taken together, wind power, solar energy and GBT represent an exciting renewable energy frontier. Exciting because they'll help save Earth by slowing, then reversing climate change. Exciting because they'll help make the United States even more energy independent. Exciting because they'll create at first hundreds of thousands, then millions of good-paying jobs. Regarding climate change, again, the statement, "There is no Planet B," may seem simplistic, trite or sound like a cliché, but the reality is….there is no Planet B, right now. And, no matter how much confidence you have in Elon Musk's various space endeavors/space travel to Mars, and Space X, the notion that humans en masse will somehow be able to move to some other planet in the next 40 or 60 years is – farfetched. But that's roughly the amount of time we have to reverse climate change, and some estimates put the time frame at an even shorter period than that. And that means renewable energies – plural – are a must. Further, few doubt the role that nuclear power and legacy fossil fuels will play in the transition, but renewable energy is vital for our planet's health, it's survival, hence progressives/Democrats must "exert every muscle" as the Old Testament says, to usher in that cleaner day and era. Obviously, the new Biden Administration will usher in that era sooner. That new Democratic administration, working in tandem with Sen. Sanders, and a Democratic Party-led U.S. Senate and U.S. House, should go full-throttle to at least double tax credits for solar, wind and other renewables, for individuals, homes, businesses and municipalities. It should also, if necessary, create a separate, new institution, a United States Renewable Energy Authority (USREA), to fund, and, as appropriate, *build entire wind farms and solar farms* in the spirit of the Tennessee Valley Authority. And the nation should have as its goal generating at least 50 percent of its electricity from renewable sources by 2030. The stakes could not be higher. The sector could not be more exciting and invigorating, regarding new ideas, creative solutions and the potential to make a major, "macro" impact on our nation and the world. In fact, it's beyond a "macro" impact: it is the stuff of a civilizational and societal advance. Seriously - what is more important than the health of Earth, as a place habitable for human life, that also protects the animal and plant world, and with self-sustaining ecosystems? In sum, in 2021, the nation is ready for progressive ideas and policies in renewable energy.

Scenario: This policy change would likely draw from scenarios 1 thru 4. In other words, like housing, renewable energy is so important and complex in the United States that it will require ideas in all shapes and sizes, and from many interest groups/stakeholders. What's clear is that, in addition to major tax credits, a new institution - such as the United States Renewable Energy Authority - will be needed to jump-start the sector, after four years of counter-productive and outright benign neglect/destructive policies by the Trump Administration. With that progressive/Democratic majority in 2021, the Biden Administration will make up for lost time, and point the nation toward an enlightened, truly populist, renewable energy era that's in the national interest.

****

The U.S. Government's Area 51

It has been called one of the most impenetrable places - if not the most impenetrable place - in the world.

The place? Groom Lake, which you know as Area 51.

Area 51 - a remote section of Edwards Air Force Base inside the Nevada Test and Training Range, approximately 83 miles (134 kilometers) north-northwest of Las Vegas - has had many names over the decades: Homey Airport (KCTA), Groom Lake, "Dreamland," "Paradise Ranch," "Home Base," and "Watertown." Area 51's current, major purpose is not in the public record. However, based on public documents describing historical use, the base most likely supports the research, development and testing of experimental aircraft and weapons systems, among other projects.

Any rigorous, systematic discussion of Area 51 must break down the base's responsibilities and functions into the confirmed, the plausible and the purely speculative.

The Confirmed

The U.S. Air Force purchased the base's site, situated on the south shore of Groom Lake, a salt flat, primarily to test Lockheed's U-2 aircraft. Other aircraft tested at Area 51 include the D-21, SR-71 Blackbird,

Area 51 - Groom Lake. (Credit: NASA)

F-117 Nighthawk and F-22, among others. Captured foreign aircraft, particularly aircraft made in the Soviet Union, such as the MiG-17F and MiG-21F-13, also were tested there.

The Plausible

It's entirely plausible that the U.S. Government is researching and testing next-generation propulsion systems for aircraft and other transport modes. It's also plausible that exotic, next-gen, energy-based weapons may be undergoing tests at the site, along with related energy research - such as advanced energy forms or energy transmission / superconductivity. It's also plausible that tests that attempt to control the weather may be occurring at / near Area 51.

The Speculative

While there are many hypotheses asserting that contact with an extraterrestrial life form(s) may have occurred at Area 51, there is no incontrovertible evidence that proves it. Similarly, regarding testimonies of reverse-engineering alien spacecraft, experiments with time-travel, the space-time continuum, and teleportation technology. However, the fact that research on the aforementioned has not been corroborated does not necessarily mean that these technologies and/or tests do not exist, only that there is nothing in the public record to confirm them.

Area 51- Restricted Area - No Trespassing

Area 51 is certainly one of the U.S. Government's most important research and testing facilities. Clearly, it's been host for several breakthrough aircraft, and probably other technologies.

Area 51 is also permanently off-limits to the public, with an array of surveillance and other systems deployed to defend it. Feel free to learn more about Area 51 from books, online broadcasts/reports and via documentaries on t.v. or YouTube.com, but do not go anywhere near Area 51.

TRIVIA TEST 4: U.S. CONGRESS

(Answers in Appendix, Page 354.)

1. The U.S. Capital was first located in which city?
a) Philadelphia
b) Denver
c) Houston
d) None of the above

2. One key, unique feature of the Senate is?
a) Limited debate
b) Unlimited debate, unless one can get 60 Senates to vote to "cloture" - limit debate
c) The Senate meets annually in Miami
d) The Senate meets only in the morning

3. Which of the following is true about a bill vetoed by the U.S. president after Congress passed it?
a) Congress must re-debate the bill
b) Congress may re-debate the bill and a simple majority vote overrides the veto.
c) Congress may re-bate the bill and a two-thirds approval of each chamber is needed to override the veto
d) None of the above

U.S. Capitol. (Credit: WikiCommons, public domain, 2007.)

4. What did Alexander Hamilton think of the new, proposed legislature, the new Congress?
a) Hamilton wanted to double the size of Congress
b) Hamilton favored a new Congress appointed by the Supreme Court
c) Hamilton believed the new Congress was too weak
d) Hamilton believed the new Congress was too strong

5. Which power does Congress have?
a) it legislates b) it appropriates c) it investigates d) all of the aforementioned.

6. Which of the following is true about the U.S. Congress?
a) Congress always has had more political power than the U.S. president
b) Congress always has had less political power than the U.S. president
c) The power relationship between Congress and the U.S. president has cycled throughout history
d) None of the above

7. In the U.S. Senate, if there is a tie vote, 50-50, who can vote to break the tie?
a) The Chief Justice of the United States
b) The U.S. Secretary of State
c) The U.S. Vice President
d) The Chairman of the Federal Reserve

8. Which federal agency provides Congress with reports regarding how much a federal program or department is likely to cost in the near future?
a) Congressional Budget Office (CBO)
b) U.S. Securities and Exchange Commission
c) The League of Women Voters
d) None of the above

9. Which of the following has been true about U.S. House districts since 1992?
a) All districts are very competitive, and either party, Democratic or Republican, can win a seat
b) Most districts are non-competitive, dominated by either Democrats or Republicans
c) All districts usually have a strong third party that frequently wins the seat
d) None of the above

10) Which of the following is true regarding campaign funding for U.S. House and U.S. Senate races?
a) It takes up little time - elected officials can raise needed funds in a few days
b) Campaign funding is provided by the U.S. Government
c) It takes up a great deal of time - with some representatives allocating more than 15 percent of their time to fundraising.
d) None of the above

(Workers pour steel, recycled from New York's World Trade Center, into a mold in September 2003; it formed the USS New York bow, at Amite Foundry, Louisiana. Credit: U.S. National Archives.)

Chapter 10: New Manufacturing Era

"It is called the Dow Jones INDUSTRIAL Average, after all." - former Oppenheimer Chief Investment Strategist Michael Metz

The tenth issue where progressives/Democrats have the philosophically stronger argument is manufacturing. Simply, the United States has to start making more goods at home – within the 50 United States. Period.

Globalization - basically the spread of capitalism and free markets to the world – ushered in an era of progress, with many positives. The chief being the lifting of more than 1.5 billion people (and counting) out of poverty, the massive increase in global trade (via exports/imports in both goods and services) among more than 175 nations, and the flow of production to lowest labor cost/lowest overall cost of production countries and sites.

However, globalization has not been without its downsides, and the analysis forwarded here argues that the major downsides for the United States have been: 1) the loss of millions of manufacturing jobs, 2) the hurting of national security, due to the offshoring of vital goods, 3) the reduction in wages paid to many job segments, primary blue collar jobs, due to wage leverage in other countries, 4) the reduction in wealth, due to the U.S. trade deficit, and 5) the undermining of health security, due to the offshoring of PPE to China/Asia and other countries. Simply, all U.S. downsides must be addressed by the Biden Administration; progressives need to go full-bore to reverse this damaging decline in U.S. manufacturing.

Further, it took 10 years for the U.S. economy to recover the more than 1 million manufacturing jobs lost during the Great Recession, 2008-2009, with the sector hitting an employment high of about 18.5 million in February 2020. Shockingly, the coronavirus pandemic in 2020 erased those gains in just three months (!!), with manufacturing employment dropping by 1.1 million to 11.7 million in May 2020, according to the Federal Reserve Bank of St. Louis. In other words, Democrats have an enormous task ahead of them – just in manufacturing: the U.S. job loss total, overall, from the pandemic has been fluid, as of mid-2020, as new data becomes available, and it will be years until we know definitively, but as of mid-year it appears at least 35 million jobs were eliminated from the U.S. economy, during the pandemic's first wave; that total includes for-contract, gig and temporary positions. Hence, few tasks will be as noble as restoring manufacturing jobs and returning sectors back to the United States: there are many sectors that need jobs. Further, pulling the lens back, the long-term story is that, due to globalization, U.S. manufacturing sector employment peaked in 1978 at about 19 million jobs. Now, to be sure, due to productivity increases, better machines, robotics and automation, and technology that's in design but hasn't been deployed yet, it's not likely that U.S. manufacturing employment will hit 19 million in the decade ahead, but, once again, U.S. public policy makers should "exert every muscle" to bring as many factory/goods sectors jobs back home, as possible.

And the reasons are obvious enough. First, again, offshoring of vital goods – including health care goods - undermines U.S. national security. That glaring U.S. weakness from globalization was laid bare during the 2020 coronavirus pandemic. In March 2020, the United States limited travel from/to China to reduce the spread of the coronavirus. Despite that action, COVID-19 infection rates exploded, and hospitals were flooded with cases, and the United States experienced shortages in surgical gloves, gowns, masks, ventilators and other vital medical supplies. Ironically – and ridiculously – the United States experienced long delays in re-stocking these items because most of the PPP sought were made in China (!!) and in other lower-cost manufacturing countries. Simply, that can never happen again, hence progressives/Democrats and the new Biden Administration should on day 1 pass a home-sourcing law for PPE: these vital supplies must be made at home, with federal funds subsidizing them, as needed. Period.

Second, defense supplies must be brought home, to maintain U.S. national security. Period. It made no sense to have PPE offshored – it created a calamity when the pandemic hit – lives were lost to the coronavirus, due to PPE shortages – hence, *it makes no sense to have defense supplies made outside the United States.* None. Relying on China to supply a U.S. defense part? That's crazy. Defense supplies/parts must be made in the 50 states. Period. U.S. national security demands it.

Third, more-broadly, the same theory should apply to manufacturing, in general: bring as many factory goods/manufactured products and processes home, as possible. Simply, the United States must start making things again. Make. It. Here. Period! High-end manufacturing. Low-end manufacturing. Wholly-assembled goods. Partially-assembled goods. Wholesale market goods. Retail market good. Consumer goods. It does not matter: bring it home. The era of companies simply "shipping tasks out to where a good can be made for the cheapest amount" must end. And it will end – if progressives/Democrats demand the change. Critics will argue that because U.S. consumers want the lowest price possible for every good, you can't home source. Nonsense! Some consumers - a segment of the market - will always pay more, and if the consumer good/item is such that its cost doubles

– such as a big-screen t.v. whose price, for example, could increase to $395 from $195. If that is case, the response should be... let the price increase to that amount to ensure that the product is made in the United States. There is no law of nature that states that, *"American consumers have to be able to afford every good or gadget imaginable."* Who created that rule? Point: They don't need to have every good at the lowest price. The notion that everything made under the Sun has to be available to U.S. consumers for pennies is an example of "rising standard of living expectations" of the very worst sort. (Further, many consumer goods do not improve one's quality of life/overall enjoyment of life: more will be said on this topic, at another time.) Also, Americans are resourceful: *they will find cheaper substitutes.* If a new, American-made t.v. is too expensive, then perhaps a used, American-made t.v. is the answer? Ditto for other appliances and big-ticket items. Further, shipping many goods half-way around the world in a container ship is not good for the environment: companies can find ways to make products and parts in the United States, and it will increase the cost of many items, but the goal of creating good-paying manufacturing jobs and supporting local/state economies is more than worth the trade-off. And once Americans realize they will not be sacrificing much from a consumption, standard of living, or quality of life standpoint, they will support home-sourcing. In addition, as noted, those citizens who cannot afford the price increase for some goods will find cheaper substitutes. Earlier, this book discussed solar/wind power as part of the renewable energy revolution/transformation: ALL components for those two, large manufacturing sectors - solar and wind - should be made in the United States. And progressives / Democrats should have as their goal adding 500,000 manufacturing jobs per year. (Minimum plan length: 10 years.) That goal may seem lofty, but to achieve great things, you have to set ambitious goals, and the return of manufacturing to the United States is a great thing: bringing home as many factory jobs as possible will boost the domestic economy and renew U.S. society in a multitude of ways, hence it's worth that ambitious objective.

Fourth, many foreign-made cheap goods...simply have to go. A colleague who has worked in business, human resources, and publishing argues that, "Much of the products that we get from China, from other countries, too, but mostly from China, are junk. It's just junk – stuff that we could do without." Indeed this "lowest price" philosophy that too many Americans have accepted is deeply flawed: it's presented as if there are no liabilities or other costs involved in the consumption choice or policy/program, but in fact there are. Too often, these imported goods are inferior-quality, cheaply-made, junk, be it a tire, a muffler, bedroom dresser, a broom, silverware, a fan, a t.v., a flashlight, dress shoes, jeans, dresses, an auto part, an electric clock, portable radio, coffee table, blender, microwave oven, or plastic food container…it's all just junk. Much of it wears out and/or breaks far too quickly, and one is left thinking, *"Why did I purchase this poorly-made item? Why did I buy with the lowest price being the primary factor?"* Moreover, if Americans truly seek some of these inferior-quality goods, there's no reason why U.S. manufacturers cannot make them here, and U.S. factories would probably do a better job of making the goods. (Further, if it sounds like the author has had several disappointing experiences with foreign-made goods, you're correct: however, time and space limitations do not permit a thorough elaboration of that topic here.) What's more, automated supply lines have reduced the production cost gap vs. foreign suppliers, hence many goods can be profitably-made in the United States, and in the process, we'll bring back hundreds of thousands of manufacturing jobs. Hence, the better policy - one progressives/Democrats and the new Biden Administration should emphasize - is to have high-quality, globally-competitive goods made in the United States: we did it for more than 100 years before globalization – the nation can do it again. In short, the analysis forwarded here argues that Americans will be willing to pay slightly more for most goods, *and substantially more for some goods*, after they know how having those goods manufactured in the U.S. benefits them – vocationally, and economically.

In sum, the analysis forwarded here argues most if not all goods, products and parts must be manufactured in the United States. Accordingly, President Biden should commit to a home-source manufacturing plan that adds 500,000 factory jobs per year for 10 years. America has so many creative ideas to reduce costs via technology, robotics, automation and other means, and dozens of sectors that can yield hundreds of thousands of good-paying jobs. And there are millions of decent, hard-working, versatile American adults who want those jobs. Imagine a United States in which all home furniture, clothing, shoes, appliances, auto parts, vehicles/trucks, buses, industrial goods, business supplies, electronics equipment, smartphones, and computers, etc. are made in the 50 states? Imagine the good-paying jobs these factories would create, and the spin-off/lateral jobs? Imagine the impact on the local and national economies, including the trade deficit and U.S. income and wealth? Imagine the increased self-sufficiency and independence for the United States? Minimally, the United States should have as its goal the home-sourcing of *all defense goods and health care service supplies and medical equipment. The United States must never again be short vital PPE at hospitals because a shipment from China was late: that was a travesty – one that cost lives during the coronavirus pandemic.* For the above national security, health and mercantile reasons, the United States must become "manufacturing self-sufficient." There is no other rational U.S. manufacturing stance in the postmodern world.

Scenario: This policy change would likely draw from scenarios 1 thru 4. In other words, like housing and renewable energy, manufacturing is so important and diverse it will require ideas in all shapes and sizes, and from many interest groups/stakeholders. Tax policy changes are likely, including incentives to home-source sectors that haven't seen the bulk of that sector's goods made in the United States in decades: televisions and clothing/apparel are two sectors that come to mind. Further, the use of tariffs may be necessary, again, on a sector-needed basis: the solar energy (solar panels) sector comes to mind regarding tariffs. The PPE manufacturing/heath care sector may also need special credits to help it expand production of all health care equipment needed to cope with a future pandemic and other threats. Finally, special Congressional attention must be paid to U.S. defense contractors so that no parts lapses occur while finding domestic suppliers.

How To Revitalize U.S. Manufacturing

This book's author grew up in All-American, middle-class / working class, industrial town – New Britain, Connecticut. And, it was there that he developed a strong interest in the national pastime – baseball. But, he also played some basketball, and one day his steel basketball rim cracked, and his Dad sent him and his Uncle Fred to a local factory to get it fixed.

At a workday end, his Uncle Fred took him to a local, huge factory, where a factory worker wearing overhauls greeted the pair. Uncle Fred gave him the hoop and he took it to a welding-iron workstation, and welded it. He did a good job welding it, Uncle Fred paid him, and the two spoke a while. The factory worker's responsibilities included cleaning up the metal shavings and other debris from industrial assembly line work – this portion of the factory-made ball bearings. It was hot, dirty work that contained other risks, but one could see from the factory worker's welding work that he was skillful, experienced and industrious. To be sure, it was not glamorous work, but it provided a living for his wife and three children, and it was good, honest toil, as we used to say. The factory worker mentioned that while growing up, he did not have the opportunity to attend high school and 7th grade was his last, completed grade. The factory worker's salary? About $32,000 per year in 2020 dollars, or about $5,600 per year in 1973.

You read correctly: an individual with a 7th grade education earned a salary high enough - $32,000 - to support a family of five, working in a factory. What's more, in some years, he made more with overtime work, bringing his wages to $35,000 in 2020 dollars.

If you read nothing else about U.S. manufacturing, the above case study would tell you much about the state of U.S. manufacturing today, and why and how it must change: it's highly unlikely that many people with a 7th grade education would be earning $32,000 in a U.S. factory in 2020.

But it occurred in 1973: a person with a 7th-grade education was able to earn enough in a factory – to be sure, toiling at hard, dirty and at times dangerous work – but work nonetheless capable of generating enough money to support his family. And it can occur again – not with the same education level – but with a similar skill set. Now, how can it be achieved?

Training And Make It In The USA

In Chapter 6, we noted how the United States must revitalize higher education and vocational training, by higher education building renovations and expansions, vocational school building, a displaced workers fund, a 21st century education

President George W. Bush greets United Auto Worker employees at a General Motors plant in Missouri, 2007. (Credit: U.S. National Archives.)

fund, and via student loan forgiveness. In short, we need to support college education and vocational training / retraining through a massive, federal re-commitment to U.S. higher education / vocational skills schools and the U.S. Congress's GI Bill after World War II is a good template / example to follow.

In Chapter 10, we noted how the United States must usher in a new industrial era by having most if not all goods – consumer, industrial, commercial, residential – made in the United States. Simply, the nation must have as many goods as possible made in the 50 states! Period! And, especially have all goods required to maintain U.S. national security made here: defense, procurement, health care goods / PPE, technology components, and general manufacturing – both high-end and low-end.

Hence, via a re-commitment to higher education and vocational training and by having factory goods made in the United States, we will both provide the skills needed for these jobs and ensure their domestic manufacture. Further, American businesses and consumers will create the demand for these home-made goods. Most of these jobs will be union jobs, and work rules will apply. Further, the philosophy of offshoring production to lower-cost production countries must be abandoned: find ways to humanely lower production costs within the 50 states!

As such, progressives / Democrats must have an ironclad commitment to have most goods made here and to adding 500,000 U.S. manufacturing jobs per year, for 10 years. High-end, low-end, robotic-based, renewable energy / green tech manufacturing: build it all here - with good-paying jobs, for everyone. Then, like that factory worker in 1973 who went home every day satisfied because he knew he was earning enough to support his family, we will also see a rejuvenated workforce – one probably as upbeat as that child in New Britain, Connecticut was, after his basketball hoop had been repaired.

(Goleta Beach, California with the Santa Ynez Mountains in the background. Credit: Antandrus via WikiCommons.)

Chapter 11: Personal Time Off

"The United States still does not have a federal vacation policy. All Western Europe nations have had them for decades." -University of Connecticut Political Science Prof. Howard Reiter

Another coming-of-age issue in which progressives and Democrats have the philosophically stronger argument is personal time off (PTO). Through

2019, the United States was the industrialized nation with the least amount of personal time off guaranteed by national (federal) law.

In fact, as of October 2020, there was no federal law requiring that companies/employers provide employees with a paid vacation. Not even one week! As a result, some employers do not. Corporate America – at least before the 2020 coronavirus pandemic – generally provided full-time employees with two weeks paid vacation, but again, they are not required to. Combine that with the proliferation of part-time, for-contract workers, "gig" workers, and temporary workers and one can see how vacation time - this very basic of employee benefits - can fail to exist for many U.S. workers, absent a change in federal law. And, that's all the more reason progressives and Democrats should make it a priority in the Biden Administration.

Federal vacation – two weeks: The federal vacation standard should be a minimum of two weeks paid vacation, with all employees having the option of carrying one week per year up to a total of five weeks, into subsequent years. (That eliminates the "use it or lose it restriction.") After five years with the same employer, the employee gets three weeks paid vacation. (The vacation time is exclusive of paid, federal holidays.)

In comparison, here are the paid vacation lengths, in days, for comparable industrialized nations, guaranteed by national law: United Kingdom, 5 weeks; France, 5 weeks; Germany, 4 weeks; Spain, 4 weeks; Australia, 4 weeks.

Paid sick time: Second, paid sick leave is another benefit area where the United States lags. Again, there is no federal law requiring paid sick days. That must change. Further, the 2020 coronavirus pandemic exposed this hole in the U.S. social safety net, and that hole, that deficiency led to horrific consequences. Workers in New York City and in nearby communities became sick, beginning in January 2020, when officials believe the virus arrived in New York state, the workers then spread the virus while working, because staying home meant not being paid. They felt forced – by a system that required one to work every day to survive – to go to work, and as a result they became additional virus spreaders, particularly in the New York City boroughs of Queens and Brooklyn. To be sure, there were other regions of New York where "superspreaders" - an individual or event spreading the virus to 20 or more people - but the bulk of New York state's initial cases stemmed from community spread - people going to work, and spreading the virus to one or two other people, who spread it to one or two others, and so on. Hospitals in these boroughs and in other areas soon became overwhelmed with thousands of COVID-19 patients arriving daily, with intensive care unit (ICU) beds and ventilators soon becoming depleted, as well. Net result: thousands of additional people died, because too many people became sick all at once, and that was largely due to infected workers forced to go to work, due to a lack of paid sick time. How many more lives would have been saved, had the additional infections note occurred, initially? We won't know for certain until systematic studies are done, in the years ahead, but undoubtedly, it's in the tens of thousands. This is known: had sick workers initially remained at home for three weeks or a month, thousands of infections would have been prevented. And that's the main reason progressives/Democrats must make at least 1 week paid sick time a federal law, starting in 2021.

Childcare/day care: Third, day care is another personal time off area that is devoid of comprehensive federal law. For individuals with incomes under $200,000 ($400,000 for married couples filing jointly), under current federal law you will receive a $2,000 tax credit for each qualifying child with a Social Security number. Up to $1,400 of the credit is refundable, meaning if a portion of the credit is left over, after you've paid your taxes, the Internal Revenue Service (IRS) will issue you a tax refund. That sounds impressive, but it simply is not enough. Hence, progressives and Democrats must work to increase this much-needed benefit.

Further, an upgrade of the benefit is long overdue. Conservatives and Republicans talk about being "pro-family" and as having "family values." Nothing could be further from the truth. Republicans 'talk the talk,' but they don't 'walk the walk.' When it comes to substantive public policies supporting childcare, Republicans generally oppose them. Further, progressives/Democrats would welcome them, if they joined the effort to adapt public policy so that it is truly pro-family by support childcare/day care tax credits.

The proposed day care expansion? A $5,000 tax credit for each qualifying child with a Social Security number. Up to $2,400 of the credit would be refundable, meaning if a portion of the credit is left over after you've paid your taxes, the IRS will issue you a tax refund. This will enable more working Moms/parents to obtain the day care they need for their kids, while maintaining their careers. It is a substantial, tangible benefit, and one that's long overdue at the federal level. And the bottom line is this: if you say you are for family values, then support families through public policies!

Maternal leave: Current federal law provides for up to 12 weeks of unpaid leave, for companies with 50 or more employees. Simply, that's not enough, either, and it excludes too many businesses – as most companies in the United States have fewer than 50 employees. Here, progressives and Democrats should provide new, creative solutions to enable Moms/parents to take up to 24 weeks off to care for a newborn. Some form of tax credit should be made available to Moms/parents, with a portion going to the employer to partially offset the company's cost of the maternal leave. Moreover, this is another family/lifestyle area in the United States – again, primarily due to the obstruction by conservatives and Republicans – that is woefully lacking in public policy. Here are the parental leaves of comparable nations: Japan, more than 60 weeks; Austria, more than 50 weeks; Germany, more than 40 weeks; Finland, more than 40 weeks; Sweden, more than 40 weeks; Poland, more than 40 weeks; Italy, more than 20 weeks; France, more than 20 weeks, and the United Kingdom: more than 10 weeks.

And the United States: 0 weeks. None. Zip. That is embarrassing! And it has to change. As mentioned, some form of tax credit should be made available to Moms/parents, with a portion going to the employer to partially offset the company's cost of the maternal leave.

Paid homemaking: This last category of PTO is a trailblazer, of sorts – at least for the United States – and progressives and Democrats should push for it in the new Biden Administration. Homemaking – a parent staying at home to care for children – has never been compensated at the federal level. Many feminists, among others, have long stated that this form of work is part of a category of work that isn't compensated, and that society should compensate it. And, the analysis forwarded here argues, the feminists have the stronger philosophical argument, on egalitarian, sustainable economy and justice grounds. Various options are possible, but progressives/Democrats should lobby for at least this: a monthly stipend, on a sliding-scale, means-tested basis, to enable both: 1) support homemakers who chose that option for that stage of their lives, and 2) have Congress and the nation at-large *finally recognize* and compensate this large category of work that has gone uncompensated. What would be a fair monthly stipend to start at? Most likely, $1,000 to $1,200 per month for couples with incomes under $80,000 per year, decreasing $100 for each $10,000 increase in annual income. Again, it does not compensate all homemaking work, but the point of the program is for society to begin to reward these tasks that have historically been completed by women. Those readers who share the perspective of this book's author will agree: this is a policy change that is long, long overdue. And the analysis forwarded here argues that all enlightened, developed democracies do this. The United States must start: just call it feminism's fourth wave.

Scenario: This policy change would likely draw from scenarios 1 thru 3. Establishing a minimum, national vacation of two weeks, an increased tax credit for childcare/day care, and maternal leave can all be incorporated via legislation and regulation changes. Paid homemaking is similar, but it is a potentially more-sweeping change, in that it may alter the workforce in a bigger way than the aforementioned changes. In other words, we don't know how many mothers (parents) would choose homemaking until that work is at least compensated in some substantial way. One could also make an argument that that scope of change represents a new economic system (scenario 3).

American Ethos: Three Americans, Three Role Models

One would think that with all the goings-on in Washington (and elsewhere) that the nation was going to you-know-what in a handbasket.

Folks, a few pointers or moderate thoughts: there's a lot that is good in these United States – there are many good, hard-working Americans who are striving for a more-perfect union. Hence, when someone starts rattling off "doom-and-gloom" statistics, just remind him or her: the United States has encountered more-serious crises, implemented reforms, and endured. (Think: U.S. Civil War, World War II, and 1968.)

In other words – stay positive – think positive thoughts. If the above doesn't convince you that better days are ahead, pull the lens back. Look at the Earth from space. Note the oceans, the wonder, beauty and enormity of the natural world itself – the diversity of animal and plant life, the ability of the environment to heal itself shortly after we humans end a polluting or eco-damaging practice. One could argue that it's miraculous; it's certainly remarkable. Consider the wonder of just two species: whales and elephants. Each pre-dates recorded human history by a long, long time. Each was around during the Roman Empire. The Roman Empire is no longer around, but the whales and elephants still are. That should tell you something about human endeavors: our landscape improvements, technology and progress must be kept in perspective – and they work best when they are implemented in harmony with nature.

Positive Thoughts – American Role Models

This profile recognizes three all-Americans – three citizens of the United States from days gone by — who serve as civic and personal role models – and as a reminder for those serving in Washington.

Dick Schaap (1934-2001)

Simply, Dick Schaap proved that you could get to the top and still be a good person.

Schaap, a sportswriter, broadcaster, and author wrote the 1968 best seller "Instant Replay" with Jerry Kramer of the Green Bay Packers, covered many other historic sporting events, and, even more important, events in American history.

He wrote a biography of and covered U.S. Sen. Robert F. Kennedy, D-New York, during his rise to national prominence, campaign for the 1968 Democratic Party nomination for president of the United States, and through his tragic assassination in June 1968.

Schaap covered the U.S. Civil Rights movement, Vietnam War and many other weighty events.

In short, no one ascended higher, from a journalism standpoint, than Dick Schaap, but through it all he remained a good person — unpretentious, considerate, reflective. Dick Schaap is a role model for anyone rising in any field.

Pete Rozelle (1926-1996)

One can say with confidence that it will be a long time before the United States – or the modern / postmodern world, for that matter, sees a sports executive like Alvin Ray "Pete" Rozelle, who was commissioner of the National Football League (NFL) from 1960 thru 1989.

Simply, Pete Rozelle proved that you could get to the top and still have lifelong relationships with all of your friends from your entire life.

There's a children's rhyme that goes, "Make new friends, but keep the old; one is silver and the other is gold." Pete Rozelle lived that rhyme. Even though he ascended to the highest levels of corporate power and privilege with an office on Park Avenue in Manhattan, Pete never forgot who he was, where he came from, Lynwood, California and Compton High School, and equally significant, the friends from his Southern California roots – from every station of his life, really.

A brilliant marketing professional who is most responsible for making the NFL one of the most successful sports leagues in the world – he regularly and routinely held parties and social events with the friends of his California youth, his college years, his early-career years as a public relations professional in Southern California, his years as the general manager of the Los Angeles Rams, and so on.

Rozelle is widely known for: 1) his executive decisions that enabled the NFL to fully-harness the promotional power of television – football is, arguably, the perfect game for television – that vastly increased per club broadcast revenue, and that enabled the league to expand, and 2) his commitment to league parity / competitive balance. But Rozelle's finest accomplishment is one you won't read about too often: if you were a friend of Peter Rozelle, you were a friend for life. In other words, despite his many accolades and accomplishments, Rozelle was still just the same "Pete from Southern California" – the same person, with the same values, who knew what friendship is. There is no finer role model for executives than Alvin "Pete" Rozelle.

Wellington Mara (1916-2005)

It's been said that a good day for Wellington Mara was morning Mass at his local Roman Catholic Church, followed by attending to all the duties and responsibilities of his station in life. That's a timeless virtue.

The co-owner of the NFL's New York Giants, Mara was instrumental in the league's revenue sharing arrangement that enabled the league to grow. A big market team with substantial revenue, Mara willingly agreed to sacrifice personal / team wealth to enable smaller market teams – such as one in Green Bay, Wisconsin – to thrive, instituting a system that paid each team the same amount of network television revenue, regardless of city / market size. Without the revenue sharing system and Mara's sacrifice, clubs in towns like Green Bay and Pittsburgh would not exist.

Mara's Giants also won two Super Bowls, in 1986 and 1990, but his enduring legacy, in addition to the revenue sharing decision, was his treatment of players and all involved in the New York Giants organization. Simply, Wellington Mara was concerned about all in his orbit, and then some. For Wellington Mara, the core value was, as the Hall of Fame Giant Defensive End Andy Robustelli poignantly remarked, "Once a Giant, always a Giant." In the roughest of all the major, organized professional sports, Wellington Mara was a gentleman, and his concern for those in his organization was the concern for each individual as a person, not as a player or employee. In other words, a Giant player's retirement marked not the end of his relationship with Mara, it marked the beginning.

Further, no concern was too small for Mara, not even the request of a mother in Connecticut who sought to give as a Christmas gift to an adolescent son, a Giants fan, two tickets so he could attend along with his Dad a Giants game that had long been sold-out that year. The tickets arrived, accompanied by a hand-written note by Mara to the boy's Mom, a week later. (The ticket request was from the author's Mom.)

Simply, there is no finer model for ownership than Wellington Mara.

Three Americans. Three Role Models.

Dick Schaap proved that you could get to the top and still be a good person. Pete Rozelle proved that you could get to the top and still have lifelong relationships with all of your friends from your entire life. Wellington Mara proved that you could be an owner and still be a person of virtue. Schaap, Rozelle, Mara - three examples of an American life well-lived.

(Construction workers. Photo credit: Shutterstock.com.)

Chapter 12: Improved Work Conditions / Universal Worker Benefits

"You need a balance of work, domestic life, and leisure to lead a healthy, happy life." -History Prof. Doris Kearns Goodwin

Another issue where progressives and Democrats have the upper hand concerns work conditions. This is a dimension of modern life/the economy that has been neglected for most of the conservative era/New Gilded Age (1981-2008). Starting in 2009, President Obama implemented a number of reforms that improved employee protections, and increased wages – including overtime provisions. (The Obama Administration and a Democratic Party-led U.S. Congress also, of course, passed the ACA in 2010.) However, many reforms have been reversed by the Trump Administration. Hence, progressives and Democrats must prioritize workplace reforms in the new Biden Administration, to reverse the backslide and restore important protections for workers.

Improved working conditions/public health: Simply, Congress must provide more funding and authorization for the Occupational Health and Safety Administration (OSHA) to substantially and radically improve food processing/meat packing worker conditions.

The 2020 coronavirus pandemic laid bare the unhealthy, poor working conditions at meat packing and meat processing plants – part of a vast army of workers categorized as essential workers: they were a superspreader source of COVID-19. The tightly-packed, cold, damp, indoor plants were perfect grounds for the coronavirus to spread, and the fact that measures weren't taken ahead of time speaks to both the nation's unpreparedness for a virus / disease and the disregard for working conditions promoted and supported by Republican-led state legislatures and a Republican-led Congress. Simply, that laissez faire stance must end with progressive legislation. Democrats should sponsor legislation that increases social distance spaces and implements other public health measures at these dangerous plants. In addition, some plants will have to be closed, due to their inherent public health/public safety risk. Further, automation/other tech advances should be deployed to increase public safety – even if substantial jobs are displaced: U.S. public health and public safety come first.

Workers injury fund: Second, progressives/Democrats must establish a U.S. Workers Injury Fund (WIF), to which all, relevant employers – particularly warehouse operators like Amazon.com and Federal Express – must contribute to. This would be above and beyond the worker's compensation fund that states administer and that employers pay to obtain insurance for. The initial fee: $75 per employee per year, increasing to 0.002 percent (two-tenths of 1 percent) per employee annual salary, depending on company size. Companies with customer service operations would be required to contribute to the fund, as well, due to repetitive-motion injuries these workers suffer. Concomitantly, companies should work with the Occupational Health and Safety Administration (OSHA) to reduce, then eliminate sources of injuries at job sites. The goal of the WIF/OSHA effort would be to encourage companies to eliminate these hazards. With e-commerce deliveries and online shopping increasing at a substantial rate, warehouses, delivery operations, customer service centers and fulfillment centers are becoming "the new factories of the 21st century" – and places where an increasing number of worker injuries are occurring. In the first quarter 2020, U.S. e-commerce sales as a percentage of total U.S. sales increased to 11.8 percent or $160.3 billion, according to the U.S. Commerce Department. Further, e-commerce sales/deliveries show little sign of slowing; in fact, given the pandemic and the quarantine that reduced indoor mall, strip mall and local merchant "store on Main Street" shopping, online shopping surged, as a goods replacement source that maintains social distancing. To be sure, some brick-and-mortar store transactions will return, post-pandemic, but the long-term trend is clear: online sales will continue to take market share away from traditional, physical store sales – which means more warehouse, delivery and customer service work, and more injuries in these lines of work – providing overwhelming evidence for the establishment of the WIF.

Benefits bank: Like the job bank described in Chapter 2, progressives and Democrats must push for a benefits bank in the Biden Administration. In the U.S. economy, there is a large and growing segment of the workforce that does not have benefits, such as health insurance, dental insurance, a 401K / 403B plan, transit benefit, vision care benefit, and medical savings accounts, among other benefits. In the best of all worlds, the trend would be that benefits would spread to these job segments; however, as of late-2020 the trend appears to be steady-state or one indicating a further decrease in the percent of jobs with benefits. (As a side note, in 2019 and early 2020, employees had started to see some increase in real incomes, with wage increases of about 2.5-3.0 percent and benefits, due to a relatively-tight labor market, with a shortage of talent in selected job segments. This occurred after roughly 10 years of sub-normal wage increases, following the Great Recession, 2007-2009.) However, the pandemic that began in January 2020 ended the tight labor market: more than 35 million people had been laid off, as of June 2020. Labor slack – a large pool of unemployed adults seeking work – resumed, and this affect not only salaries offered, but also benefits offered in new jobs in 2020 and early 2021. Hence, the creation of a benefits bank is most timely.

The benefits bank would cover all Americans who work full-time of part-time, regardless of hours per week. If you do not receive benefits at your company, and you work 40 hours per week or 1 hour per week, you are still eligible for the benefits bank. The benefits bank would direct you and help you sign up for ACA health insurance or, at age 55, Medicare, (after it has been expanded from age 65); and provide you with group dental insurance coverage. Equally important, it will offer a 401K/403B program, sponsored and administered by the U.S. Government, so that you can obtain the tax deduction for retirement savings beyond an IRA that every other employee with benefits has. Similar funds would be established for a transit benefit. Basically, the goal of the benefits bank is to ensure that every person working in the United States has the benefits that have become the modern world's standard. Having a benefits banks creates a more-fair workforce system and a more perfect union.

Further, one little-discussed plus from a benefits bank would be more career flexibility and less "job lock." Job lock occurs when an adult in a given job, such as insurance sales, would like to switch fields to, for example, graphic design, at a content firm or art studio, but fails to do so because he/she does not want to go without benefits because the new job doesn't have any. The benefits bank would go a long way toward eliminating that concern/risk. Think about how much workforce efficiency, better-matching and movement would occur – as people seeking jobs that are a better-fit or that tap new skills, knowing that they can change jobs without losing most benefits? The U.S. economy is likely to be enhanced, including the unlocking of worker value-added from new skills deployed and creativity exercised, as a result of more skills being used and more adults in jobs/fields they want to be in.

Another potential benefits solution: have every worker in this category serve as an extended federal employee (EFE), for a set period of time: for example, 5 years. The EFE status would end after the adult obtains a job in the private, public or non-profit sectors or enters college or vocational school for retraining. (However, if after school completion, the adult did not obtain a job in the sectors mentioned, EFE status would resume, for up to 5 years.) The EFE option for the above-mentioned workers would help end the two-tier benefits structure, but it would probably cost more than the benefits bank. It is an idea for the individual 50 states to consider – and state programs would be superseded only by a superior federal program, be it the benefits bank or EFE.

For too long, a two-tier U.S. benefits system has existed. That has to end: all workers should be eligible for the same benefits permitted by the U.S. tax code. It is a matter of basic fairness – intrinsic to democracy, when you think about it. Moreover, in addition to workers in warehouses, delivery operations, customer service centers and fulfillment centers mentioned above, there is an entire mega-field, if you will, of workers in the "gig economy" that historically have lacked benefits, as well, or at least most have lacked benefits, up to late-2020. These workers would greatly benefit from this benefits bank, as well. (Pun intended!). In addition, many for-contract and temporary workers in restaurants, offices, home care/nannies/maids/au pairs, babysitting, landscaping, garbage collection and in other sectors, would receive benefits for the first time, as well.

In sum, the U.S. workforce has been neglected and abused for far too long. Eliminating unsanitary and unsafe working conditions in meat processing and meat packing plants is just the tip of the iceberg. Conditions that endanger public health and worker safety must be eliminated, everywhere they exist. Further, a workers' injury fund must be established for those higher-risk, 21st century economy jobs where workers compensation does not cover them. Third, progressives/Democrats must start a benefits bank to create a universal benefits system for all who work – one that would also help eliminate job lock. All of the above changes will create a more-egalitarian system and a more perfect union.

Scenario: This policy change would likely draw from scenarios 1 thru 3. Many improved work conditions can occur from regulation revisions; others will require new legislation. The workers injury fund would require a new institution, and the benefits bank would require both.

[There is no better sign of the U.S. EPA's effectiveness than these two: wildlife is returning, everywhere, even near the nation's biggest city. Just 28 miles north of New York City, in Novo-Diveevo Russian Orthodox Cemetery in Spring Valley, N.Y., a buck (right) waits for his doe (left). Credit: Joseph Lazzaro.]

Chapter 13: The Environment – Re-thinking Our Relationship With Nature

"Live in each season as it passes; breathe the air, drink the drink, taste the fruit, and resign yourself to the influence of the Earth." - Henry David Thoreau at Walden

Incontrovertibly, another issue where progressives/Democrats have the stronger philosophical argument concerns the environment. Led by the urgent, No. 1 issue of our time - climate change - environmental reform encompasses so many topics, one chapter cannot address them all: time and space do not permit a thorough elaboration here, hence we'll focus on 5 primary topics.

In his 2020 encyclical on the environment, entitled, *"Laudato Si – on Care For Our Common Home,"* published in June 2020 after the coronavirus pandemic had spread to Europe, North America, and South America, and killed more than 200,000 globally, Pope Francis, bishop of Rome and head of the Roman Catholic Church, said his work's goal is to encourage a restoration of the climate and the achievement of justice, and seeks "to enter into dialogue with all people about our common home." The poor and the marginalized in society are Pope Francis's greatest concerns, as they are the ones who suffer the most from economic and environmental injustice. And by extension, an economy and society that focuses on the common good will also be one that lives more in harmony with nature and ensures that everyone lives a dignified life. He makes clear that excesses in consumer consumption, manufacturing, and pollution of the environment, including the fossil fuel-use buildup of greenhouse gases, must be eliminated. We must, the pope said, create a sustainable economy. In fact, the analysis forwarded here argues that Pope Francis's themes are a good outline for progressive environmental policy. A word on each:

The common good: Certainly public policies, and many progressives / Democrats would argue, many private sector policies, should have as their primary goal the common good. Further, climate is a common good: there's very little that humanity can proceed with, if it does not ensure the health of the Earth. Therefore, corporate policies, public policies and individual actions must be aligned with the common good, as often as is possible. Further, Pope Francis is careful to point out that future generations are part of the common good; hence, by extension, policies must be sustainable for the decades ahead. In addition, the pope is also clear in that an economy (nation) where poverty exists is not one that operates for the common good. All of the above implies substantial changes in business and public operations in the United States, and the outline is clear: just wages for everyone, less or no pollution, less consumption, more recycling, an end to fossil fuel use, and policies that serve the interest of all (the common good).

Greenhouse gases: The scientific consensus is specific and well-known – human burning of fossil fuels is a major source of greenhouse gas buildup and the climate's warming in the 20th century/21st century, and especially in the last 80 years (roughly since the end of World War II). True, other factors contribute to climate change, but fossil fuel use is the major one and one humans can reduce, then eliminate. It is no mystery that as China, among other nations, industrialized - and repeated the mistake of the West and burned fossil fuels pervasively - the climate warmed even more in the 20th century's second half than it did in the first half. The policy Democrats should follow here is clear, one in-sync with Pope Francis: society must shift to renewable sources of energy, over time – and the sooner, the better. How much time does humanity have to make the shift? Time and space do not permit a full debate here about the possible "tipping point" period/year for climate change; that point - when the Earth's oceans and atmosphere warm to a point where it cannot cool to pre-fossil fuel burning temperature levels, causing all ocean ice to melt, with massive sea level rises – is not precisely known, but the important point is that that decade (year) is approaching, hence global warming must be reduced, then reversed by phasing-out fossil fuel use. This book has discussed a myriad of renewable energy sources (Chapter 9) – from wind to solar to tidal – and on to that, we add: "All of the above, and more." On to the aforementioned "rainbow of renewable technologies," the analysis forwarded here argues the United States must deploy extraordinary creativity to develop the renewable energy systems (and energy storage systems) that will finally break the nation's and then the world's reliance on and use of fossil fuels. Progressives/Democrats and the Biden Administration will be ready for the task, and in no way should they let the standard Republican rhetoric of easily-available oil and coal distract them. Finally, natural gas and nuclear power can play a role, but only as a transition to the renewable energy world and future.

Manufacturing, consumption, residential changes: Major changes, obviously, also must occur in manufacturing, consumption, and residential life. Business executives, scientists, researchers, policy wonks, homemakers, and consumers, in general, must find ways of reducing chemicals and plastics, and increase recyclable material use, among many other changes. In addition, there has to be a shift in resources away from consumption and more toward quality-of-life. To be sure, there won't be a 'one-size-fits all communities' formula – i.e., a White Plains, New York lifestyle may differ substantially from one in Missoula, Montana - but some examples would include: 1) a town that chooses to attract a community college/vocational skills school as part of a chamber of commerce-led grand list expansion program, instead of trying to attract a logging company; 2) a county that sells land leases to wind farm/solar farm operators; 3) a county that invests in a technology park, in an effort to attract a critical mass of robotics / machine learning / artificial intelligence, data storage and fuel-cell technology firms; 4) a city that chooses to ramp-over a center portion of a 3-mile interstate that travels directly through the city's center, to create a tree-ringed park, recreation fields, walking/cycling and jogging paths, picnic areas, and other outdoor recreation points connected to nature; 5) a town that develops a 500-unit condominium complex for all age groups, with a 100 percent renewable/self-sufficient energy plant, with solar energy sold back to the power grid; 6) a state that builds 5 regional vocational skills schools teaching electrical repair, plumbing, carpentry, solar panel construction, auto repair, home construction, masonry/bricklaying, interior design and comparable vocational skills to state residents, tuition-free; 7) a shoreline town that installs 50, 300-foot windmills, positioned so that they capture the most wind, but do not interfere with the activity or enjoyment of the town's beach; 8) a town that combines a high school football/baseball/soccer/lacrosse/track field that also features a sliding roof in the winter that has solar panels, and creates a hockey/recreation skating rink; 9) a county aquatics center that is part winter aquatics and summer botanical garden, including solar heating for both, and 10) a city that features an electric bus network that is fully-automated, and can take any resident to any point in the city, at any hour.

Again, the possibilities for reform are almost limitless. The key is to implement progressive ideas that achieve sustainable communities, that enhance the quality of life of all, while reducing, then eliminating pollution and waste; in other words, policies in the common good.

Soil, mountain, vegetation, fresh water and sea preservation: Here, the task for reform is as large as the oceans, literally. Everything from massive tree replanting, habitat restoration, cleaning the seas of debris, limitations on fishing to enable the oceans to replenish themselves, limiting river water use to enable ecosystems to regenerate, and reducing/eliminating mining to restore natural landscapes, must be undertaken. Concerning oceans, numerous studies have confirmed that with changed practices, the oceans can recover by 2050. These changed practices include: 1) protecting species, 2) harvesting wisely, 3) protecting spaces, 4) restoring habitats, 5) reducing pollution, and 6) mitigating climate change. What's more, the 2020 coronavirus pandemic's initial stage (January-June 2020) created a fishing hiatus, as demand for seafood collapsed globally, after restaurants and hotels closed. Scientists and researchers believe the hiatus will help regional fisheries recover, with the extent of the recovery depending on how long fish boats are idled, and the long-term consumption patterns for fish. The last major fishing hiatus occurred during World War II (1941-1945) and that led to a major rebound in fish stocks. The moral and the logic of the above is clear: oceans can recover, with best practices, including no over-fishing. The coronavirus pandemic-induced hiatus will give us a hint of the recovery possible for oceans/other water bodies, and progressives/Democrats should leverage these insights to encourage more-sustainable fishing and consumption patterns.

Similarly, progressives/Democrats should fervently push for tree planting, and other natural landscape restoration projects. On the former, trees are not the only factor in increasing oxygen/decreasing carbon dioxide, and they should not be viewed as an excuse for nations, including the United States, to not reduce greenhouse gases from fossil fuels: every nation must reduce fossil fuel use. Combined with decreased fossil fuel consumption, adding trees, in addition to increasing oxygen and providing wonderful areas for ecosystem development and biodiversity, will, at minimum, buy time for humans to reduce/eliminate fossil fuel use. On the latter, there are always tensions between undisturbed landscapes in their original form and parks/land used for recreation, but progressive planners will need to identify the restoration model that best suits that particular national park/state park or recreation area. Again, one park restoration plan will not fit every location/case study.

A sustainable economy is a just economy: Pope Francis was adamant in that there cannot be a just, sustainable environment or economy, if social justice does not prevail. A sustainable economy is one that enables everyone to live a dignified, humane life. The pope is clear in arguing gross domestic product (GDP) must not prevail over human life, health and dignity.

Further, Pope Francis on April 2020 said the coronavirus pandemic revealed both our individual and collective sins/mistakes against the Earth:

"We have sinned against the Earth, against our neighbors, and ultimately against the Creator, the benevolent Father who provides for everyone, and desires us to live in communion and flourish together." Being made in the image of God, he said, means "we are called to have care and respect for all creatures, and to offer love and compassion to our brothers and sisters, especially the most vulnerable among us, in imitation of God's love for us, manifested in his Son Jesus, who made Himself man to share this situation with us and to save us." He added: "We see these natural tragedies, which are the Earth's response to our maltreatment. I think that if I ask the Lord now what he thinks about this, I don't think he would say it is a very good thing. It is we who have ruined the work of God."

Progressives/Democrats know that marginalization and alienation of workers, of the poor, of anyone, eventually destabilizes society – and has sometimes led to extreme reform movements, when only minor reforms were needed to create a more-just, more egalitarian society in which all can flourish. Accordingly, the pope's environmental encyclical should energize and motivate progressives/Democrats to seek policy changes that sustain the environment and that enable all citizens to develop their talents, abilities and skills and to be compensated fairly for them with a living wage/just wage.

In sum, through the actions of progressives/Democrats, those who share the perspective of this book know that we must re-think and re-envision our relationship with nature: there must be a change in humanity's relationship with nature, so that the economy is more-just and sustainable; the two are linked, as Pope Francis underscored. Further, being a steward of environment is inadequate: we saw in the previous 120 years, how that stance led to terrible environmental mistakes. Progressives/Democrats must push for U.S. public policies that enable humans to live in harmony with nature. Policies must be focused on the common good, eliminate greenhouse gases, implement major changes in manufacturing/consuming/living, protect and sustain every Earth asset, and enable all members of society to live a decent, dignified life, with universal recycling and without depleting resources. That is an awesome environmental task, one that obviously won't be accomplished in the first four years of the new Biden Administration, or in one or two decades, for that matter. But with the election of progressives/Democrats in 2020, that wholesale shift in U.S. environmental policy – an environmental policy transformation, really – must begin, as there is no alternative. As noted earlier, *"There is no Planet B."* Climate change is real. We must implement sustainable resource use policies. Doing so creates the better world that we seek and that we require, and also, for the United States, creates a more perfect union.

Scenario: This policy change would likely draw from scenarios 1 thru 4. It's implied that the aforementioned reforms for the new stance toward the environment will require ideas and programs of all shapes and sizes, and from every sector - public/private/non-profit. We will need to pass new regulations, revise current ones, and change the tax code (including tax credits). And, it's possible that a new institution (scenario 4) will have to be created to help with the transition by families/individuals, work sites and leisure opportunities to live and exist more in-harmony with nature, to let nature blossom - policies that appreciate nature for its splendor and diversity, and that above all do not harm it. (On a personal note, it is hard for yours truly to look at nature, both the animal world and fauna/vegetation and not think of a creator God. That does not mean yours truly does not accept evolution – he does – it's just that with nature's life, beauty, diversity and awesomeness – it's hard not to think that a supreme being, a creator God, set it in motion. Basically, yours truly is in-sync with Pope Francis regarding that.) And there are other insights on the environment that Pope Francis expands on that, the analysis forwarded here argues, progressives/Democrats and the new Biden Administration would be wise to incorporate into the U.S. environmental policy. Those insights will help the United States, and hopefully the world, make the 21st century, the century when humanity repaired the damage it had done to nature and began to live in-harmony with the beautiful environment that is Earth.

TRIVIA TEST 5: U.S. HISTORY

(Answers in Appendix, Page 354.)

1. A key moment in U.S. revolution history was:
a) Washington crossing the Connecticut River
b) Washington crossing the Delaware River
c) Washington crossing the Mississippi River
d) None of the above

2. Which of the following did not write one of the Federalist Papers?
a) Ben Franklin
b) Alexander Hamilton
c) James Madison
d) All of the above wrote a Federalist Paper

3. Which most accurately describes why Washington, D.C. became the capitol of the United States?
a) The Potomac metro area was well-developed when the capitol was moved there
b) The climate is cool and dry - ideal for politicians
c) It was a compromise between Ben Franklin and Sam Adams
d) It was a compromise between Alexander Hamilton and Thomas Jefferson

4. Which chief general of the Union Army did President Lincoln replace in 1862?
a) Jim Smith
b) Dave Smith
c) George McClellan
d) Roger Sherman

5. When Pearl Harbor was attacked on December 7, 1941, what function did the Hawaii location serve?
a) It was a tomato farm
b) It was a U.S. Navy base
c) It was an iron and steel commerce area
d) All of the above

6. World War I was billed as which of the following?
a) The war to end all wars
b) The war to end poverty
c) The war to develop Latin America

d) None of the above

7. The president who created the Central Intelligence Agency (CIA) was?
a) Woodrow Wilson
b) Ronald Reagan
c) Jimmy Carter
d) Harry Truman

8. What can we say about President John F. Kennedy's Vietnam policy at the time of his assassination in November 1963?
a) Kennedy definitely would have escalated the war had he lived
b) Kennedy in 1961 supported advisors for the war, but by the end of 1963 had pretty much decided against escalating the war with U.S. troops
c) Kennedy favored putting together a United Nations coalition to end the war
d) None of the above

President John F. Kennedy, March 1962. (Credit: U.S. National Archives.)

9. The last president to balance the U.S. Government's budget was?
a) Ronald Reagan
b) George W. Bush
c) Bill Clinton
d) Jimmy Carter

10) Which of the following is true regarding the Washington, D.C. Metro subway system?
a) It was paid for by France
b) It was paid for by Cuba
c) It was paid by Spain
d) None of the above

(The Pentagon, the U.S. Department of Defense Headquarters in Arlington, Virginia. Photo credit: U.S. Department of Defense.)

Chapter 14: U.S. Department of Defense / Defense Policy

"I would be proud to lead you fine men into battle, anytime, anywhere." –U.S. Army General George S. Patton

Historically, U.S. defense policy has not been an issue where progressives and Democrats have had the advantage, but that will change in the decade ahead.

Aided by progressives/Democratic majorities in Congress, the first thing the new Biden Administration should do is restore the good word of the United States abroad, with our democratic allies/alliances and treaties. Under Trump, our allies could not count on us to defend democracy and human rights abroad. In fact, our allies could not count on the United States even defending them against our adversaries, particularly Russia. Hence, the first repair work task is the North Atlantic Treaty Organization (NATO). The United States must convince NATO members that the U.S. will defend them against any threat - conventional, nuclear, terrorist/asymmetrical, cyber or otherwise – and reaffirm our commitment to this historic, democracy-supporting alliance. And the United States should add troops to Germany and in other nations and increase military aid to Europe to do so. Additional missile deployments should be considered, as required, to telegraph to Russia that NATO is getting stronger and there is no turning back the clock on democratic gains in Western Europe or Central Europe. Further, the United States must also triple aid to Ukraine – both economic aid and military aid – to enable it to defend its democracy from Russia-supported rebelling provinces in eastern Ukraine. The U.S.'s goal should be a firm commitment to free markets and democracy in Ukraine, with the hope of a negotiated settlement; but under no circumstances will permanent Russian troops be tolerated as part of any agreement. To be clear: the goal is a peaceful Ukraine, but one does not cede land, nor seek to take more land in the east or 'surround' Russia.

Second, progressives/Democrats must inform our key allies in the Pacific – Japan, Australia, South Korea, Taiwan, India, New Zealand, the Philippines, and Malaysia – that the era of "unchecked China expansionism" is over. China, by building man-made islands that serve as military bases, is attempting to claim that international waterways are Chinese waterways. China is also undertaking other non-peaceful measures that have increased tensions in the region. The United States must make clear on day 1 of the new Biden Administration that the United States seeks the peaceful, mutually-agreeable resolution of all differences in the region, but under no circumstances will China be able to block international waterways, or claim land that is not their's. And the United States should be prepared to deploy additional U.S. Navy assets to let China – and any other party – know that free, safe waterways under international law will prevail in the 21st century.

Third, regarding South Korea/North Korea, progressives/Democrats should obviously push for a resumption of multi-lateral talks (North Korea, South Korea, China, Japan, United States), aimed at independent monitoring of North Korea's nuclear program. The program must remain for civilian use, only. (Electric power generation.) The United States should make it clear that no change in international sanctions can occur, so long as North Korea does not agree to the aforementioned.

Fourth, concerning the Middle East, the United States should re-affirm its commitment to a two-state solution for Israel and the Palestinian Authority. The goal is two states, contiguous, living in peace, hopefully with trade occurring between the two - to enable all citizens of each country to fulfill their potential and flourish. Regarding the Syrian Civil War, the United States should re-affirm its commitment to a negotiated settlement among all parties.

Fifth, concerning Central America, the United States should provide aid to Mexico to help it prevent border crossings and to enable all refugees to live dignified, humane, lives either in Mexico, their home country, or in the United States. This will not be a simple or quick policy change: it will require at least $20 billion per year and address fundamental issues that create poverty in Latin America, and that prevent Mexico from stemming the flow of immigrants to both its country and the United States. But do not misunderstand: the U.S.-Mexico border must remain secure, however the United States under the Biden Administration must end the policy of separating children from parents at the border. Migrant families must remain intact and *the United States must remain an asylum for refugees* who are fleeing poverty, drug wars, gangs, other violence and political persecution in their home countries. In other words, the United States must re-commit to its role as a beacon for all, as "the Mother of Exiles," as poet Emma Lazarus so aptly phrased it in her sonnet, "The New Colossus" – which is located at the base of the Statue of Liberty in New York Harbor. The United States is *the nation of nations* and must remain the last refuge for all seeking asylum.

Below is a breakdown of each U.S. Department of Defense operation by branch, with comments on strategy and operations:

U.S. Army: Proposed Fiscal 2022 (F2022) budget: $230 billion.

In the modern era, the U.S. Army's philosophy has been to be strong enough and equipped enough to fight two, major, regional wars at the same time. Progressives/Democrats should modify that doctrine, slightly: propose a budget that can fight one, major, regional war, and ramp-up to fight a second one, within three months. The above is not to imply that major threats are decreasing – Russia and China can at any time present a major threat to Central/Western Europe and South Asia, respectively, but the more likely scenario is one or no major wars, hence the doctrine modification. In addition, the resources made available from this shift can be deployed to more rapid-response, commando groups. Future armed conflicts and skirmishes are likely to take that shape: jump in with 2,000 or 5,000 troops/paratroopers/special operations forces, get the job done, then jump out, after a week, a month, or few months, etc. Another change concerns tech: U.S. troops should have every, essential tech option to help them win and survive in battle, but that technology *must be durable.* One Soviet/Russian Army equipment characteristic that the United States should mirror concerns durableness. During the Cold War, rarely did the Russians have the most sophisticated weaponry, but the durability of their machine guns, tanks, armored carriers, intercontinental ballistic missiles (ICBM), and rocket launchers, was renowned. The classic example: the automatic machine gun, the AK-47: its reliability under harsh and extreme conditions set the standard for modern equipment. U.S. Army tech improvements should follow the same theme: tech needed to win in battle, but tech that requires little maintenance.

U.S. Navy: Proposed F2022 budget: $240 billion.

Without question, progressives/Democrats should lobby for the U.S. Navy to deploy more ships – and if necessary, shift a carrier group – to the Seventh Fleet in the Pacific Ocean, and by extension, bolster the Third Fleet off the Pacific Coast of the United States. And the reason is obvious enough: China's aggressive stance. China must be discouraged from attempting additional, aggressive actions in international waters next to its country. That, obviously, will require additional U.S. assets in the region. Further, at least initially in the 21st century, the U.S. Navy must be capable of fulfilling both modern and postmodern roles: large-scale warfare and special operations/strike missions in regional conflicts, respectively. How many ships will be required to fulfill this complex, dual role? More than the roughly 355-ship fleet the U.S. Navy is currently operating – probably closer to 375 ships. The Gerald R. Ford-class upgrade of aircraft carriers will proceed, as scheduled - with at least two more deployed during the 2020-2029 period. The submarine force would remain at a minimum of 71, with Virginia-class replacements proceeding as scheduled. Further, the analysis forwarded here argues that progressives/Democrats should let the U.S. Navy determine the number of aircraft carrier groups, as long as the aforementioned shift to the Seventh Fleet occurs, for the China concern, with total carrier groups topped at 10. To be sure, in the decade ahead, debate will invariably continue on the effectiveness and utility of aircraft carriers in an increasingly-connected, high-tech world. True, aircraft carriers are big, expensive assets. But in terms of force projection and the ability to send a signal to all within 1,000 miles that "peace should prevail" – few defense assets match the aircraft carrier, including its strike group. The bottom line for the U.S. Navy? It is likely to play an enhanced role in the initial decades of the 21st century, as ocean-defense comes to the fore, assuming China continues to try to assert itself, and attempt to seize territory from what is international territory/water. Of course, the hope is that China won't, and instead choose to seek international dialogue and United Nations debate to peacefully resolve all international disputes. But China probably won't, hence the tack here is, "Hope for the best, but prepare for the worst, regarding the Pacific," and that means equipping a roughly 400-ship U.S. Navy.

U.S. Air Force: Proposed F2022 budget: $230 billion.

The U.S. Air Force's mission is not likely to change in the decade ahead, but it will continue to evolve. The five core tasks: 1) air superiority, 2) global integrated intelligence, 3) rapid global mobility, 4) global strike and 5) command and control.

The U.S. Air Force boasts 5,369 aircraft and about 330,000 active-duty air personnel, and 145,789 civilian personnel. It's been said that we've been asking the Air Force to do too much, with too little, for decades, but the Air Force continually outperforms….and few expect that pattern to change.

That said, in the decades ahead, absent a bump up by Congress in the Air Force's budget beyond the $230 billion called for in this book, the Air Force may finally receive the additional material support needed to fulfill its mission - via technology. Notwithstanding the F-22 raptor and F-35 Lightning II fighter planes, look for technology - and in particular drones and other non-manned aircraft (NMA) - to play an increasing role in air defense and conflicts. Don't misunderstand - this is not to undervalue the manned-mission: the manned-mission is a staple and will remain vital to Air Force operations. But know that in the decade ahead, where NMA and drones can successfully perform missions and tasks, they will be deployed. The key is the result - success – and few would disagree with the theory behind it: why risk a casualty, possibly a death, when a drone and/or NMA can complete the mission/task? Moreover, as in other fields where technology has been deployed, in the Air Force it will produce the added benefit of freeing up personnel for other tasks. That, plus the versatility and enhanced human safety make the deployment of the new technologies worth their weight in gold.

Further, that new technology will help the Air Force continue to do what it does best: projection. Along with the U.S. Navy's aircraft carrier, no aspect of U.S. defense projects to a potential aggressor/adversary nation than the sight of a B-52 bomber in flight, or, in the case of the B-2 stealth bomber, the sight of the B-2 at one of its home bases, as it's invisible to radar in flight. A potential adversary knows that the U.S. can strike from the air quickly, can defend its territory, and can deploy air assets to forward zones relatively quickly. That does not provide 100 percent protection – no defense strategy can provide that – but it does send a signal to adversaries that an attack on a U.S. interest is ill-advised and will likely result in unacceptable losses and damages to the aggressor. That is not a small factor in preserving the U.S.'s peace and security. The other factor is "the unknown." As with the other branches of the U.S. Department of Defense (DOD), potential adversaries must not overlook the unknown – a heretofore unknown Air Force technology or aircraft unseen in previous conflicts. Like the U.S. Navy's submarines, the Air Force's non-discussed new aircraft and/or weapons systems combine with projection to plant in the mind of potential adversaries that, if they strike, they are not only fighting weapons they know about, but they'll likely be fighting against an as-yet, unpublicized, next-generation technology.

U.S. Coast Guard: Proposed F2022 budget: $15 billion.

Regarding the "Fifth Side of the Pentagon," the analysis forwarded here argues the U.S. Coast Guard (USCG) deserves a substantial increase in funding. The Coast Guard is the "unsung hero" or "unsung branch" of the U.S. Department of Defense. In the post-September 11 world, the Coast Guard has taken on increased homeland security roles, hence they are better-known now, but they still perform tasks that often receive too little recognition, given the risks and danger involved. The Coast Guard is involved in coastal defense, maritime law enforcement and search and rescue. Unlike other branches of the U.S. Armed Forces, the USCG is authorized to carry firearms and to make an arrest, without a warrant, for any offense against the United States committed in the officer's presence, or for a felony; the USCG also is authorized to perform any other law enforcement duty that the Secretary of Homeland Security may designate. Moreover, even though defense and law enforcement tasks have increased in the postmodern era, it is the search and rescue role many Americans may see them perform. And the analysis forwarded here argues that latter reason makes the USCG's F2021 $11.5 billion bang for the buck, and it's why yours truly would like to see progressives/Democrats increase it to at least $15 billion in the new Biden Administration in F2022.

There is no finer sight than a U.S. Coast Guard helicopter or ship rescuing another person at sea or in/near another body of water. Readers have probably watched t.v. news reports of an adult or a family that may have made an unfortunate choice, or perhaps the weather changed or luck turned against them, and they were in distress. But here comes the U.S. Coast Guard, sometimes in 10 F / -12 C degree weather, or colder, or in a snowstorm, or amid rough seas: a Coast Guard service person in a metal rescue basket is lowered by the helicopter, to gather adults and children into the basket to safety, and transport them to other, attending rescue personnel/first responders on the mainland, and from there to medical attention, as needed. It is a sight that never gets old! It is always exhilarating! Truly, it is a sight that is always uplifting, always gratifying, and that restores one's faith in humanity.

And know this, the men and women of the U.S. Coast Guard will risk their lives to protect you and your family – placing themselves in extreme danger – even amid the worst weather one can imagine - to save your life, and the lives of your loved ones and friends. And, yes, if they can reasonably undertake it, they'll even save your dog / pet.

The USCG operates about 250 coastal and ocean-going vessels, 1,650 smaller boats and 201 helicopters and fixed-wing aircraft. In fact, if counted as a separate navy, the Coast Guard would be a top 15 global navy.

As of 2018, the Coast Guard had 40,992 active-duty personnel, 7,000 reservists, 8,777 full-time civilian employees, and 31,000 auxiliary members.

Together, they form a dedicated, cohesive, close-knit community that, again, does not receive a great deal of publicity/notoriety – at least not compared to the U.S. Army, Navy, Air Force and Marines. But, as described above, their work is invaluable. The USCG goes where many won't or can't: it is the selfless work the nation relies on.

U.S. Marines, U.S. Navy Seals, U.S. Army Green Berets and other Special Operations Forces: Proposed F2022 budget: about $80 billion.

Due to their highly specialized operations, progressives/Democrats will leave reviews of and revisions for these forces in the hands of the experienced military service professionals who manage them, save one: as noted, it is highly likely that in the postmodern, pos Cold War era, asymmetrical warfare, such as commando-style operations and raids, will occur more than conventional conflict. Combat and force use is likely to be more-focused, with less time commitment and overall force deployed, as in the elimination of terrorist cell: "Go in, kills the bad guys, capture those bad buys that survive, jump out." Or: "Deploy a select number of troops to neutralize an insurrection or an aggressor group against an ally, eliminate the threat, or at minimum eviscerate its capability, then return home."

Nuclear Triad: Proposed F2022 budget: undetermined.

The United States's nuclear triad originated in the 1960s. Progressive / Democratic reforms for the triad proceed from President Dwight D. Eisenhower's adage/instruction in his farewell address: *"Every gun that is made, every warship launched, every rocket fired signifies, in the final sense, a theft from those who hunger and are not fed, those who are cold and are not clothed."* No truer words were spoken by a U.S. president regarding both the defense budget, its role in a democratic republic, and the impact of excessive defense spending. That said, we still must have an adequate defense. Accordingly, progressives and Democrats in the new Biden Administration should push for a new strategic arms reduction treaty (START) – call it START V. The United States currently has about 6,200 nuclear warheads; Russia, about 6,500. The parties should seek to reduce these totals to 5,000 in 2022, then 3,000 in 2024. In other words, the U.S. goal should be a nuclear force adequate to deter, while avoiding a senseless, costly, counter-productive nuclear arms race. Accordingly, any action or summit that gets the United States closer to President Eisenhower's goal is a victory for the nation.

U.S. Cyber Warfare Force: This proposed, expanded branch of the U.S. DOD will be discussed in Chapter 15.

Scenario: The policy changes listed above would likely draw from scenarios 1 and 2. There are enough institutions, processes and demonstrated contractor relationships within the U.S. Department of Defense to implement the aforementioned reforms, except for the U.S. Cyber Warfare Force, discussed in Chapter 15.

U.S. Veterans Of The Korean War: Forgotten, No More

By Joseph Lazzaro

It has been called "the forgotten war." However, after long-delayed recognition and a Washington, D.C. memorial, the Korean War - and more important - the U.S. Veterans who fought on the Korean peninsula to keep South Korea free and the United States safe - one can finally say that these men and women who fought so nobly, 1950-53, are getting their richly-deserved credits.

U.S. At Mid-Century

Perhaps because it came after the tectonic World War II that encompassed the existential threat posed by Adolph Hitler and Nazi Germany and imperialist Japan, and perhaps because it was initially described as a "police action," Americans did not fully appreciate the sacrifice of the U.S. Armed Forces in the Korean War. The term police action was a distortion - it was not about catching petty thieves and cars traveling above the posted interstate highway speed limit. It was a civil war between free South Korea and communist North Korea that served as a proxy war between the United States and Soviet Union during the Cold War. In all, 54,246 U.S. servicemen and women were killed in the war, with another 92,134 wounded.

U.S. Armed Forces at Chosin Reservoir, N Korea. (Credit: USNA.)

What's more, Allied deaths totaled 178,426; the North (China, North Korea, and the Soviet Union) lost 367,283. Hardly a "police action."

Korean War Vets: Fulfilled Their Mission

But when the Armistice was signed on July 27, 1953 at Panmunjom, North Korea, the U.S.'s/Allies' objective had been achieved: South Korea remained free and democratic, with the 38th Parallel separating a still-free South Korea from communist North Korea. North Korea's goal to unite the peninsula under communism had not been achieved. Quite the opposite: under democracy and free markets, South Korean went onto become a dynamic, strong, vibrant economy – one of the "Asian Tigers" that continues to register impressive GDP growth and product / service innovation today. To be sure, there would be many more conflicts and flashpoints during the Cold War (most notably in Vietnam, Cuba, and Berlin) as the decades

Korean War Veterans Memorial. (Credit: Library of Congress, Carol Highsmith.)

progressed, but readers should know this about the Korean War: U.S. Veterans achieved their mission – the United States and the West's goal that there would be no communist expansion outside China and North Korean into broader Asia, except in Vietnam, was achieved. Japan, Australia, the Philippines and many other nations remained free. Communist China and the Soviet Union were further put on notice: the U.S. and West will fight you for every block and farm field, if you try to expand further in Asia.

By Familial Tie, A Personal War

For this book's author, the Korean War was a personal topic of considerable interest, by virtue of his father, Joseph S. Lazzaro, who fought in it as a member of the U.S. Army. However, save for a story or two about basic training and Korea's terrain, Dad didn't talk about the Korean War very much while my sister and I were growing up in the 1970s. But I sensed…I knew that his service - like thousands of other U.S. Veterans – was no picnic: far from it. Through the early 1970s he did not discuss anything about combat, about what it was like to be on the front line. Perhaps the generation gap played a role in that during the early 1970s - I was in my teens, and like many boys my age, was influenced by the culture of my generation, the 'me' generation that emphasized youth, not parents. Perhaps it was also due to the fact that the United States was involved in another war - this one highly controversial - the Vietnam War - and it wasn't the time to talk about the past. It certainly wasn't trendy, or hip. How could one? The Vietnam War bitterly divided the nation and became the nation's most serious internal crisis since the Civil War. That lack of discussion during the very now-oriented "me generation" times of the early-1970s to mid-1970s further obfuscated the sacrifice of U.S. Veterans in the Korean War.

Further, I and my Dad's discussion about the war and his role in it probably never would have occurred were it not for the creation and broadcast of what would become a landmark television series: M*A*S*H (CBS Television: 1972-1983). The show, which, as I recall, my Dad started watching regularly, was like the final drill bit that releases the oil: Dad, once reticent to talk about any Korean War incident in detail, now effused with analysis of various scenes. He astutely, and with context and perspective, pointed out to me what scenes in M*A*S*H accurately portrayed Korean War situations, or what he termed "what was real" and what was fake, or what he called, "That's Hollywood. That didn't occur." And I asked him dozens of questions during the show's original broadcast, and during reruns. "What about that helicopter evacuation of a wounded U.S. soldier on the front line? Did it occur like that? With the enemy shooting at the helicopter" I asked. "Yes, it did," Dad said. "And the faster trip to the M*A*S*H unit saved thousands of lives, including men from my unit." Almost no Korean War subject was off-limits. Korea's cold winters? "Bitter cold," he said. Terrain? "Dominated by near-endless hills, for the most part rugged and rough terrain." Those discussions deepened our father-son relationship. And without question, the show signaled to my Dad, and I trust to all Korean War Veterans, that their sacrifice was real, their sacrifice was enormous, their sacrifice would not be overlooked any longer.

'That Was Us'

Of course, for my Dad, included in that recognition was: catharsis. It seems counter-intuitive, but it took a t.v. series - based on true stories, but often embellished and adapted for situation comedy / drama - to convince my Dad that what he participated in during the Korean War wasn't a myth, or easy, or inconsequential. Yes, that was us, Dad would say, "I ran up a hill like that with our unit just north of the 38th parallel, and man, were we glad when we saw those F-86 U.S. Sabre Jets coming."

The author is convinced that most of my Dad's healing from the Korean War occurred during a "welcome home party" from the war, hosted by his sister, when he met his sister's friend, Gloria Tarvaian, who would become his wife and kindred spirit, and my Mom. But part of it also occurred during those years when he and I talked about various situations in the Korean War portrayed during M*A*S*H.

The Korean War Veterans Memorial

Further, a groundswell to finally recognize the sacrifice of all U.S. Veterans who fought in the Korean War, slowly but steadily built, and on July 27, 1995 the Korean War Veterans Memorial in Washington, D.C. was dedicated. The memorial, on the National Mall's south side, is a walled triangle containing 19 stainless steel statues representing a squad on patrol, drawn from each branch of the U.S. Armed Forces. They are dressed in full combat gear, with terrain resembling Korea's rugged terrain. Yours truly highly recommends that every reader, certainly every American, visit the memorial. The sacrifice of the U.S. Veterans of the Korean War, my Dad's sacrifice among them, is forgotten no more.

(A Facebook page in the United States. Photo credit: Joseph Lazzaro.)

Chapter 15: Social Media in the United States, U.S. Cyber Warfare Force

"Social media in the United States will change because it has to change. There are too many bad actors, chiefly selected nations." - Washington, D.C. source

Simply, as our source noted above, social media in the United States will change because it has to change: there are too many bad actors. Chief among these bad actors: the Russians, but also China, Iran and North Korea, among others.

First, some background: the United States Intelligence Community (USIC), in its assessment, concluded that Russia interfered in the 2016 U.S. presidential election, Russia helped Republican Party nominee Donald Trump, hurt Democratic Party nominee Hillary Clinton, swayed voters to vote for Trump and discouraged other voters - largely Democrats and Independent / Unaffiliated voters - from voting for Clinton, resulting in a slight electoral college win for the Republican nominee. Clinton won the popular vote by a large margin, nearly 3 million votes: 65,853,514 to 62,984,828 and should have become the 45th president of the United States, but because Trump eeked out wins in Pennsylvania, Michigan and Wisconsin, he entered the Oval Office. Russia, using special cyber warfare operations and Russian Intelligence – KGB/FSB and GRU – deployed disinformation thru social media channels, especially Facebook, Twitter and Instagram, to both motivate likely Trump voters to vote, and to discourage probable Clinton voters from voting. According to the USIC assessment, the Russian cyber operation was an overwhelming success – and represented its biggest covert operation success versus the United States since the end of the Cold War in 1991. The evidence of Russia's success and their expertise in social media is documented in the Mueller Report. In fact, one could make an argument that the 2016 Russian cyber warfare operation was its biggest covert operation success versus the United States in the modern era – or since the 1917 Bolshevik Revolution. Further, many cyber analysts argue Russia's cyber warfare operation is 3 to 5 years ahead of the United States' operation, that the Russian intelligence presence in social media continues to this day, that the United States is not doing enough to counter it, and it will be a factor in future elections. (Again, all of the aforementioned points are documented and addressed at length/in detail in the Mueller Report.)

Now, given that Russia is ahead in cyber warfare and its disinformation and related covert campaigns to influence elections and achieve its objectives continue to this day, the question is, "What is to be done? What can be done to counter it/prevent it?" Certainly – based on the Trump Administration's woefully inadequate response though the 2020 election – a lot more. In fact, an incredible amount more. Further, it's no stretch to say the Trump Administration has done very little to counter Russian intelligence and the Russian disinformation operation's assault: as of August 2020, Trump indicated he still did not believe Russia interfered in the 2016 election (!!), despite overwhelming evidence to the contrary. Given his track record, it reasonable to conclude Trump is lying – that he believes they did, but is not countering the Russian operation because he knows that Russian interference helped him in 2016, helped throughout his prior 3 years in the Oval Office, and that would help him again in the 2020 U.S. presidential campaign and election. I.E., it's reasonable to conclude that Trump and other elected / influential Republicans know about Russia's past and current interference, and they just don't care, as long as that interference benefits Republican candidates and goals/policies. Regardless, the most important fact is this: Russia's cyber warfare continues, they are a big, bad actor in 2020, and are likely to remain a cyber force for a long time, and they must be countered and checked. That will take a large, ongoing effort. Short term, due to the Trump Administration's failure to allocate a large amount of federal dollars to U.S. cyber warfare, the work has to be done by the Democratic National Committee, and by U.S. social media sites, to root-out Russian disinformation and propaganda; and work also has to be done by U.S. news organizations to guard against the same. Long term, the United States Government has to establish an entirely new branch of the U.S. Department of Defense: a U.S. Cyber Warfare Force (USCWF). A word on each, follows. [Also, it should be noted that the U.S. Intelligence Committee, led by the Central Intelligence Agency (CIA), in coordination with the Federal Bureau of Investigation (FBI) and the National Security Agency (NSA), and other intelligence organizations, will do what it can to counter the ongoing Russian cyber operations, until a USCWF has been established. Moreover, ultimately only the new Biden Administration, united with Congressional Democrats, may be the only activators capable of advocating for and deploying the massive amount of funds required to wage and win this ongoing, long-term asymmetrical form of warfare against Russia.]

Social media: As we entered late-2020, social media giants Facebook and Twitter had taken steps to root-out disinformation, as well remove hate speech and speech that incites violence, and speech inciting an insurrection against the United States Government. Twitter has disabled hundreds of thousands of fake accounts and accounts by extremist groups, and like Facebook, permanently banned Trump's account after the November 2020 election. Most extremist groups / domestic terrorists are on the far-right of the U.S. ideological spectrum – groups that Russia often tries to feed disinformation and propaganda to – but radical left groups also have been banned. One example of group banned: such as the Boogaloo group – a group that seeks to incite a second U.S. Civil War/race war, which they believe will undermine the government, lead to anarchism, and then (eventually) lead to a return to society in its so-called "natural" state – before modern civilization and government. These two steps by Twitter and Facebook, respectively, and others undertaken by Buzzfeed and other social media outlets, are a start, but it's going to take more: much more. Given that Russia has – at minimum – 12,000 intelligence officers working in cyber warfare, the above steps are just opening volleys.

U.S. social media organizations' effort: Right now, social media in the United States is like the nation's Wild West Era from 1869-1899, and it's a major reason Russian intelligence was able to sway so many voters in 2016 and achieve their objective of seeing a very-Kremlin-friendly candidate enter the Oval Office. On the social media platform, or in the social media arena, if you will, there is no sovereign. [There could be one, right now, in the Federal Communications Commission (FCC) given that cable t.v. operators are involved in providing internet service, but we'll save that discussion for later.] Media outlets and social media platforms live in a hyper-competitive environment for viewers/readers/unique visitors, and by extension, advertising dollars. The result is that often bad actors slip their way into the system. Example 1: A reader in Kansas finds a link on an international news web site operated in another country, it's a false story about a Russian achievement and an alleged error by the United States, the content agrees with the Kansas reader's point of view, so he posts it on

Facebook. It's then shared by more than 1,500 readers via his network of Facebook friends. As a result, potentially more than 1,500 voters learn something that's wrong – patently false, it's disinformation – about an American topic. Example 2: A reader in Texas sees a YouTube video that appears to be authentic, but it's a deep fake – a high-quality propaganda video that astutely approximates a real news story. As a result, that person's view of a candidate changes, based on disinformation. Other examples abound, and the Russians, in particular, are experts at creating very strong, false news stories that contain an ounce of truth, that lure the reader into the story, which results in the adult reading lies, disinformation or propaganda that helps achieve the Kremlin's objectives.

Further, there are so many entry points for disinformation on social media and social news aggregation sites that the major companies – Facebook, Twitter, YouTube (Google), Reddit, Buzzfeed and Instagram must take a more-assertive role. As noted, as of mid-2020, Facebook and Twitter had commenced this effort. But it's exactly that: just a beginning. What's needed: a comprehensive system of monitoring committees among social media platforms to self-monitor, discern, and reject content that's disinformation, hate-speech, that incites violence, that incites insurrection, represents extremism and/or is content from a bad actor. The most efficient committee system would be those established and managed by the social media outlets, themselves. Further, social media outlets will have to establish dozens, if not scores of committees – committees for each content vertical or section – given, the sprawling nature of their operations. Concerning federal oversight, the analysis forwarded here argues that at least initially, progressives and Democrats should not require formal, federal report-filing – but that remains an option – perhaps quarterly reports – in the years ahead. The key is to have the social media outlets become more aware of the originators of the content that's published by users on their pages. Russia has taken advantage of U.S. freedoms to gain entry to U.S. web sites and, by extension, to gain entry to U.S. readers' minds. I.E., *"In 2016, the Russians did not hack voting machines, they hacked U.S. voters' minds."* China, Iran, North Korea and Venezuela also have been involved in disinformation/propaganda operations, but Russia was the major bad actor in 2016, and remains the top threat, as of early 2021. U.S. social media outlets have to reduce that vulnerability as much as they can, while still allowing space for a diverse discussion that is a hallmark of a free, democratic society.

To be sure, the above will not be a quick and simple, nor inexpensive task: the committees will add a layer of cost to social media operations, but, again, it's the logical first step, and in many ways, the least expensive option. The alternative would be to have the federal government and/or the states establish monitoring committees, and at this stage, that does not seem practical. The best, first solution is monitoring committees established by social media outlets: they are closer to the action.

U.S. Cyber Warfare Force: Further, as noted, long term the United States Government has to establish an entire U.S. Cyber Warfare Force (USCWF) and branch in the U.S. Department of Defense. There are no two ways around it. Here's why:

Russia has – at minimum – 12,000 intelligence officers working on disinformation, propaganda and other cyber operations designed to achieve the Kremlin's objectives, be they foreign policy or domestic policy. That staff total probably is closer to 20,000 as of late 2020, and even though the U.S. DOD has assets deployed to counter it, and the U.S. Intelligence Community does, as well, the United States is not doing nearly enough. (We will leave for another time, and perhaps another book, the reasons why the Trump Administration did not substantially counter the KGB/FSB and GRU cyber operations; for now, know this: they must be countered in a big way, and the new Biden Administration must prioritize it.)

In fact, in the first few months of the new Biden Administration, the administration should consider an executive order establishing a U.S. Cyber Warfare Force, one that would only be supplanted by Congress passing a law creating a U.S. Cyber Warfare Department (USCWD) branch of the U.S. DOD. The threat is that big. Russia scored, arguably, its biggest covert operations win versus the United States with its "active measures" campaign to help Trump in the 2016 U.S. presidential election. Russia's active measures campaign continues to this day, and in mid-2020, U.S. intelligence officials said it was working to defeat Democratic Party candidates, including the presidential nominee, and help Trump again; all the aforementioned provides evidence that the Russian cyber warfare operation never stopped. Further, China, Iran and North Korea were also intervening with disinformation and propaganda in the United States – attempting to sway public opinion to achieve various political/propaganda goals. Hence, the evidence is overwhelming for the need for a USCWD at the Pentagon. The USCWD would coordinate with the CIA, FBI, NSA and NRO to devise the best plan to both counter and thwart Russia's active measures, counter the bad actors, and also neutralize other nefarious cyber campaigns by the U.S.'s adversaries. The USCWD should also work in coordination with U.S. news organization and social media outlets to both help harden their cyber systems, intranets, and to alert them to attacks and/or tactics they may not have noticed.

The proposed, initial F2022 budget for the USCWD: $50 billion. Again, this effort will not be cheap, and it must match the commitment of the Russians; they are long-term thinkers – *Russia thinks and measure time in decades, not years.* Moreover, resources have to be adequate to thwart multiple, simultaneous threats – from China, Iran, and North Korea, etc. Further, as noted, in theory the FCC can intervene, given that it regulates cable t.v. providers/broadband providers, but at this stage, the FCC does not appear to be the best mechanism – given the extra layer (cable companies, then social media outlets) it would require. That's not ideal; hence the best tack is news site/social media site monitoring committees and the USCWD.

The 2016 U.S. presidential election laid bare the vulnerabilities of the U.S.'s free system. It was far too easy for Russia's KGB/FSB and GRU to push disinformation onto social media platforms, and then into the minds of the American people. The social media platforms were wide open and there weren't enough people in the civil service dedicated to stopping the

Russians. Now, there must be, and the political coalition is there, now that President Biden has won and the Democrats/progressives have won majorities in both chambers of Congress. In 2021, Democrats/progressives must establish both the social media policies and the USCWD to not only check the Russians and other bad actors, but also to take the propaganda war to them – as we did during the Cold War. Russia President Putin, a former KGB director, using asymmetrical warfare, leveled the playing field between Russia and the United States by effectively deploying a weapon – or fighting in an arena - where he has the advantage: cyber warfare. That is an active weapon, Putin has not stopped using it, and it will play a role in future elections, as well, hence the United States must counter it: that is incontrovertible. Russia will not attack the United States conventionally or directly. Why would Putin? When you're winning with asymmetrical warfare (in Crimea, Ukraine, pressuring NATO, in Syria, even in the United States) why would you stop riding that train? Accordingly, U.S. news/ social media companies must establish monitoring committees and the U.S. Government must fund a new branch of the U.S. DOD: the USCWD to counter the massive Russian/bad actors' threat. Only then, will the United States begin to turn the tide against those who oppose democracy, the Bill of Rights, and government based on the consent of the governed.

Scenario: This policy change would likely draw from scenarios 1 thru 3. Most of the aforementioned reforms can be implemented by private sector companies, including the major news / social media outlets. The USCWD would require a new institution within the U.S. DOD, obviously.

In Dealey Plaza, It Is Always November 22, 1963

It can be called the textbook example of a horribly botched criminal investigation. And we mean horribly botched. Further, it may ultimately represent something far, far worse – but as of the late-2020, there still isn't incontrovertible evidence to prove it. The botched criminal investigation? The investigation into the assassination of President John F. Kennedy on November 22, 1963 in Dealey Plaza, Dallas.

Of course, what you choose to believe regarding who murdered President Kennedy is up to you, but consider this: almost nothing - *nothing* about this case - is normal. Here are the known facts in the case:

1) Lee Harvey Oswald was in the Texas School Book Depository (TSBD) before the assassination.

2) Nightclub Owner Jack Ruby killed Oswald with a handgun, two days after the assassination.

That's it. Those two facts. Hundreds of other facts are up for debate, i.e. assassination researchers differ regarding the record on the other points.

Consider: One witness, Howard Brennan, standing near the TSBD, said he saw a man with a gun in the

Dealey Plaza, Dallas, Texas. (Credit: WikiCommons, public domain.)

sixth floor window. But Brennan is an especially unreliable witness: he claimed the man was standing up when aiming the rifle (a sash window to the waist made this physically impossible); and he said he could identify the shooter, but he failed to pick Oswald out of a lineup.

Consider: Victoria Adams, "the girl on the stairs" of the TSBD, failed to see Oswald as she traveled down the back stairs immediately after the 12:30 p.m. shooting at 12:31 p.m. CT. The Warren Commission (WC) said she had to see Oswald, because Oswald had to travel down those stairs to get to the building's ground floor. Adams didn't, which strongly suggests Oswald was where he said he was at the time of the shooting: in the lunchroom on the second floor, getting a drink.

Consider: Doctors examining JFK at Parkland Hospital in Dallas described an entrance wound on his throat - inconsistent with rear shots.

Bethesda, Maryland autopsy doctors said this was an exit wound. Most Parkland doctors also described a large, rear head wound; Bethesda doctors did not.

Consider: The WC concluded that 3 rifle shots were fired from the rear, with one missing the limousine, another causing throat injuries to Kennedy and multiple injuries to Texas Gov. Connally, followed by a fatal head shot to Kennedy. But at least 20 witnesses saw or heard a shot from the front, from somewhere near the Stemmons Freeway Overpass to the grassy knoll.

Consider: Oswald, a purported communist, was handled curiously by the U.S. Government. A traitor to his country, Oswald was allowed to return from the Soviet Union, at the height of the Cold War, and with a Russian wife no less, despite having threatened to reveal important military information to the Soviets. And he wasn't punished. And the U.S. State Dept. paid for his travel return to the United States.

And there are at least a dozen more substantive questions that underscore that while a plot has not been proven, a mystery still resides at the center of this case. Chief among these include the 1,100 JFK files - still classified by the Central Intelligence Agency (CIA) 50 years after the assassination - due to national security. The CIA says making the files public will jeopardize national security by revealing means, sources and methods. Assassination researchers believe the files will help determine the whole truth regarding what happened on November 22, 1963 by providing evidence on the actions of CIA officers prior to the assassination, and info regarding how the CIA treated Oswald's file, among other answers.

(Microsoft Headquarters, Redmond, Washington. Photo credit: Shutterstock.com.)

Chapter 16: Technology and the U.S. Workforce

"The pace of technological change is accelerating." -Former Microsoft CEO Bill Gates

Another issue that progressives/Democrats have the stronger philosophical argument concerns technology and the U.S. workforce. As discussed in Chapters 6 and 11, the nation's workforce will encounter several stresses or hurdles in the decades ahead – substantial changes that will leave many adults scrambling – and one major change concerns technology. Technology – artificial intelligence (AI), machine learning, data analytics, robotics, automated systems, self-driving vehicles and drones – will cause substantial job cuts and job consolidations, in many sectors. The job losses have only just begun, and concerning sectors, as mentioned, perhaps a better statement is – name a sector that won't be affected by technology and incur job losses? You'd be hard-pressed to find several. What's more, those individuals who think the major period of tech dislocation is over are, simply – wrong: as automation becomes cheaper and, equally significant, as self-driving vehicles become much better at what they do, and operate safely, they will proliferate. And that implies massive jobs losses – in the millions.

And, as noted in Chapter 6, those massive jobs losses will require a comprehensive worker retraining program that progressives and Democrats must lobby assertively for in the new Biden Administration: 1) a massive $750 billion public sovereign wealth fund to pay for public higher education facilities expansions and new facilities, 2) $100 billion for public vocational training facilities expansion, 3) new, modest grants for students attending private colleges, 4) a $100 billion special fund for adults displaced by industries that disappear (due to globalization, technology or other reasons), and/or that do not yield strong prospects of a new job and 5) a $50 billion 21st century education fund to identify those new, innovative sectors that are likely to give our nation a strategic advantage and/or that are likely to yield significant social/cultural benefits. In a summary, it's an "uber-sized re-training program" to meet the demands of the super-competitive, globalization-/regionalization-buffeted job market in the immediate decades ahead. American adults – adults young and young at heart – are going to need all the help they need, given the sheer number of jobs that are likely to be automated or disappear in the next 20 years, and progressives/Democrats have to be ready with the skills-training and career-training ideas and programs to meet the needs of the day.

Now, how many jobs are likely to be eliminated by technology? The McKinsey Global Institute estimated that 73 million jobs will be eliminated by 2030. Jobs that are likely to see large reductions include: truck drivers (due to self-driving trucks), couriers (due to increased drone use), bookkeepers, mortgage loan originators, receptionists, secretaries, medical diagnosticians (due to productivity increases and artificial intelligence), market research analysts, bank branch managers (banking apps are reducing the need for local bank branches), bank tellers, benefits managers, financial planners, (selected) construction workers, (selected) advertising salespeople, fast-food workers, retail sales clerks, bus drivers, street cleaning personnel, window cleaners, security guards, and dish washers, among many others.

As one can see, the breadth of jobs eliminated cuts across almost all categories – white collar and blue collar. Nor will the cuts affect only entry-level or minimum wage jobs: one example - many mortgage loan originator positions that gross more than $100,000 per year will be eliminated. In the future, it will no longer be the case that only modest-training, low-education, low-skill jobs will be automated/displaced: many significant-training, college education-required jobs will be phased-out.

Further, progressives/Democrats should place themselves decidedly in the pro-technology camp. The analysis forwarded here argues that the problem is not technology, but how technology is managed. Hence, progressives and Democrats should be in the pro-technology camp, but argue that technology must be re-directed, or at least re-focused. In other words, there is some truth to the assertion that, *"Technology is a two-edge sword."* In its purest form, one can see the benefits of technology: and how could one not? The story of human development and the quest to meet basic needs is, in part, a story that involves tools and technology. However, late in the 20th century and early in the 21st century, the globalization era has demonstrated that technology incorrectly applied or with flawed premises can do tremendous harm: it can make problems worse, not better. Examples abound. For now, we'll focus on the issue of sudden, large job dislocation. Examples: the U.S. steel worker displaced by a new, automated steel mill that requires one-tenth the blue-collar and white-collar workers as the previous generation; the retail employee displaced by Amazon.com, which substantially decreased the retail chain store's sales; the truck driver displaced by the self-driving, 18-wheel tractor trailer truck. Moreover, as noted, we are only at the start of these large technological changes – and that means their dislocation potential is only going to magnify with scale and with tech deployment in dozens more countries.

That is, that dislocation potential will magnify if we do not manage technology better. Progressives/Democrats must identify ways public policy officials and corporate executives can manage technology so that it serves the common good/public interest and that also continues to offer all (or almost all) of the benefits we've reaped from technology, including: rising productivity and incomes, expansion of the middle class, economic development, increased efficiency, and the cheaper international connections that are at the heart of global trade and the global economy (and will be at the heart of a regional economy, if regionalization becomes the norm in the post-coronavirus pandemic era). For lack of a better term, progressives/Democrats need to create a *"Technology with a human face."* Further, progressives and Democrats should not view the problem as being one the market alone will solve. The answer will require a shift in mindset in corporate, public policy and companion circles – it will be a synergy.

Andrew Yang's idea: To be sure, the worker retraining issue is a daunting task, but as noted it's one progressives and Democrats must steadfastly undertake, because of the enormous social consequences job losses cause, the worst of which is personal bankruptcies, small business failures, a decrease in household formation, a decrease in national income and lost GDP. However, as comprehensive as any worker retraining program can be, in the decades ahead there will still be adults who – through no fault of their own – will be without an income. The U.S. Social Security Disability system provides a modest income for those who have been legally-defined as disabled. However, many whose jobs have been displaced and are unable to find suitable employment or otherwise cannot be retrained will not qualify as being legally disabled, hence there will be a gap in the social system, even with the programs mentioned in Chapters 6, 11 and here. American Entrepreneur Andrew Yang, a former 2020 U.S. presidential candidate, has offered a potential solution: a guaranteed minimum income (GMI), also known as a universal basic income (UBI).

The GMI has been unpopular for at least some in U.S. culture (primarily conservatives, Republicans and libertarians), and perhaps for other groups, as well, for decades. Those that oppose it often oppose many government programs and services, at the federal level, and sometimes at the state and local levels, too. (Or: they opposed government programs that do not benefit their constituencies, and favor those that do.) Still, given the likely large number of adults whose jobs will be displaced by technology, increasing U.S. wealth/income inequality, the recession (start date: February 2020) caused by the coronavirus pandemic, high U.S. poverty levels, and the our ageing population, the time may have arrived for a U.S. GMI. Of course, most Republicans will likely oppose The analysis forwarded here argues Democrats should try to pass a modest GMI, at least, even though it will require 60 Senate votes to be approved. Sen. Sanders may not be happy with this proposal - he's favored a larger GMI in the past - but a good U.S. GMI starting point is $1,200 per month. Again, opponents will cite various reasons for not starting one, but the fact remains that a GMI has the potential to deliver a minimum income benefit more-efficiently than many other programs.

Further, ideally the GMI would start at $2,000 per month, but that doesn't seem likely, given the U.S.'s political culture - at least given the political culture to 2020 - hence the more-modest $1,200 start. Yang called for a $1,000 GMI paid for by a 10 percent value-added tax. (Some goods, such as yachts/luxury goods, would be assessed a higher VAT than 10 percent, under Yang's program.) Further, progressives and Democrats should ask the Congressional Budget Office to score every GMI proposal, and find one that strikes a balance – i.e. that represents a happy medium – between an adequate, starting monthly stipend and the best fit for the proposed F2022 or F2023 budget. In addition, ideally, the GMI would continue, even if the person holds a job. A gradual phase-out should start at about $12,000 in annual income, with $50 per month deducted from the GMI for every $1,000 in income above $12,000. Hence, the GMI stops at $36,000 in income, assuming a $1,200 GMI start; $32,000 in income, assuming a $1,000 GMI start. The GMI would also be per individual, with the same sliding scale applying to each person in a couple, individually, if they are married.

Paid homemaking: As discussed in Chapter 11, paid homemaking would be a trailblazing, large step for the United States. Progressives and Democrats should lobby for it, as it would represent Congress and the nation at large recognizing and compensating this large category of work that has gone uncompensated in the United States, in terms of federal funding. What would be a fair monthly stipend to start at? Most likely, $600 per month for couples with incomes under $60,000 per year, decreasing $50 for each $1,000 increase in annual income. At incomes below $36,000 ($1,200 GMI start) or $32,000 ($1,000 GMI start) the GMI would supplant the paid homemaking stipend. However, above, those incomes, the homemaking stipend ensures that domestic work is compensated, even after an individual (or couple) leaves the GMI program, up to $48,000 ($1,200 GMI start) or $44,000 ($1,000 GMI start).

These and other ideas should be a part of progressives'/Democrats' policy palette for the U.S. workforce in the new Biden Administration. To be sure, they'll be opposed by many, but the Democrats have much going for them, not the least of which is: 1) Republicans have few credible ideas to solve the nation's problems, and 2) the march of technology will continue, and with it, it's a two-edged sword. In other words, ignoring technological change and automation won't make them disappear: better to shape them, to create a *"Technology with a human face"* as the nation ventures further into the competitive 21st century economy.

Scenario: This policy change would likely draw from scenarios 3 and 4. Both the GMI and paid homemaking are new systems, and the latter, at least for some Americans, will seem like "change even beyond a new system." It's hard to envision a system that pays the homemaker – historically that has been women – for the work performed at home. That it has gone without direct compensation in most societies says something about how we structure societies. But this work should be compensated! Think about it: how will we truly know who wants to stay at home, undertake housework, and care for children, if it isn't paid for? A better test of our society's priorities would occur when this work is compensated.

TRIVIA TEST 6: U.S. History, Part 2

(Answers in Appendix, Page 354.)

1. The president who established the U.S. Environmental Protection Agency (EPA) was:
a) Theodore Roosevelt
b) Franklin D. Roosevelt
c) Herbert Hoover
d) Richard Nixon

2. In which federal organization did President Nixon try to establish a mini-CIA to counter the CIA?
a) Drug Enforcement Agency
b) Securities and Exchange Commission
c) Federal Emergency Management Agency
d) None of the above

3. In April 1968, President Johnson did something no one thought he would do. He:
a) Started bombing Cambodia
b) Said he would back a plan to move the U.S. Capitol to Omaha, Nebraska
c) Said he would back a plan to give each American 5 weeks paid vacation per year
d) Announced that he would not seek, nor accept, the Democratic Party's nomination in 1968 for another term as U.S. president

President Dwight Eisenhower, 1956 (Credit: U.S. National Archives.)

4. Which highways in Europe so impressed General Eisenhower, that when he became U.S. president he proposed a U.S. interstate highway system?
a) Sweden's secondary highways
b) Britain's highways

c) France's country roads
d) Germany's Autobahn

5. Which of the following is true about the U.S. stock market as measured by the Dow Jones Industrial Average?
a) It fell under President Clinton and rose under President Obama
b) It fell under both Presidents Clinton and Obama
c) It rose under President Clinton and rose under President Obama
d) None of the above

6. The Cold War was:
a) A winter war between England and France
b) A winter war between Argentina and Mexico
c) A winter war between Canada and Mexico
d) The post-World War II struggle between the free world (led by the United States) and the communist world (led by the Soviet Union)

7. Which U.S. general famously recited the following? "Old soldiers never die, they just fade away."
a) George Patton
b) Dwight Eisenhower
c) Douglas MacArthur
d) Norman Schwarzkopf

8. Which event in the Soviet Union in 1957 prompted the United States to improve training in math and science?
a) The development of a nuclear bomb
b) The development of a main frame computer
c) The development of a transistor radio
d) The launch of Sputnik 1, an unmanned space satellite

9. The first American to orbit the Earth was?
a) Neil Simon b) Edgar Winter c) John Glenn d) Mitch Miller

10) The first person to walk on the Moon was?
a) Buzz Aldrin b) Michael Collins c) Neil Armstrong d) none of the above

They Said It: Presidential Humor 2

It's not directly in the category of U.S. presidential humor, but when you think of what he implied behind it, it certainly sounds presidential. FBI Director J. Edgar Hoover, who presided over the bureau like no other director, and served the longest term, 1935-1972, used to greet visitors to the FBI Headquarters Building in Washington, D.C. with the following:

"Welcome to the seat of the United States Government," Hoover said.

**

President Harry S. Truman enjoyed public life, was the model of virtue and did not abandon his Midwestern Missouri sensibility and simplicity, despite decades in Washington, D.C. And his relationship with the Washington community was one of a keen, arms-length observer.

President Truman: "If you want a friend in Washington, get a dog."

President Truman, announcing the end of World War II in August 1945. (Credit: U.S. National Archives.)

**

President Truman, like all presidents, received many reports from Cabinet officials that had an upside and a downside. Economists were famous for their, "On the one hand, if we act our policy will have these positives; on the other hand, it will have these negatives."

President Truman: "What I wouldn't do for a one-armed economist."

President Truman also disliked the U.S. presidency's incapacitation clause in the Twenty-Fifth Amendment, Clause 4, which allows the U.S. vice president, together with a majority of the Cabinet or "such other body as Congress may by law provide" to declare the president disabled by submitting a written declaration to the Senate president and House Speaker. The U.S. president can resume his duties by submitting the same.

President Truman: "The first thing I would do, upon regaining capacity...is to fire every son-of-a-bitch who voted to incapacitate me in the first place."

**

U.S. Sen. Howard Baker, R-Tennessee, observed many high-level meetings between President Richard Nixon and CIA Director Richard Helms.

U.S. Sen. Baker: "Nixon and Helms have so much on each other, neither of them can breathe."

**

During the October 1962 Cuban Missile crisis – one of the most serious nuclear crises during the Cold War between the United States and Soviet Union - the tension was high, to say the least. One wrong move, or misinterpreted act, and who knows what would happen? The U.S. wanted the Soviet Union to remove nuclear missiles from Cuba. President John F. Kennedy ordered a U.S. Navy blockade around Cuba to turn away any new missiles on incoming Soviet ships to Cuba. At a meeting with President Kennedy, U.S. Secretary of Defense Robert McNamara, and U.S. Navy commanders, there was concern / doubt about how the U.S. Navy would respond to the approach of a Soviet ship.

U.S. Secretary of Defense Robert McNamara: "So, if a Soviet ship starts getting close to the blockade perimeter, admiral, what's your response?"

U.S. Navy Admiral: [silence.]

Secretary McNamara: "Admiral?"

U.S. Navy Admiral: Mr. "Secretary, it's all right there...it's all in the Navy Manual."

Secretary McNamara: "I'M NOT TALKING ABOUT WHAT JOHN PAUL JONES WOULD DO!! I want to know what YOU would do, TODAY, in the event a Soviet ship approaches the blockade."

(President John F. Kennedy addresses the first Peace Corps class in 1961. Photo credit: U.S. National Archives.)

Chapter 17: U.S. National Service Program

"Men and women will be expected to work and live alongside the nationals of the country in which they are stationed—doing the same work, eating the same food, talking the same language." – President John F. Kennedy, on the Peace Corps, 1961

Now, for a discussion about a challenging but important issue/subject, but another one in which progressives and Democrats have the philosophically stronger argument, as well.

The United States must implement a national service requirement, call it the United States National Service Program (USNSP) primarily for its youth, but also for selected others who are suitable for and can benefit from the program.

For too long, national service has been neglected. It's time to reverse that incorrect, counter-productive trend. Progressives and Democrats should support and promote the new, positive, constructive standard: national service. The idea of national service increased in stature when President John F. Kennedy created the Peace Corps in 1961, however the Peace Corp placed serving Americans internationally – outside the United States. Later, in 1965 President Lyndon B. Johnson started VISTA (Volunteers In Service To America). Since that time, the Peace Corps has flourished, VISTA, less so. The USNSP will not affect the Peace Corps, but it will augment VISTA.

Required service: One major difference regarding USNSP will be its national service requirement. Adults, ages 18 to 22, must be available to undertake and complete two years of national service, and adults ages 23 to 30 serving 1 year, in the United States, including its territories. Initially, the top-end age limit will be 30, with lotteries for ages 23-30 so that they comprise 1/5 of the that year's class of 25,000 adults (5,000), and ages 18-22 comprising 4/5 of the adults (20,000). Adults ages 18-22 will have an open-enrollment period: if the 20,000-adult minimum is not met, a lottery will occur for that age group, as well. Adults ages 18-22 can delay their service for up to 4 years. The exceptions to the lottery entry requirement would be if the adult enters U.S. military service, has a legally-defined disability or if an extreme family hardship exists. (There will also be selected personal hardship exemptions granted, including for health: a young adult who has recently recovered from cancer, or another serious illness, such as the coronavirus/COVID-19, will be granted exemptions, if USNSP medical personnel determine that it is not in the interest of the adult's health or safety to continue with national service.) The program's goal is to increase the skill level of poor/less-fortunate members of society – and enrich the poorest communities – through service. Candidates serving in the USNSP will help the nation achieve these goals, and in the process also learn that becoming a success means more than earning a high income or buying a home, and acquiring material possessions, as important as those goals are: it's about service to the nation. Further, too often service programs draw from middle-income and lower-income ranks: the USNSP will ensure that upper-income groups and the wealthy do two years of national service. In other words, *"There is no free lunch."* With the USNSP, the era of the free lunch will be over, at least regarding national service. All able-bodied, sound-mind members of American society will contribute to the betterment of the United States via helping to solve some of its social problems, and other concerns.

What skills will USNSP adults teach? For grades 4-8, the program will emphasize basic skills: reading, writing, arithmetic, and social interaction skills. A special set of teachers will instruct grade 9-12 students in test preparation for the scholastic aptitude test (SAT), and in vocational skills: computer skills, science, basic construction, art, design, and basic environmental skills/conservation skills/national park skills. In the lower grades, the goal is to ensure that all students have the basic reading-writing-arithmetic skills to keep pace and excel in school; in the higher grades, the goal is to not only introduce a student to a practical job skill, but also to introduce them to interests they may not have thought about – and perhaps in the process discover a hidden talent for science, music, art or design, that they hadn't thought about before. In other words, along with basic skills, the USNSP will hopefully help elementary and especially middle-school and high-school students discover talents (perhaps even expertise) in fields they hadn't dreamt of considering. And surely within these communities there are future prodigies and gifted students waiting to discover what they have; certainly all can and will benefit from the skills training.

Further, as with the Peace Corps and VISTA, USNSP teachers/tutors will learn, too. It's been said by college professors and teachers that, "When you teach, you learn a second time." That may very well be the case with the USNSP, or the instructors may learn for the first time. However, in any event, it will often be a mutual learning experience, for teachers and students alike. Teaching imparts to the mentor many benefits, including mastery of subject knowledge, preparation skills, presentation skills, production experience, the ability to summarize information into understandable points, patience, and perseverance, among other skills. One often finds that one had a talent or two that one wasn't aware of, hence in instruction, if past is any prelude regarding skills, the USNSP will be a mutual learning experience.

As noted, other USNSP semesters for high school students (grades 9-12) will be established in selected physically-challenging settings, such as training in basic environmental skills/conservation skills/national park skills – where student interest/capability exist and where teacher/mentor talent enables the tutoring programs. Still others will occur at housing construction sites. Again, the goal of these programs - geared toward high school students - will be to teach a basic skill and familiarize the student with the tasks performed and the various jobs/career paths in a field or at a work site. At minimum, the program will introduce the student to a field's mission and vocabulary, as well as to the various talents and abilities required to enter the field. For example, at new home construction sites – the goal would not be to merely find out if a student has an interest in and a talent for carpentry, but also to familiarize him/her with the many, different roles performed by construction workers on a home construction site. Hence, students should take away from every USNSP semester not only a set of marketable skills, but also the realization/conclusion regarding whether his/her talent for and interest in that field suggests that he/she could excel in it.

Underscoring, there is no free lunch. For too long, a portion of the U.S. adult population, largely from upper-income groups, but not exclusively, has been able to escape national service, if they did not choose to enter the U.S. Armed Forces or choose public service/foreign service. That policy must end, as it represents "a free lunch," and lets the benefits of democracy and self-government accrue to more-fortunate individuals, without them fully realizing its costs. The USNSP will help end and reverse that social phenomenon. All able-bodied, sound-mind American citizens ages 18-30 will provide national service in the fields noted above, and progressives /

Democrats are encouraged to offer other vocations and professions: the number of career paths/apprenticeships is almost limitless. The important point is to have adults of means sharing their knowledge, skills and time with those who show aptitude and/or are eager to learn – a program that gives strong indications of benefiting all involved: the student, the nation, and U.S. civil society.

Scenario: This policy change would likely draw from scenario 2. It's a reform within the system – but some, particularly conservatives and Republicans, who are not used to this type of program in which all must serve, may consider it a new system. (Scenario 3.)

No Finer, Gratifying Sight: U.S. Coast Guard Rescue At Sea

There are some dimensions of the United States Government, including the U.S. military, that get considerable publicity and recognition, and there are others that get not nearly enough. Put the United States Coast Guard decidedly in the latter category.

Readers know about the U.S. Army, Navy, Air Force, and Marines - and rightfully so: those pronouns role-off like the rhyming lyrics in a familiar and enjoyable song.

But that other branch - the Coast Guard – is sometimes left out, and this should never be the case.

The Coast Guard is a maritime, military and multi-mission service that's unique among U.S military services in that it has a maritime law enforcement role - with jurisdiction in both domestic and international waters. As such the Coast Guard is involved in homeland security, maritime law enforcement, search and rescue, marine environmental protection, and river / intra-coastal maintenance and offshore aids to navigation.

What's more, the USCS does all of the above with just 40,992 active-duty personnel, 8,777 civilians, 244 cutters, 1,850 boats, and 205 aircraft. Its fiscal 2019 budget was $11.6 billion. You read correctly: just $11.6 billion for all of the aforementioned services. The Coast Guard Academy is in New London, Conn.

No Finer Sight

And, the view from here argues there is no finer, more-relieving sight than that of a Coast Guard rescue by one of its ships, or those orange helicopters. Consider: in fiscal 2017, the Coast Guard responded to 15,951 search and rescue missions, and saved 4,188 people and saved millions of dollars in property.

U.S. Coast Guard MH-65C Dolphin. (Credit: U.S. Coast Guard.)

All rescues involve risks, but winter rescues of boats stuck at sea or of travelers who ventured out into a frozen wilderness - not realizing how harsh, and how quickly conditions can become life-threatening – have to rank among the most heroic. Again, there can be no finer sight than seeing Coast Guard personnel place another rescued person in that basket, securing it, then giving the "thumbs up" sign to helicopter personnel to lift another person to safety. Seeing it happen lifts one's spirit, every time. (Pun intended.)

Postmodern Era

Since the September 11, 2001 terrorist attacks, the Coast Guard has taken a more-prominent role in national security and now has armed helicopters operating in high-risk areas, for both law enforcement and anti-terrorism measures. In addition, the USCG now has unmanned aerial vehicles (UAV) for both security and search/rescue operations.

Motto

"I am a Coast Guardsman.

I serve the people of the United States.

I will protect them.

I will defend them.

I will save them.

I am their shield.

For them I am Semper Paratus.

I live the Coast Guard core values.

I am proud to be a Coast Guardsman.

We are the United States Coast Guard."

-The Coast Guard Ethos

U.S. Coast Guard NSC Bertholf (Credit: U.S. Coast Guard.)

U.S. Sen. Frank Church - Public Servant, Extraordinaire

In the pantheon of U.S. public service, inscribe the name of the late U.S. Sen. Frank Church, D-Idaho.

Although his political career had many highlights, if readers remember only one Church accomplishment, it should be the Church Committee.

Formally the 1975 U.S. Senate Select Committee to Study Governmental Operations with Respect to Intelligence Activities - the committee investigated an area of U.S. public policy that few committees had evaluated before: the Central Intelligence Agency (CIA), National Security Agency (NSA) and the Federal Bureau of Investigation (FBI)

The Church Committee, which led to the permanent Senate Select Committee on Intelligence, formed after a series of disturbing revelations involving the intelligence community came to light. These included the CIA's use of various actors to plot assassination attempts against foreign leaders and covert attempts to subvert foreign governments, with both occurring in the 1950s, 1960s and 1970s; and the U.S. Army's spying on the civilian population.

A Nation Stunned By Strange Activities

U.S Frank Church (Credit: U.S. National Archives.)

The nation was stunned - particularly about the CIA's extra-legal (some call it supra-constitutional) efforts to assassinate foreign leaders. In-tune with this public pressure, the Church Committee recommended that U.S. President Gerald Ford ban U.S-sanctioned assassinations of foreign leaders. President Ford did so in 1975, issuing Executive Order 11905. (President Ronald Reagan's Executive Order 12333 in 1981 replaced and reversed EO 11905.)

The committee also learned that the CIA and FBI had intercepted, opened and photographed more than 215,000 pieces of mail prior to the program - called "HTLINGUAL" - being stopped in 1973.

The Ford Administration, led by his intelligence / foreign policy advisers (Henry Kissinger, Donald Rumsfeld, Philip Buchen, and John Marsh) opposed efforts by the Church Committee to have CIA Director William Colby testify before the committee, arguing that the committee's work was jeopardizing all

Church speaking with President Jimmy Carter in 1977. (Credit: U.S. National Archives.)

legitimate, secret intelligence operations. Colby testified, and enough information was revealed to trigger reforms of selected intelligence community programs, but the CIA achieved a victory, as well: it and the other organizations in the U.S. intelligence community prevented the committee's dismantling of the agencies.

Church: Oversight Matters

In sum, Frank Church and the Church Committee "got the ball rolling" regarding some semblance of oversight regarding the U.S. intelligence community - the U.S.'s secret organizations. Further, regarding civil protest to the Vietnam War, for Church anti-war citizens represented "the highest concept of patriotism" - which argues, when your country is right, support it; when it is wrong, make it right.

Finally, as Edward Snowden's revelations regarding the recent NSA violations of privacy demonstrate, Congress in 2020 still is not on-top of every intelligence operation - CIA, NSA, FBI or otherwise. In fact, until the Church Committee, one could characterize the relationship as the U.S. intelligence community guiding, if not overseeing Congress, not Congress overseeing the intelligence community. Further, the U.S. is still a nation where national security prevails over privacy, and few would want it otherwise. But at least, thanks to Frank Church, Congress is asking, "Is this sacrifice of privacy truly necessary to maintain national security?"

(President Franklin D. Roosevelt signs the U.S. Social Security Act of 1935 in August 1935. Photo credit: U.S. National Archives.)

Chapter 18: Etatism – The Positive State

"What we need is a federal government of fraternity, not a government of strangers," -Washington, D.C. colleague

"Don't focus on what America is, focus on what it can become." U.S. Rep. Shirley Chisholm, D-New York

This is not an issue, per se, but a discussion on a theoretical/abstract topic – but, like the issues, it is one that progressives and Democrats have an advantage over conservatives and Republicans. Or, in other words, the Democratic Party's corner of theory contains the philosophically stronger argument than the Republican Party's. Yours truly was reluctant to include it in the initial or early chapters because: 1) it's an abstract topic and harder to understand/grasp/comprehend, and 2) the book is a practical guide to a

New Progressive Era and a call to action for it, given that the Democratic Party won the U.S. presidency, and majorities in both chambers of Congress in November 2020. Hence, yours truly did not want to bog-down readers with a theoretical/abstract topic and discussion in a work that is a pragmatic work - a call to action and guidebook for economic and social change in the United States. However, by now, some readers may be asking, *"Where did the author get the idea for the book and why does he advocate for progressivism, for a New Progressive Era, with the Democratic Party leading and governing the United States Government?"* That's another good question.

In a nutshell, liberals/progressives and Democrats believe that, in addition to the benefits produced by the free market/private sector, the state can play *a positive role in peoples' lives* – that the state can be a positive force for change for the typical person, or man or woman in a typical American town. Academics call this "the positive state" – or *etatism*, a French word. Conservatives and Republicans do not, in general, believe this. Republicans – and certainly the Republican Party in 2020 – have a negative view of the state, at all levels, and certainly at the federal level, and its impact on the lives of the typical person and citizen. In fact, some conservatives and Republicans want the private sector or the free market to solve all problems: as noted earlier – they assign a near metaphysical certitude or power to the market, arguing the market can best decide what goods should be produced, what value should be paid for labor, and what's right and wrong. Liberals call these folks "market absolutists," - some people call them "market fundamentalists" - and argue their theory amounts to economic and social Darwinism. What's more, without state intervention – without some standard or floor regarding what constitutes a decent, humane life - Republicans' market absolutism will lead to people - whole sectors - being impoverished – living in poverty, and also, eventually, if standards are not maintained, to immiseration and destitution for entire classes of society.

An extension of progressives' positive state stance is the tenet that progressives/Democrats, in general, want to eliminate needless human suffering and pain. Some bad things are bound to happen in our fallen order, the author's favorite Roman Catholic nun taught him as a youth, but humans should strive to eliminate needless human suffering and pain: they are called to do this, my favorite nun argued. Conversely, conservatives and Republicans, in general, do not want to eliminate needless human suffering and pain, or if they do, they don't believe the state has any role in it. (Some Republicans allow the state to eliminate some human suffering, but the important point here is that Republicans' intervention call and stance pales – it is almost ridiculously small – compared to progressives' and Democrats.')

Further, it is this positive role for the state and the tenet at all levels of government (town/city, county, state, federal) that can reduce and then eliminate needless human suffering and pain *that served as the genesis for this book.* To be sure, there were other factors, as well, in the life of the author, but it was the failure of conservatives' and Republicans' ideas to solve problems in the United States over a 40-year period, (since the election of U.S. President Ronald Reagan, a Republican, in 1981), that led yours truly to seek answers for our nation's economic and social problems. However, this is not to say that no conservative ideas work: some do, but the majority do not. In fact, many Republican ideas make problems worse. One major example: too low a federal income tax for upper income groups that creates even larger income and wealth inequality and that underfunds public assets, public needs and the federal government. Another example: A so-called small business with 150 employees and $300 million in annual revenue that nevertheless does not pay its lowest-ranked employees a living wage (!!) - to the point where those employees' health insurance premiums must be subsidized by the ACA: that's called *social cost transferring,* and it unjustifiably shifts the business owner's cost to U.S. taxpayers. What's more, what may appear to be shocking to some readers, is in fact, a conservative/Republican tenet: some Republicans do not want to solve selected economic and social problems - some of these elected officials don't even consider economic problems to be...problems. (!!) They are a group of lawmakers that is so callous, so cruel, it is practically criminal; it is certainly inhumane, does not serve the common good, and goes against everything yours truly was taught while growing up in an all-American town.

To be sure, this is not to overlook the benefits of a free market: yours truly favors the free market - he believes in U.S. corporate capitalism with a legitimate safety net/social welfare state. Further, the market's/private sector's benefits are many. As noted earlier, without question, the U.S. economic system has many benefits, the chief among these being: entrepreneurship, innovation, ingenuity, dynamism, reward for work, risk taking, wealth building, a more-efficient deployment of resources and the primacy of science-led commerce. (The relatively wide freedom science and scientists have to operate in the United States – and the benefits that freedom has produced - is a major virtue of the U.S.'s system, and it's worthy of a discussion, but that is a subject for another time.) However, few would deny the harshness of the U.S.'s current economic system - corporate capitalism. To deny the harshness of the American economic system - a system that's much more harsh than the European economic system - is to refuse to accept a matter of incontrovertible fact. In conservatives' and Republicans' world, that harshness that exists is something that should exist - the state is not capable of reducing suffering and should not be permitted to do so - and if the individual/corporations/free market do not reduce suffering, so be it. That aforementioned Republican view is the antithesis of the common good – what yours truly has been taught.

Further, it was the piling up or the aggregation of economic problem after economic problem, social problem after social problem, over 40 years – largely under conservative/Republican rule and by using their system - supply side economics (low taxes, few regulations, little support for education/job training, health care, housing and the environment) that convinced yours truly that the answers/solutions to problems had to be found elsewhere and that the United States was overdue for a New Progressive Era.

Oh, conservatives/Republicans do favor some government – some role for the state: defense spending, agriculture subsidies for farmers who generally vote for them, some support for stock/bond market to provide liquidity and keep the markets functioning, and state enforcement of contracts. That's about it. After that, Republican support for the state is virtually zip. Niet. Nothing. Nada.

And conservatives' and Republicans' stance toward the poor? The working poor? Underpaid workers? The elderly? The vulnerable? The marginalized? The homeless? The stance of Republicans is unacceptable. Callous. Uncaring. The current system they have largely put in place, as a result of the 2017 Trump tax cut that primarily benefited the top 10 percent of income earners, is harsh and is making U.S. economic and social problems worse – not better. And, had they won the November 2020 election, Republicans would have made the economic system even more harsh: they would have pushed/regressed economic and social conditions back to the level of the inhuman conditions in Dickens' England, which was so accurately and articulately chronicled by British author Charles Dickens. (Dickens wrote: "A Christmas Carole" and "A Tale of Two Cities.") For those reasons alone, the victory of President Biden and the Democratic Party in Congress is a minor miracle – a saving grace for the experiment called the United States of America, this "last, best hope for mankind," to cite President Lincoln.

Underscoring: the United States has many economic and social problems, the chief of which are: 1) poverty, 2) stagnant or flat wages for too many job segments, especially blue-collar jobs, 3) a lack of a universal health insurance system and too high health care insurance premiums, 4) enormous – inequalities in income and wealth, and 5) a workforce in need of new skills from higher education and vocational skills schools. As this book has outlined: *there is a progressive solution* - one where the state plays a role in varying degrees - *for all of these problems and issues.*

Conservatives and Republicans either don't believe the federal government can play a positive role, can't solve these problems, and others, or *they don't care to try to solve them.* Progressives and Democrats do care, and they want the federal government, and state and local governments too, to take action to solve them. Progressives and Democrats believe in the positive state. They believe the federal government can improve peoples' lives and help people: it is as simple as that. Moreover, there's a documented history of federal and state intervention solving economic and social problems: the list is voluminous. Example: In 1935, President Roosevelt's establishment of Social Security as the nation's first retirement pension: it substantially reduced senior citizen poverty levels. In the 1950s: President Eisenhower lobbying for and securing passage of legislation to build the U.S. Interstate Highway System. In 1964 and 1965: President Johnson doing the same for the U.S. Civil Rights Act and U.S. Voting Rights Act, respectively. In 1965, President Johnson doing the same for Medicare, the health care insurance program for senior citizens. And of course the Affordable Care Act (ACA)/Obamacare expanded health care insurance to tens of millions of U.S. adults who did not have it before; it also lowered the U.S. uninsured rate to less than 10 percent by the end of 2016, from a high of about 18 percent in 2010. (For some ACA enrollees, it was a first time in their life they received regular health care services, including an annual visit to a personal physician.)

Further, as one might sense, it's not easy for many Republicans to accept progressive reforms. Moreover, it seems almost impossible for current Republicans in 2020/2021 - those Republicans currently in the U.S. House and U.S. Senate, and in state-level offices - to accept progressive programs. It's almost as if by accepting a public policy program or regulation change to solve an economic and/or social problem, they are admitting that either U.S. corporate capitalism, corporate capitalism in general or capitalism outright has failed. For some issues, and in some cases, that is an accurate statement; for others, it most certainly is not, as economic and social problems frequently have multi-factor and often layered causes. Not every issue is, "X causes Y" or "If we stop doing X, Y occurs." Even so, Republicans are mistaken in thinking public policy changes weaken U.S. corporate capitalism: on the contrary, public policy changes strengthen corporate capitalism by making its system that much more humane *and* one that's more-attractive for talented people, as well as for innovative, dynamic and promising companies. The reason upcoming reforms will make the American system more-attractive is because, in many ways, the United States is a "reform cycle" or social cycle behind Western European democracies. Germany's public pension system – it's base system – is vastly superior to the U.S.'s system. France's health care system – including its public option – provides better health care services at *substantially lower cost* for every French citizen. The United Kingdom's higher education systems provide college degrees at a remarkably lower cost to students. (Also, Canadians pay higher income taxes than Americans, but their economic/social outcomes - income distribution, education levels, quality of health are rated higher than the U.S.) All across Europe, and in other modern democracies, one can find examples and case studies where the United States is trailing its sister, western, developed democracies. The question is - why? A major reason is we've been in a roughly 40-year conservative policy cycle that began in 1981 that's resulted in a New Gilded Age – many breakthroughs in business, but also huge economic and social inequalities, and all of the problems associated with it. That New Gilded Age appeared to end in November 2008 and a New Progressive Era appeared to start with the election of President Obama, a centrist-to-liberal reformer. [As noted, it would have continued (and should have) had Madam Secretary Hillary Clinton entered the White House's Oval Office after the November 2016 election.] The events of November 2016, including Russian intelligence interference in the election, prevented that; with the election of President Biden and the Democratic-led Congress as result of their victory in the 2020 U.S. presidential election, the analysis forwarded here argues the nation did enter a New Progressive Era in 2008, and Biden and the Democrats in 2021 – a more-progressive party than in 2008 - will continue reforms begun in 2008 – addressing many economic and social problems discussed in this book.

All of the above points to the obvious (but don't expect many elected Republicans to change): Republicans have to accept that the state is capable of positive things – the positive state. (As noted, it is known as *etatism* in

France.) And, if the initial decades of the 21st century are any indicator, it looks like this century, even as the private sector expands and achieves unprecedented technological breakthroughs, will require more state invention/ public services, as well as smarter state intervention/public services – not less. Wash, rinse, repeat! This will be hard for conservatives and Republicans to accept because it is against their culture, which is private sector first, public sector second, and any public sector intervention must be local first, not state-level or national-level. The U.S.'s culture is anti-government and anti-central state; the problem is – that culture is flawed. Save for Alexander Hamilton, the system of government the Framers/Founding Fathers devised did not anticipate the industrial revolution, and they certainly did not anticipate the rise of the modern transnational corporation (also called the multi-national corporation). Those production changes created a new super-actor, what yours truly calls "nations unto themselves" or "corporate nations" that have, to be sure, produced many economic and social benefits, but that have also created many economic and social problems and other challenges, not the least of which are: 1) wealth concentration and 2) what happens to those who are not part of a corporation? And regarding the latter: what happens to them - the others? Those not part of a corporation? Some are left to fend for themselves, and if their means are modest, and the social safety net / social welfare state is inadequate, poverty and other awful social problems occur. Republicans don't seem to care, or say *"The free market will take care of it."* Well, the analysis forwarded here argues, the market won't care, the market won't solve those problems, the market won't take care of it: the people, through the positive state, can and will.

In other words, Conservatives/Republicans don't seem to care if the private sector results in conditions akin to Dickens' England, or something Medieval or something even more barbaric. To paraphrase the late author Gore Vidal, "Conservatives' ideology is near-perfect in its immorality." Well, progressives/Democrats do care: they believe in the United States Government as a tool for good, as a solver of problems – and above all they believe in a United States Government that has in the past, and can and will in the future eliminate needless human suffering and pain. And that positive state - that *etatism* - is the New Progressive Era, and it is the theoretical foundation and practical goal of this book – the reason it was written.

Scenario: This policy change - really, a shift in worldview/outlook - would draw from scenarios 1 thru 3, but again, it's more a shift in one's view of the state. Hence, progressives and Democrats, thru both educational and program means, should do everything within their power to promote this outlook, as the sooner most Americans adopt it, the sooner the nation will support public policy solutions to address longstanding problems and pass them into law.

American Ethos: Kenneth Feinberg – America's Chief Mediator

The law-based, impartial, diligent service that is the U.S. civil service is filled with role models for the ages. These are heroic figures who combine impeccable character, stellar intellect and informed, judicious reasoning, along with experience, wisdom and other attributes to telegraph to all the motto that applies always: "fairness and equal treatment under law." The names Dr. Anthony Fauci, Eliot Ness and Joseph Califano immediately come to mind, among others.

Further, regarding U.S. Government assignment appointees for mediation services, the standard – certainly in the modern era – is Kenneth Feinberg, a Massachusetts lawyer and former U.S. prosecutor for the U.S. Justice Department. Just call him, "America's Chief Mediator."

In 2001, Feinberg was appointed by the U.S. Attorney General to be special master of the September 11 Victim Compensation Fund. He worked for almost three years pro bono (without salary), and developed the regulations regarding the fund's governance and administration and administered all program aspects, including evaluating applications, determining appropriate compensation and disseminating awards. The fund was established by the U.S. Congress shortly after the September 11, 2001 terrorist attack on New York,

Ken Feinberg. (Credit: Miller Center for Public Affairs, 2010.)

Washington, D.C. and Stonycreek Township, Pennsylvania, to compensate the victims of the attack (or their families) in exchange for their agreement not to sue the airline corporations involved.

The federal law Congress passed authorized the fund to disburse a maximum of $7.375 billion, including administration costs.

In toto, $7 billion was awarded to 97 percent of the families, with Feinberg presiding over 900 of the 1,600 hearings. Families unhappy with their settlement offer were allowed to appeal in a non-adversarial, informal hearing to present their case in any manner they chose. A non-negotiable clause in the acceptance papers was: that the families were to never file suit against the airlines for any lack of security or otherwise unsafe procedures.

What Is Life Worth?

In his book, *"What Is Life Worth?,"* Feinberg described the eight-part plan which was applied to the September 11th Victim Compensation Fund. Feinberg had to make decisions regarding how much each family of a September 11th victim would receive, including estimating how much each victim would have earned in a lifetime.

"It's a brutal, sort of cold, thing to do. Anybody who looks at this program and expects that by cutting a U.S. Treasury check, you are going to make 9/11 families happy, is vastly misunderstanding what's going on with this program," Feinberg said to ABC News in 2003. "There is not one family member I've met who wouldn't gladly give back the check, or, in many cases, their own lives to have that loved one back. 'Happy' never enters into this equation."

Difficult work that, in the analysis of many, can never, ever be sufficient: but monetary compensation had to occur to begin to provide for the dependents whose life circumstances were changed forever by the terrorist attack. Feinberg's ability to evaluate each case and arrive at impartial, independent decisions has won praise from many, and his services have been actively sought. Feinberg has also served as special master for TARP Executive Compensation, as government-appointed administrator of the BP Deepwater Horizon Disaster Victim Compensation Fund, and as administer of the Commonwealth of Massachusetts' One Fund, a victim assistance fund established after the 2013 Boston Marathon bombings.

Feinberg's work has been praised and recognized by numerous organizations and he's received many awards for his civil service and public service, including the Hubert H. Humphrey Humanitarian Award (2011), the Thomas Jefferson Foundation Medalist in Law award (2014), the Yale University Legend in Leadership Award (2014), and the "Lawyer of the Year" (2004) award by the National Law Journal.

TRIVIA TEST 7: U.S. – 1776-Present

(Answers in Appendix, Page 354.)

1. Which person did not sign the U.S. Declaration of Independence?
a) John Adams
b) John Hancock
c) Thomas Jefferson
d) Abigail Adams

2. Who was the first president to use an airplane on U.S. official business?
a) Kennedy
b) Carter
c) FDR
d) None of the above

3. Which is true about both President Lincoln and President Obama
a) Each is from Illinois, each is tall and thin, and each had most of his policies opposed by the South
b) Each is a fan of soccer
c) Each was against the right of the people to elect representatives to the U.S. House
d) None of the above

President Barack Obama and First Lady Michelle Obama, 2009 Inauguration. (Credit: U.S. National Archives.)

4. Name the four presidents whose faces appear on Mount Rushmore:
a) Washington, Jefferson, Lincoln, Theodore Roosevelt
b) Washington, Jefferson, Lincoln, John Adams
c) Washington, Jefferson, Lincoln, Roger Sherman

d) Washington, Jefferson, Lincoln, Alexander Hamilton

5. President Theodore Roosevelt:
a) Enjoyed the outdoors and supported the development of a national park system
b) Is the president most responsible for the Interstate Highway System
c) Is the president most responsible for the U.S. Department of Education
d) None of the above

6. True or False: President Theodore Roosevelt used to swim in the Potomac River, next to the White House.
a) True
b) False

7. The "whistle-stop tour" using a train to campaign across the country was first used by which U.S. president?
a) Woodrow Wilson b) Calvin Coolidge c) Herbert Hoover d) Harry S. Truman

8. President John F. Kennedy's economic and social program theme was:
a) The New Frontier b) The New World c) The New Day d) The Modern Day

9. President Lyndon B. Johnson's economic and social program theme was?
a) The Great Society
b) A Great Event
c) The Big Event
d) The Big Picture

10) The Democratic Party's victory song is:
a) "There's No Business, Like Show Business"
b) "Good-day, Sunshine"
c) "Day Tripper"
d) "Happy Days Are Here Again"

First Lady Jacqueline Kennedy: The Strength Of The Nation

First Lady Jacqueline Kennedy, who helped define the modern United States with her contribution to the arts, culture and fashion – and did this all with elegance, grace and style – will nevertheless be remembered by most Americans for her strength. The strength to shepherd the nation through its saddest, most horrific and stunning period in the 20th century: the assassination of President John F. Kennedy, her husband, on November 22, 1963.

Dealey Plaza, Dallas, Texas

Further, there is no way to overstate First Lady Kennedy's fortitude. It's a strength that's truly hard to fathom, when one considers what Mrs. Kennedy endured. One moment, at noon she's riding in a motorcade with President Kennedy on a brilliant, sunny, fall day through a downtown packed with people who came to see the president and the first lady on that day. Thirty minutes later, as the motorcade reaches its end in Dealey Plaza preparing to attend a luncheon at the Dallas Trade Mart, shots ring out. How many shots? More than 50 years later, we still don't know if three gun shots - or more than three gun shots - were fired. The president of the United States - your husband – is dead of a severe gun shot wound to the head. His blood and head parts are sprayed all over you and the back of the presidential limousine in a ghastly, horrific trauma – a nightmare for the nation and for the first lady.

Who could possibly remain composed after such a horrific act? Who could possibly function after such a horrific act? Who could possibly move forward after such a horrific act? The brutality, horror and shock of the act *still is difficult to deal with, reading about it today.* It is impossible to fathom what Jacqueline Kennedy went through on that ghastly day.

But incredibly, and miraculously, First Lady Jacqueline Kennedy remained composed, and continued to function. And she helped the nation move forward. There is no greater strength than what she exhibited in Dallas on that horrific day, and in the days that followed during President Kennedy's funeral.

JFK Funeral

Monday, November 25, 1963 arrived too quickly for a stunned nation – still trying to fathom how their young, intelligent, charismatic, liberal-reform-minded president could be dead – taken away from them in the prime of his life. And how the alleged-accused assassin, Lee Harvey Oswald, could not be protected by law enforcement authorities: Oswald was shot and killed by nightclub owner Jack Ruby, as Oswald was being transferred from Dallas police headquarters to the county jail two days after President Kennedy's assassination.

First Lady Jacqueline Kennedy in 1961. (Credit: U.S. National Archives.)

The two events are dizzying in their magnitude, and in their ability to switch a nation filled with confidence...to uncertainty and suspicion.

But once again, at the state funeral Jacqueline Kennedy was a tower of strength. She planned the funeral to follow protocol and historical precedent – planning a procession that duplicated the funeral of President Abraham Lincoln, another liberal reformer who also was assassinated while in office. Her face, hidden with gray veil until her beloved's casket approached, is forever etched in our memory.

Then, after a funeral service at Cathedral of St. Matthew the Apostle in Washington, D.C., walking along with the president's brothers, Attorney General Robert F. Kennedy and U.S. Sen. Edward M. Kennedy, she led the procession to Arlington National Cemetery, and lit the Eternal Flame gravesite for President Kennedy – a flame created at her request.

Post-White House

After the funeral and residing for a short time in Washington's Georgetown neighborhood, Jackie moved to New York. In April 1968, in Atlanta she attended the funeral of the Rev. Martin Luther King, Jr. - another liberal economic and social reform leader - who was assassinated in Memphis. Later that year, Jackie encouraged U.S. Sen. Robert F. Kennedy to run for the presidency, after President Lyndon B. Johnson said he would not seek re-election, due to the controversial Vietnam War, a war that had substantially lowered LBJ's public approval rating and divided the nation. Despite her concerns about RFK's safety, after seeing the political opposition's hatred for him being, in her opinion, as bad or worse than it was for President Kennedy, she supported RFK's decision to run for the presidency and campaigned for him.

RFK Assassination

The nightmare that is the JFK and MLK assassinations continued on June 5, 1968 when Robert F. Kennedy - another liberal economic and social reformer - was assassinated in Los Angeles after winning the California Democratic Party presidential primary. Jackie immediately flew to Los Angeles and, joined by Coretta Scott King, widow of Rev. King, then flew back to New York for RFK's funeral services.

Onassis Marriage

Jackie was criticized, by some, for marrying Greek shipping tycoon Aristotle Onassis in October 1968. But the logic and rational for her decision is obvious. Her husband, a president, was assassinated. Her brother-in-law, a close confidant to her husband and his attorney general, also is assassinated while running for the presidency. The Rev. Martin Luther King, a liberal reformer whose goals were similar to JFK's and RFK's, also is assassinated. You have two children. What will happen next? Meanwhile, Aristotle was able to provide the privacy and security Jackie sought in a land away from the United States. Or, as she put it: "If they're killing Kennedys, then my children are targets....I want to get out of this country," Jackie said.

New York Publishing

After Aristotle's death in 1975, Jackie returned to New York. With her children older, and the nation's political temperature cooler, (after the end of the controversial and unsuccessful Vietnam War), if not normal, following the 1974 Watergate scandal, Jackie accepted a job in a field she always found to be satisfying: writing and literature - an editor job with a New York publisher, before transferring to a second. She spent much of her working life editing books, in addition to her philanthropy work.

Saving Grand Central Terminal

While in New York, residents, still angered by the controversial demolition of the landmark train station, the Beau Arts-style Pennsylvania Station on 34th Street, sought to build political pressure to prevent the demolition of the city's other landmark train station, Grand Central Terminal on Park Avenue and 42nd Street. Jackie led a protest effort to block Grand Central Terminal's demolition and her prominent role played a part in its renovation / preservation. Jackie wrote, in an op-editorial column:

"Is it not cruel to let our city die by degrees, stripped of all her proud monuments, until there will be nothing left of all her history and beauty to inspire our children? If they are not inspired by the past of our city, where will they find the strength to fight for her future? Americans care about their past, but for short-term gain they ignore it and tear down everything that matters. Maybe...this is the time to take a stand to reverse the tide, so that we won't all end up in a uniform world of steel and glass boxes."

A plaque inside Grand Central Terminal recognizes her prominent role in its preservation. Once again, Jacqueline Kennedy showed us what true strength is.

(Central Intelligence Agency Headquarters, Langley, Virginia. Photo Credit: CIA.)

Chapter 19: U.S. Intelligence Community

"A secret organization is a risk in any society. I believe it is a risk that we must take for the net-gain, because I believe it is always going to be there. Now, let's say that we abolish the CIA, it's done so many bad things, let's don't ever have this kind of intelligence organization again. Do you know what will happen then? American presidents are strong-willed men. They wouldn't be in that office if they weren't. If they don't have an intelligence service, they're going to create their own. It may not be very big. And they may reach into the loony bin to find the people to run it. And they may call it 'The Plumbers.' But they will have it."

–CIA Western Hemisphere Director David Atlee Phillips, from the documentary film, "On Company Business: The CIA."

Intelligence gathering and the science/art of spycraft were not invented in the modern era (post-1932), but they certainly expanded during that period. In the 2020-2029 decade ahead, progressives/Democrats can retain the philosophically stronger argument regarding public policy for the U.S. Intelligence Community (USIC) by being strong backers of intelligence community oversight – but oversight that is totally and steadfastly committed to defending American values and American interests.

In the United States, two factors served as the major impetus for the establishment of a large, permanent intelligence community: 1) the failure of U.S military intelligence to detect the surprise, major attack by then Imperialist Japan on the U.S. Naval Base at Pearl Harbor, Hawaii on December 7, 1941, and 2) the unwillingness of the Soviet Union, today Russia, to de-mobilize after the end of World War II in 1945.

Truman's Vision: President Harry Truman's vision and response to the fragmented, disorganized intelligence gathering process was to create one, central organization to both collect and assess data/intelligence, a centralized intelligence agency, hence the name of the CIA. Further, it is important to note that Truman's original plan did not call for the new organization to conduct covert operations or paramilitary operations. Truman would later draw attention to his admonition against CIA covert/paramilitary operations, during his retirement in 1963.

Passed by Congress, Truman signed into law the National Security Act of 1947, which dissolved the original Office of Strategic Services (OSS) – and transferred its functions to the U.S. State Department and U.S. Defense Department – in favor of the new Central Intelligence Agency, headed by a director, appointed by the president, subject to Senate approval.

However, despite Truman's vision/outline for the new intelligence organization, almost from its inception the CIA engaged in both intelligence gathering and covert operations. Truman would admonish the latter in his 1963 op-editorial column, referring to them as "strange operations," that he never intended the agency to conduct.

CIA Intelligence Performance: What's more, the Agency's intelligence performance over the decades has been mixed. The Agency did not predict North Korea's attack on South Korea in 1950; nor the subsequent intervention by China into the Korean War; nor the September 11, 2001 terrorist attack on New York City, Washington, D.C., and Pennsylvania; nor the re-unification of Germany/tearing down of the Berlin Wall in 1989; nor the declaration of independence by former Eastern-Europe Soviet satellite nations; nor the break-up of the Soviet Union in 1991; nor the social change/unrest associated with the Arab Spring in 2011. And, perhaps most glaringly - and catastrophically - the CIA failed to detect substantial and broad-based support for Communist Cuba Leader Fidel Castro during the Bay of Pigs invasion by anti-Castro Cuban rebels in 1961. (Much controversy still surrounds the Pay of Pigs fiasco: the CIA either misjudged Cuban support for Castro, or gambled and thought that President Kennedy, seeing the outmanned and outgunned Anti-Castro rebels facing likely defeat, would mobilize the U.S. Air Force to support the rebels. Kennedy did not. Kennedy later accepted full blame for the invasion failure, despite the fact that the record shows that the CIA under Director Allen Dulles went forward with the Bay of Pigs invasion in direct disobedience to Kennedy's order. Kennedy subsequently fired Dulles.)

CIA Covert Operations: The Bay of Pigs incident in Cuba can be categorized as both an intelligence and covert operation, and regarding the latter, CIA's performance over the decades also has been mixed. CIA covert operations played a role in the overthrow of the leaders of Iran, Guatemala, and Chile. (In Chile, a 1973 coup d'etat sponsored by the CIA resulted in the ouster and death of Salvador Allende, the first democratically-elected Marxist/Democratic Socialist of a Latin American country, and the start of a military junta led by Chilean Army General Augusto Pinochet.) More-recently, the CIA has been criticized for extraordinary rendition (the extrajudicial transfer of terrorists/enemies of the U.S. to nations for interrogation and possible torture); enhanced interrogation techniques - which most human rights groups consider to be torture; the training of militants, and other actions.

Church Committee: The above underperformances in both intelligence and covert operations, combined with activities that violate human rights, U.S. law and/or actions that were deemed not in the national interest of the United States, among other issues, led to a 1975 U.S. Senate investigation of intelligence activities, the U.S. Senate Select Committee to Study Governmental Operations with Respect to Intelligence Activities, commonly known as the Church Committee. The committee was chaired by U.S. Sen. Frank Church, D-Idaho; the committee served as a precursor to the permanent U.S. Senate Select Committee on Intelligence. (Today, there is also a U.S. House Committee on Intelligence.) The Church Committee investigated reports of illegality during intelligence gathering by the CIA, FBI and NSA, after several activities were made public, as a result of the Watergate investigation in 1974.

The Church Committee evaluated the U.S. intelligence community's alleged violations of law and abuses of power, and issued reform recommendations; selected recommendations were implemented. The Church Committee investigated attempts to assassinate foreign leaders, including Democratic Republic of Congo Leader Patrice Lumumba, the Dominican Republic's Rafael Trujillo, the Diem brothers of Vietnam, Chile Gen. René Schneider, and also investigated CIA Director Allen Dulles's plan - approved by President Eisenhower - to use the Sicilian Mafia to attempt to kill Cuba's Fidel Castro.

As a result of the committee's work, President Gerald Ford issued Executive Order 11905, that banned U.S.-sanctioned assassinations of foreign leaders. In 1981, President Ronald Reagan's Executive Order 12333 reversed and ended the ban.

The Church Committee represented the most extensive, systematic and public review of U.S. intelligence operations in the nation's history. A considerable amount of information remained classified, but more than 50,000 pages of intelligence material were declassified under the Assassination Records Collection Act of 1992.

Intelligence In The Postmodern Era: In the postmodern era, 18 agencies form the U.S. intelligence community, led by the Office of the Director of National Intelligence (DNI). One key qualifier: the DNI has no authority to direct or control any agency in the intelligence community, except his/her own staff.

The 18 agencies:

Central Intelligence Agency (CIA), Office of Intelligence and Counterintelligence (OICI), Office of Intelligence and Analysis (IA), Coast Guard Intelligence (CGI), Bureau of Intelligence and Research (INR), Office of Terrorism and Financial Intelligence (TFI), Defense Intelligence Agency (DIA), National Security Agency (NSA), National Geospatial-Intelligence Agency (NGA), National Reconnaissance Office (NRO), United States Army Intelligence and Security Command (INSCOM), Marine Corps Intelligence Activity (MCIA), Office of Naval Intelligence (ONI), Federal Bureau of Investigation, National Security Branch (FBI/NSB), Drug Enforcement Administration (DEA), Sixteenth Air Force (SAF), Office of National Security Intelligence (DEA/ONSI) and the U.S. Space Force (USSF).

The Church Doctrine: As former CIA Western Hemisphere Director David Atlee Phillips outlined, a secret organization is a risk in any society - that's incontrovertible. But what's also incontrovertible is the need to develop a capacity to know what enemies - current and potential - of the United States are doing. How best, then, to proceed?

The answer was offered by the late, great U.S. Sen. Frank Church, D-Idaho, in what is called here, "The Church Doctrine" – and it's one progressives/Democrats should push for in the new Biden Administration.

Church, who left this life far too soon, believed the key – whether it's CIA, NSC, DIA, NRO etc. – is oversight, or what he called "proper supervision." All government organizations - indeed all organizations, private and public – display a tendency to emphasize "organization interest" over a larger, non-selfish interest. Hence, regarding U.S. Government institutions, lawmakers on Capitol Hill must be ever-vigilant to ensure that the intelligence community, and in particular the CIA, is: 1) not violating the law and 2) is implementing the administration's directives/obeying administration policy. And when that "proper supervision" as Church outlined, is not occurring, Congress and the president must implement changes to see that it resumes.

One issue for the president and lawmakers on Capitol Hill concerns what constitutes effective oversight of the CIA, of the NSA and the intelligence community more-broadly. Although recent attention has centered on the NSA, historically, because it has been at the apex of the intelligence community, the focus has been on the CIA. One argument - one backed by President John F. Kennedy – argues that the problem is the CIA's independent agency status – that it inherently repels oversight/proper supervision. This line of reasoning would break up the CIA, with various units distributed to the State, Treasury and Defense departments, arguing that placing these units under direct cabinet-level control restores oversight by the president. Others say the problem is not with the CIA's independent agency status, so much as it is with too many Congressional intelligence committee members not doing their jobs – i.e., that lawmakers who become 'successfully co-opted' by the Agency, and align their interest with the Agency, to the detriment of oversight. As of late-2020, there was no overwhelming consensus among lawmakers on Capitol Hill regarding how to reform oversight.

Accordingly then, progressives and Democrats should take up that gauntlet and lobby for enhanced, closer oversight, led by the president and vice president in the new Biden Administration. To be clear, Democrats must emphasize their close, daily dialogue with the USIC, led by CIA.

Further, the new U.S. president should resume at least monthly meetings with the CIA director; ideally the two should meet every two weeks, but due to the time demands of each, monthly meetings may be the most practical schedule. The U.S. president–CIA director meeting lapsed during the 2017-2020 period, and it needs to resume, as does the president's regular reading of the President's Daily Briefing (PDB) – the classified intelligence brief that CIA submits early each morning to the president. Democrats must also insist that the president designate one person in his inner circle of close advisors – it could be U.S. Vice President Harris – as the go-to point-person for liaison to the U.S. Congress on intelligence matters, specifically for whomever is the leader of the Democrats in the U.S. Senate and the U.S. House. (Now that the Democrats have majority status in the Senate, and retained their House majority, that would be U.S. Sen. Charles Schumer, D-New York, and Speaker Nancy Pelosi, D-California, respectively.) Both Senate and House Democratic leadership must know who the White House go-to person is for CIA and USIC-related matters, in order for the legislative branch to exercise proper oversight, from the party in power. This is in addition to statutory communications for the "Gang of Eight" - the eight leaders within the Congress who are briefed on classified intelligence matters by the executive branch. In short, Democrats must re-establish the classified, close, continual dialogue between the president and the USIC, led by CIA – a vital, ongoing dialogue that is intrinsic to maintaining U.S. national security.

Scenario: This policy change would likely draw from scenario 1 – reforms within the system. Reiterating, Democrats should re-establish the national norm that went absent 2017-2020: emphasize their close, daily dialogue with the USIC, led by CIA.

American Ethos: Dan Hardway – Congressional Investigator Extraordinaire

There are great lawyers, and then there is the beyond-stellar lawyer Dan Hardway. There are great investigators, and then there is the uber investigator Dan Hardway. And there are morally and institutionally courageous individuals serving the public interest, and then there are the beyond heroic deeds of Dan Hardway.

Isn't it time for the truth? The American people want the truth.

Isn't it time for the facts? The American people want the facts.

If it is, then it's time for Dan Hardway.

From 1976 to 1978 lawyer Dan Hardway and lawyer Edwin Lopez were assigned by the U.S. House Select Committee on Assassinations (HSCA) to re-investigate the assassination of President John F. Kennedy on November 22, 1963 in Dallas, Texas. Robert Blakey was HSCA chief counsel. Hardway, a Cornell law student at the time, and Lopez began their work for the HSCA in July 1977. Specifically, Hardway's primary assignment / responsibility on the HSCA's Task Force 5 was: research the Central Intelligence Agency's (CIA) awareness of accused assassin Lee Harvey Oswald's activities in Mexico City during the fall 1963. Oswald, a purported communist, was arrested about 90 minutes after the shooting in Dallas's Dealey Plaza on November 22 and charged with both the murder of President Kennedy and the murder of Dallas Police Officer

Attorney Dan Hardway. (Credit: Assassination Archives and Research Center, Maryland, United States.)

J.D. Tippet. In September 1964, the Warren Commission concluded that Oswald fired three shots in Dealey Plaza from the Texas School Book Depository building, killing JFK, and wounding Texas Gov. John Connally, with a bullet fragment striking the cheek of bystander James Tague, across the plaza.

Oswald Defects, Returns To U.S.

Oswald, a former U.S. Marine who had defected to Russia (then the Soviet Union) in the 1950s, but returned, had been a pro-Castro Communist Cuba supporter and had other trappings of being a communist, but many assassination researchers argue he was "sheep-dipped" – made to appear to be a communist, when, they argue, he really was a U.S. intelligence agent trained to be a false defector deployed in the Soviet Union.

Hardway's and Lopez's work was dependent on gaining access to CIA records, and initially Hardway and Lopez had it, as Blakey had negotiated a very good agreement with CIA that gave Hardway and other investigators unprecedented access to its files.

Blakey initially ruled out investigating whether there had been a plot / conspiracy to assassinate President Kennedy, as the HSCA's budget and time was limited, and Blakey considered a plot / conspiracy investigation "putting all our eggs in one basket" – i.e., searching for conspirators when you haven't even determined if there was a conspiracy. From the fall 1977 to mid-summer 1978 Hardway and Lopez had an office at CIA's Langley, Virginia headquarters. Hardway's research confirmed that the Agency had photos of Oswald in Mexico City – or at least someone claiming to be Oswald. Based on Hardway's research, Hardway became convinced someone had impersonated Oswald during calls to the Russian Embassy, if not in person at the Russian and Cuban embassies in Mexico City. Hardway thought the assassination bore the earmarks of an intelligence operation, and he thought that the best way to research the operation was to look at the disinformation portion of the assassination and work backward. In his research, Hardway determined the sources of post-assassination, pro-Castro news stories on Oswald.

CIA Changes HSCA Research Rules

However, that's when the CIA changed HSCA's research rules. CIA closed Hardway's and Lopez's office, and brought retired CIA Officer George Joannides back to serve as liaison to the HSCA and Hardway / Lopez: the latter two no longer had direct access to CIA files, and all requests had to go through Joannides, in writing. Basically, at that point the Agency shut down the Hardway / Lopez investigation, according to Hardway, but before it did, Hardway said he was able to document many links between CIA Officer David Atlee Phillips and most of the sources of the news stories that came out immediately after the assassination with detailed information on Oswald and his pro-Castro activities. Hardway confronted Phillips with those links at an interview at CIA on August 24, 1978. Phillips was extremely agitated by that line of questioning, but Phillips was forced to admit that most of the sources were assets he had managed, and were managing in the fall 1963. Phillips, a high-ranking CIA officer and as cool an intelligence official as there ever was, had 3 cigarettes lit at the same time when Hardway questioned him on his assets information / disinformation campaign.

And About Mr. Joannides...

Further, the Agency also violated an agreement with the HSCA: the Agency promised not to have any liaison to the HSCA be a CIA officer who was active in 1963. But it not only assigned someone who was active in 1963 to be HSCA liaison – George Joannides – about two decades after the HSCA investigation, Author / Researcher Jefferson Morley found in a CIA 201 Intelligence File that Joannides was overseeing the propaganda operation at JMWAVE in Miami and had direct responsibility for the DRE, the Directorio Revolucionario Estudantil or Student Revolutionary Directorate, a group of anti-Castro Cuban exiles whose officers had contact with Oswald – and was the main source of pro-Castro Oswald stories in 1963 - stories both before and after the November 22, 1963 assassination. CIA has since admitted, in court filings, that Joannides served in a covert capacity at least twice: in Miami in 1963 and as CIA liaison to the HSCA in 1978.

In other words, according to Hardway, the Agency knew where to not let Hardway and Lopez look, and it shut the pair's investigation down. HSCA Chief Counsel Blakey has called what the Agency did "obstruction of justice." From an outside reviewer / reader standpoint, at minimum, it certainly was audacious.

Hardway still believes there was intelligence operation involvement in the assassination. Readers can evaluate the facts and discern for themselves what they think it means, and what would represent a prudent, next step. Investigator Morley argues that it asks whether the Warren Commission in 1963-1964 had the basic facts - the basic material - to reach an informed verdict/conclusion regarding the JFK case, and according to Morley's analysis, they didn't.

According to yours truly (Lazzaro), the author of this book, and I state my name here so that the reader knows this is my analysis – not anyone else's – whether Oswald was a double-agent or legally insane, I'm not sure. The case is complicated by numerous unknowns, the most important of which may be regarding who Oswald was. There are still classified flies regarding Oswald, hence one good starting point for additional research would be to make public those files. Nearly 60 years after the most shocking assassination of the modern era, and one of the worst days in American history, we still don't know exactly what happened and who Lee Harvey Oswald was. If you're a younger reader or someone who has never heard about November 22, 1963 and you learned nothing else, after reading this profile you essentially know the status of the case today: it's an unsolved murder, with scores of unanswered questions remaining.

**

Note: This profile is primarily based on HSCA reports and research by Hardway and Lopez, and Hardway's narrated report, Episode 44 – "50 Reasons For 50 Years," produced by Len Osanic, Black Op Radio, Canada, 2013.

American Ethos: Victor Marchetti On The CIA And 'The Cult Of Intelligence'

Just call Victor Marchetti "a trailblazer."

Patriotic, loyal, talented, industrious - few intelligence professionals - let alone the general public - will understand the role, operational structure, effectiveness and impact of the nation's chief intelligence organization, the Central Intelligence Agency (CIA), as well as Victor Marchetti, who joined the CIA in 1955 and rose to special assistant to CIA Director Richard Helms. Marchetti was a specialist on the Soviet Union's military capability, especially regarding Cuba, and, equally significant, became the CIA's leading expert on aid given to Third World countries, today known as emerging markets / the developing world.

A Reassessment

A valued and star performer, Marchetti became disillusioned with the Agency's policies and practices and resigned in 1969. After writing a novel, entitled "The Rope Dancer," his second book, "The CIA and the Cult of Intelligence," published in 1973, made front-page news, to say the least. In it, Marchetti outlines the CIA's not-so-slow walk from collecting intelligence, to an obsession with clandestine operations in other countries (and in some cases, inside the United States – something that's prohibited by the National Security Act of 1947). Many of these operations involved interference in the internal affairs of sovereign countries. And Marchetti is very clear regarding where he stands on the CIA's effectiveness and impact: "I had come to the conclusion, as a member of the CIA, that many of our policies and practices were not in the best interests of the United States, but were in fact counter-productive, and that if the American people were aware of this they would not tolerate it," Marchetti wrote.

Vietnam: A Focal-Point For Many

Marchetti left the CIA in 1969, amid the Cold War and during the most intense period of the highly-controversial Vietnam War – the U.S.'s greatest internal crisis since the Civil War.

Marchetti's Breakthrough Work

Marchetti cited the false, propaganda incident that the CIA had a role in publicizing - the 1964 Gulf of Tonkin incident - with influencing his decision to leave the Agency. In the Tonkin incident, North Vietnamese motor torpedo boats had allegedly attacked two American destroyers, and that persuaded Congress to give President Lyndon B. Johnson a blank check to pursue the war in Southeast Asia. The CIA confirmed the attack. But the attack never occurred, Marchetti said: the boats did perform threatening maneuvers, growled a bit, but never fired. There were no

(Credit: Alfred A. Knopf Publisher, 1974.)

torpedo hits, or reports of any torpedoes whizzing by the U.S. ships. Most readers know the rest of the story: LBJ used the 'attack' to get the resolution passed in Congress, escalated the Vietnam War, the U.S. was nearly torn apart in civil and social strife, and more than 53,000 U.S. Armed Forces members were killed. Further, one could make a case that the tumultuous 1960s that included a major counter-cultural movement would not have been as questioning or as disruptive had the Vietnam War not occurred. It was a war that was fought for the wrong reason, and a major impetus was an attack, publicized by the CIA, that - in fact - did not occur.

Marchetti's message from "The Cult of Intelligence" is clear: the CIA has abused its authority, its secrecy too often is a cloak by which it evades responsibility / accountability, it's wielding disproportionate and in some cases unilateral influence on foreign policy, and most covert operations are not maintaining national security – they are weakening the United States by turning the hearts and minds of citizens in foreign countries against the United States. He is not bashful in his analysis.

'A Master At Distorting History'

"It [The CIA] has unwittingly and, often, deliberately deceived itself - and the American taxpayer. The CIA is a master at distorting history - even creating its own version of history to suit its institutional and operational purposes. It can do this largely because of two great advantages it possesses. One is the excessively secret environment in which it operates, and the other is that it is essentially a private instrument of the presidency," Marchetti wrote.

Marchetti: "The real reason for the official secrecy, in most instances, is not to keep the opposition [the CIA's euphemistic term for the enemy] from knowing what is going on; the enemy usually does know. The basic reason for governmental secrecy is to keep you, the American public, from knowing -- for you, too, are considered the opposition, or enemy

-- so that you cannot interfere. When the public does not know what the government or the CIA are doing, it cannot voice its approval or disapproval of their actions. In fact, they can even lie to you about what they are doing or have done, and you will not know it."

Marchetti continued: "As for the second advantage, despite frequent suggestion that the CIA is a rogue elephant, the truth is that the Agency functions at the direction of and in response to the office of the president. All of its major clandestine operations are carried out with the direct approval of or on direct orders from the White House. The CIA is a secret tool of the president -- every president. And every president since Truman has lied to the American people in order to protect the Agency. When lies have failed, it has been the duty of the CIA to take the blame for the president, thus protecting him. This is known in the business as 'plausible denial.' "

"The CIA, functioning as a secret instrument of the U.S. government and the presidency, has long misused and abused history and continues to do so. I first became concerned about this historical distortion in 1957, when I was a young officer in the Clandestine Services of the CIA," Marchetti wrote.

Marchetti: Villain Or Patriot?

Another, former officer, the late CIA Officer David Atlee Phillips, 1950-1975, who was head of Western Hemisphere Operations, would probably put Marchetti in his "the kiss and tell boys" category because Marchetti wrote a book that revealed CIA secrets, which violated the CIA's secrecy oath. Phillips said he would always honor the CIA's secrecy oath.

Postmodern U.S. Intelligence

Marchetti's criticism of the CIA poses questions for which there are no easy answers. How can the United States collect intelligence and reign-in/eliminate the abuses associated with secrecy? How can it make the CIA more-accountable, with stronger oversight, without reducing its ability to complete operations? More broadly, how can it prevent the CIA from guiding policy - and in some cases from implementing policy - on its own? [There's no better example of the CIA guiding policy than Cuba in the 1960s, when, in Marchetti's interpretation, the U.S.'s failure to accept initially-modest reforms by President Fidel Castro pushed Cuba into an alignment with the then-Soviet Union (now Russia).] And should the CIA's operations be transferred to federal departments where there is more-direct oversight, such as the U.S. Department of Defense? Each question requires input from many experts, and will take years for Congress to formulate an answer. Marchetti argues that reform is needed because, as he astutely outlined, the U.S. intelligence community is not prompting citizens in other countries to think well of the United States.

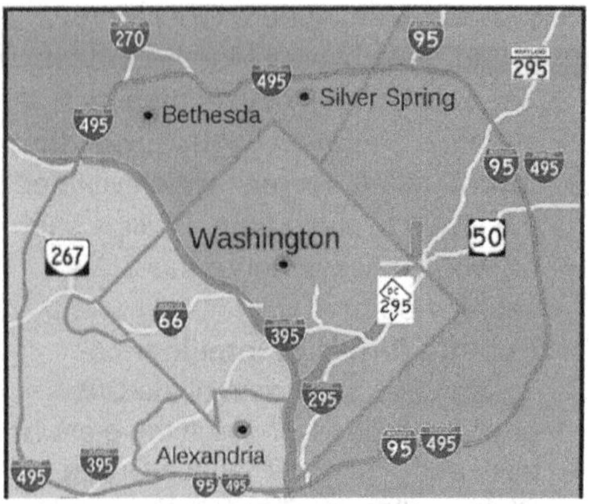

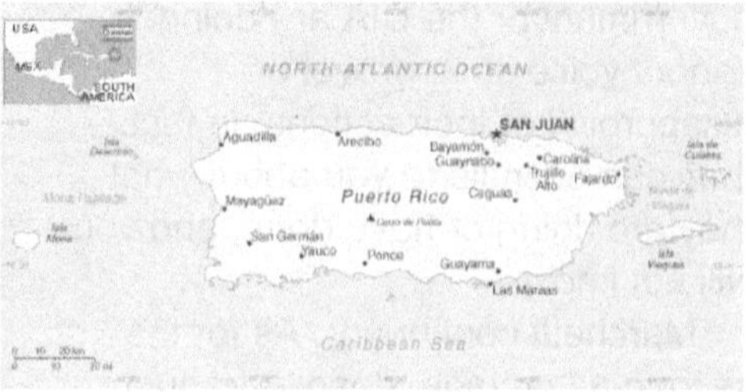

(Washington, D.C. and Puerto Rico. Photo credit: Washington, D.C. WikCommons and Puerto Rico: CIA World Factbook.)

Chapter 20: 51st and 52nd States - Washington Douglass Commonwealth and Puerto Rico

"No taxation without representation," -Founding Father/Framer Benjamin Franklin

Another issue where progressives and Democrats have the philosophically stronger argument is: creating the 51st and 52nd states in Washington Douglass Commonwealth (currently Washington, D.C.) and Puerto Rico (currently U.S. territory Puerto Rico).

On June 26, 2020, the U.S. House passed the D.C. Statehood Bill, 232-180. The bill now heads to the U.S. Senate; further, given that the Democratic Party hold a majority in the Senate in 2021, the bill may receive a vote, but Republicans will likely filibuster any Democratic Party effort to vote on the bill, and it takes 60 votes to end a filibuster, a parliamentary move called "cloture." However, if Democrats choose to eliminate the filibuster, it will only take 51 votes, not 60, to approve statehood. As noted, with the Senate split 50-50, Vice President Harris is the tie-breaking 51st vote for the Democrats. (In fact, as noted, look for many 51-50 Democratic Party win votes in the next two years, and probably for longer.)

Meanwhile, Puerto Rico in a November 2020 referendum (52.3%) asked to be admitted to the union as a state.

With the ballot measure is approved, Puerto Rico's governor will appoint a seven-member commission to represent Puerto Rico in matters and negotiations related to achieving statehood. The commission would develop a transition plan, which the governor would approve or reject, and present the plan to Congress and the president.

Arguments for statehood: The arguments for statehood for each are manifold.

-Full and equal Congressional rights. Currently, the residents of D.C. and Puerto Rico have no voting representation in Congress. Yet in D.C., they bear the same responsibility of citizenship, including paying U.S. income taxes. (Puerto Rico citizens are exempt from U.S. income taxes, except for those adults who work for the U.S. Government.) D.C. has a Congressional delegate, who can sponsor legislation and vote on committees, but not on the U.S. House floor; Puerto Rico has a non-voting resident commissioner in Congress, who serves a four-year term – the only elected House member who serves four years.

-No taxation without representation: In the case of D.C., it's literally a case of "taxation without representation" – in other words in direct conflict with the reason the United States, formerly British Colonies, revolted from the British Empire. It is rank hypocrisy, according to the analysis of many, including yours truly. At minimum, it is a double standard of the egregious sort. Every citizen in these United States deserves equal representation in Congress.

In the case of Washington, D.C., the injustice has occurred for more than 200 years: Congress passed the District of Columbia Organic Act of 1801, which placed the District under the exclusive control of the federal government. After the Organic Act's passage, citizens living in the District were no longer considered residents of Maryland or Virginia, and that ended their representation in Congress. In the case of Puerto Rico, it's been 122 years, since the United States claimed the island as a territory after its victory in the Spanish-American War. Then, in 1917, the U.S. Congress passed the Jones–Shafroth Act (popularly known as the Jones Act), which granted Puerto Ricans born on or after April 25, 1898, U.S. citizenship.

With statehood, the proposed Washington Douglass Commonwealth and Puerto Rico, will each have 2 U.S. Senators, Washington would have 1 U.S. Representative and Puerto Rico at least 4 and possible 5 U.S. Representatives. (Puerto Rico's population is larger than 21 states; D.C.'s population is roughly equal to Vermont, Wyoming or Alaska.) In Washington, D.C.'s case, the District of Columbia's federal area (containing the U.S. Capitol, Supreme Court, National Mall, and other federal properties) would remain the smaller District of Columbia; Douglass Commonwealth would encompass the residential and commercial areas of D.C. Also, with statehood, D.C.'s electoral college votes in U.S. presidential elections would remain 3; Puerto Rico would have electoral college votes for the first time, totaling 6 or 7, depending on its population at the time, according to the equal apportionment of electors based on the U.S. Census. (Electors for the states are allocated based on population, plus an elector for each state's 2 U.S. Senators).

Further, to some readers, statehood may seem like merely an abstraction or an academic debate. Nothing could be further from the truth: statehood is an important issue, for its practical impact on the typical person's daily life, for its substance and for its principle/symbolism. Consider this: without statehood, residents of D.C. and Puerto Rico do not receive full benefits during crises, such as hurricanes, earthquakes, the coronavirus pandemic, fiscal emergencies, other act-of-nature events, and unexpected problems. Statehood literally will eliminate second-class citizenship status for these citizens. In the case of Puerto Rico, all island residents, not just federal employees, would have to pay U.S. income taxes, but the analysis forwarded here argues the above benefits far outweigh the liabilities. It goes without saying that there is something inherently unfair about a citizen of a nation not having the same rights, responsibilities and benefits as any other citizen: flawed as the U.S. Constitution was, Thomas Jefferson spoke to this inherent equality in his famous sentence in the U.S. Declaration of Independence. Jefferson: *"We hold these truths to be self-evident, that all men are created equal, that they are endowed by their Creator with certain unalienable Rights, that among these are Life, Liberty and the pursuit of Happiness."*

Another reason for D.C. and Puerto Rico statehood concerns local rule / home rule. Citizens of these future states want to end Congressional interference in their local governments. Republicans are for states' rights, but here again – this is another issue where Republican hypocrisy is blatant: they like states' rights when it favors red or Republican states, they don't like it when it favors blue or Democratic states. That, too, is rank hypocrisy and a double-standard of the very worst sort. With D.C. and Puerto Rico as states, local governors, state legislators and town mayors will have much more freedom and discretion to manage local issues and concerns – and to formulate/adapt solutions so that they meet local interests and needs: the people of these states will be closer to their government. Progressives and Democrats should continually hammer away at this powerful point: new states mean more local control, local control, local control! And home rule. (A phrase favored by residents of Connecticut.)

In addition, those that argue statehood creation is a special, extraordinary or non-traditional process present a very weak argument: in a summary – they are wrong. The U.S. Congress can create the 51st and 52nd states by simple majority votes. Along with the 13 original colonies, all 37 states since the original 13 have gone through the same process. It's called an Admission Act. Unlike the states, Washington, D.C. is mentioned in the U.S. Constitution (Article 1, Section 8), but that only sets a maximum size for the District ("not exceeding 10 square miles") for the "Seat of the Government of the United States." Congress can reduce the District's size, as it did in 1846, when Congress returned the District's portion south and west of the Potomac River to Virginia, after residents in that state convinced Congress that that portion of the District was not necessary for the successful operation/function of the federal government. In other words, from a legislative or parliamentary standpoint, creating a state is easy. Politically, however, it is hard. As noted, for decades, the Republican Party and conservatives have opposed D.C. and Puerto Rico statehood because these two areas are disproportionately comprised by Democrats. Moreover, it appears that no fact or argument will change the Republican Party's stance in Congress – at least it won't change that party's stance anytime soon. Hence, progressives and Democrats should expend little or no energy trying to do so because it would be a waste of time. Rather, given the "no taxation without representation" philosophically stronger argument, progressives and Democrats have already won that debate, and, now that they control Congress and the presidency after the November 2020 election, they should proceed directly, with confidence, to work to pass two Admissions Acts, on a timetable of their choosing. Progressives and Democrats can refute any protest by Republicans by simply saying, "Republicans denied D.C. and Puerto Rico statehood for decades because they had the votes in Congress, now we progressives/Democrats are passing D.C. and Puerto Rico statehood because we have the votes in Congress."

Arguments against statehood: The arguments against statehood are philosophically weak, to say the least. For example, some argue that Puerto Rico should seek independent nation status. That would bestow several benefits – Puerto Rico could cut all ties with the United States and remove all U.S. Navy installations and related armed forces facilities from the island, as some seek, if they choose to do so. But independent nation status would probably affect the interest rate and terms of its debt. As of late-2020, Puerto Rico's public debt totaled about $74 billion. In all probability, the debt will have to be restructured, and the analysis forwarded here argues that remaining as a state in the United States will lead to more-favorable refinancing terms. Whether one is a strong supporter of U.S. investment banks (as yours truly is) or less of a fan, the fact remains that these banks generally offer more-favorable terms when a bond issue or deal is connected to or supported by the United States Government. And that does not mean only debt offerings guaranteed by the federal government – which almost always receives the lowest interest rate among U.S. jurisdictions:

additionally, a debt offering *coordinated or encouraged by the U.S. Government* almost always nets a lower interest rate for the borrower(s) from the investment banks. And, needless to add, if a major restructuring has to occur, for example, if $35 billion in short-term debt is written-off/cancelled in exchange for $40 billion in longer-term debt – which would result in a substantial cash flow improvement for the borrower(s), once again, the investment banks are much more likely to approve it if the United States Government, either through moral suasion, or "Do one in our favor, do one for the good of the team," asks the U.S. investment bank(s) to approve the deal. Fiscally, and with the public at large, that has to count for something, hence the benefit of statehood status.

Similarly, the arguments against statehood for D.C. are also weak. Some argue that the District should merge with either Maryland or Virginia. The problem is, neither Maryland or Virginia residents favor D.C. inclusion, and their respective elected state officials show no inclination to go against the public on this issue. Others want the District to retain the status quo, but as noted, that continues the awful "taxation without representation" policy that should not have been allowed to start. Further, linking up the District with other territories is not practical. Hence, the strongest philosophical and operational argument is D.C. as the 51st state – the Douglass Commonwealth.

The 51st and 52nd states: In sum, progressives and Democrats, with the new Biden Administration, should move forward with statehoods for Washington, D.C. and Puerto Rico. These reforms will give the citizens of these new states a government based on the consent of the governed, local control / home rule, and equal representation in the U.S. Congress.

Scenario: This policy change would draw from scenario 3 (new system) – the creation of two states.

TRIVIA TEST 8: U.S. – 1776-Present, Part 2

(Answers in Appendix, Page 354.)

1. How many jobs did Presidents Carter, Clinton and Obama create? (Obama thru March 2016.)
a) 39,631,000
b) 20,521,000
c) 17,410,000
d) 14,950,000

2. How many jobs did Presidents Reagan, George H.W. Bush and George W. Bush create?
a) 15,831,000
b) 14,750,000
c) 12,990,000
d) 11,450,000

3. Which is true about President George W. Bush '43'?
a) He was the first U.S. president to visit the Soviet Union
b) He did not like baseball
c) He did not attend Yale
d) He came close to becoming the first president in the modern era to end his presidency with no, net new jobs created

President George W. Bush, with U.S. Attorney General Alberto Gonzales, 2004
(Credit: U.S. National Archives.)

4. Which is true about President Harry S. Truman?
a) He did not enjoy going for a walk
b) He opposed any attempt to expand public health care in the United States
c) He opposed plans to create the Central Intelligence Agency

d) When he left office in 1953, President Truman had no presidential pension and under $200,000 in wealth

5. President George H.W. “Poppa” Bush can call 4 states home: Connecticut, Texas, Maine and?
a) Idaho b) Alaska c) North Dakota d) Virginia

6. True or False: President Eisenhower had a White House putting green installed in 1954.
a) True b) False

7. The only former president whose wife has won an election to the U.S. Congress is?
a) Woodrow Wilson
b) Calvin Coolidge
c) Herbert Hoover
d) Bill Clinton

8. Which president said, "The only thing we have to fear is, fear itself." ?
a) President Eisenhower
b) President Nixon
c) President Reagan
d) President Franklin D. Roosevelt

9. Which presidential candidate received the most votes in the 2016 election?
a) Smith b) Mathews c) Green d) Clinton

10) As of March 2016, President Obama’s national health insurance plan, the ACA / Obamacare had increased the number of Americans with health insurance by how many?
a) 20 million b) 10 million c) 15 million d) zero

(The Earth, as seen from Apollo 8. Apollo 11 would later land on the Moon in July 1969. Credit: NASA.)

Chapter 21: NASA, U.S. Postal Service, Amtrak and PBS & NPR

"Houston, tranquility base here. The Eagle has landed." -Apollo 11 Astronaut Neil Armstrong, after the lunar module landed on the Moon in July 1969.

Another issue that progressives and Democrats have the stronger philosophical argument concerns not so much an issue as it is the restoration of key public organizations and public assets, following four years of degeneration and deterioration from malign neglect, underfunding and hollowing-out: NASA, the U.S. Postal Service, Amtrak and PBS & NPR. A description and analysis of each, follows.

National Aeronautics and Space Administration

First, progressives and Democrats and the new Biden Administration must jump-start the National Aeronautics and Space Administration (NASA).

NASA's vision: "We reach for new heights and reveal the unknown for the benefit of mankind."

NASA's mission: "Drive advances in science, technology, aeronautics, and space exploration to enhance knowledge, education, innovation, economic vitality and stewardship of Earth."

The NASA F2020 budget is $22.6 billion and its proposed F2021 budget was $25.2 billion. With Democratic Party control of Congress, and with the new Biden Administration in place beginning in January 2021, Democrats should propose a $30 billion F2022 budget with three goals: 1) a plan for at least 1 return flight to the Moon, 2) a plan to fly an un-manned, but human-capable flight to Mars by 2030, and 3) full U.S. participation in the International Space Station through F2040. However, there is a caveat:

Given the number, variety and complexity of NASA programs, and their cost, House/Senate Democrats should let the new Biden Administration indicate its space priorities, before lobbying for the above three programs. Moreover, they should adjust the above three to accommodate the administration's preferences and needs. It is entirely possible that President Biden may have a different priority or two, and that's reasonable. Doing so will enable Democrats to unite/merge White House/Capitol Hill legislative goals – which will increase both Capitol Hill and public support for the NASA program – something that will aid passage of NASA's budget.

In 1961, President John F. Kennedy, whose "New Frontier" represented the start of new era in American purpose, achievement, and contribution to civilization, challenged the nation to do better in the business world, in education, in diplomacy, in international relations, and in space:

"I believe that this nation should commit itself to achieving the goal, before this decade is out, of landing a man on the Moon and returning him safely to the Earth." -President John F. Kennedy, address to Congress, May 1961.

The Space Race - the Cold War in outer space between the democratic United States and the communist Soviet Union (now Russia) – was on.

"We choose to go to the moon in this decade and do the other things, not because they are easy, but because they are hard." -President John F. Kennedy, Rice University speech, September 1962.

Dallas - November 22, 1963: Kennedy's brutal and sudden death, murdered in a flurry of bullets on November 22, 1963 at 12:30 p.m. CT in Dealey Plaza in Dallas, Texas — stunned and numbed the nation. And without question, it deepened the national resolve to meet his goal – as a lasting tribute to him, to his policies, and to his leadership. After the nation's most horrific murder of the modern era, Americans were now not only racing to land a man on the Moon to beat the Soviets: they were doing so to honor President John F. Kennedy.

And race the nation did, and in retrospect, the nation, at least initially, moved too fast. Astronaut and U.S. Sen. John Glenn's, D-Ohio, became the first American to orbit the Earth in February 1962. Soviet Union Cosmonaut Yuri Gagarin was the first human to orbit the Earth, in April 1961 – and with the U.S. pushing hard to achieve a different space exploration first before the Soviets, a tragedy occurred. Apollo 1, a planned low-Earth orbital test of the Apollo rocket program, never made its target launch date of February 21, 1967. A cabin fire during a launch rehearsal test on January 27, 1967 at Cape Canaveral Air Force Station Launch Complex 34 killed all three crew members: Command Pilot Virgil "Gus" Grissom, Senior Pilot Edward White, and Pilot Roger Chaffee. U.S. manned Apollo flights were suspended for 20 months until program's design and construction flaws were corrected.

Problems corrected, the first, successful, manned Apollo mission was Apollo 7 in October 1968. Two months later, in December 1968 Apollo 8 became the first manned spacecraft to leave Earth's orbit, obit the Moon, and return safely to Earth. In March 1969, Apollo 9 successfully tested the command/service docking, and a spacewalk, the latter of which the Soviet Union achieved first in January 1969. In May 1969, Apollo 10 represented a full, dress-rehearsal of every task needed to land on the Moon, it orbited the Moon, with the lunar module coming within 8.4 nautical miles (15.6 kilometers) of the lunar surface, during practice maneuvers.

Man lands on the Moon: Then, on July 20, 1969, Apollo 11, with astronauts Neil Armstrong, Buzz Aldrin and Michael Collins on board, became the first spacecraft to land on the Moon. Mission Commander Armstrong and Aldrin piloted the lunar module to its landing on July 20, 1969 and at 20:18 UTC (Coordinated Universal Time) or 4:18 p.m. New York, N.Y./Washington, D.C. ET (Eastern Time), Armstrong descended the lunar module's stairs to the Moon, saying:

"That's one small step for [a] man, one giant leap for mankind."

Armstrong, made a mistake and did not pronounce the word 'a' before 'man.' But his oversight, in retrospect, gave the statement a symmetry that is as timeless as the trip itself.

Apollo 11 then completed many tests and collected many samples of Moon rocks and soil, among other tasks, then rocketed home, returning safely to the Earth via a splashdown in the Pacific Ocean on July 24, 1969.

The United States had fulfilled the national goal proposed by its slain leader, President John F. "Jack" Kennedy, of landing a man on the Moon and returning him safely to the Earth by the end of the 1960s. Their fallen leader, who left this life far too soon, had been honored. And the United States had won the Space Race vs. the Soviet Union.

Space, the final frontier: Of course, the moon landing was an enormous achievement by NASA. Further, there have been many other successes by the U.S. space program, including space station Skylab, the Space Shuttle, the nation's participation in the International Space Station, and numerous civilian, military and commercial satellite launches, including satellites that have been launched to explore the universe. And as with the manned missions before them, these achievements have not come without a human cost: 2 space shuttles failed. In January 1986, Space Shuttle Challenger disintegrated shortly after launch, killing all seven astronauts on board. In February 2003, Space Shuttle Columbia disintegrated on re-entry, killing all seven astronauts in its crew.

Further, despite a constituent lobby that would like the U.S. to speed-up its goal of a mission to Mars, a segment of Congress is opposed to increasing NASA's budget, which currently is a fraction of its Apollo-era budget, in percent of GDP terms. These critics argue the federal money is better-spent on other priorities, or not at all. Are they correct? The analysis forwarded here argues they are not.

NASA's work has benefitted civilian life in so many ways: miniaturization of electronics, photovoltaic cells, smoke detectors, high-density batteries, scratch-resistant lenses, shock-absorbing helmets, freeze-dried tech, flat panel televisions, digital imaging, cool-temp lasers and numerous other products and services either were invented for the space program, or are an adaptation of technology used in the space program. And there have been many other environmental/green applications that have not been mentioned here.

In sum, NASA, the government agency that saw its modest start get caught up in the Cold War in space, is at the forefront of research and exploration benefiting not only U.S. life, but all of civilization. The analysis forwarded here argues that a vote against NASA is a vote against human progress, which is why progressives and Democrats should re-commit the nation to space exploration. NASA is another example of your federal government at work – another example of the good the United States Government does.

U.S. Postal Service

Second, simply, progressives/Democrats, united with the new Biden Administration, must push for a fully-funded U.S. Postal Service (USPS). Postal Service officials have been hampered by Republican underfunding efforts, for decades: Republicans have not allocated enough funds to enable USPS technological and operational improvements; equally harmful, they have forced the USPS to prefund too much of its retirees' pension and health care benefits. Those payments accounted for about 75 percent of the USPS's $78 billion in operational losses in the past 13 years. What Democrats should do is have the U.S. Senate pass the USPS Fairness Act, which passed the U.S. House, 309-106, in 2019. If passed by the U.S. Senate, the bill would shift the Postal Service to a pay-as-you-go model that's similar to how other federal agencies and businesses fund their retirement benefits.

Further, any effort to raise package delivery fees above the prices by private delivery services - such as what UPS, FedEx, DHL and Amazon delivery charge - should be opposed. Raising USPS package delivery rates above the private carriers' rates will simply (obviously) result in Postal Service business lost to the private carriers; i.e. a price hike would be short-sided and, ultimately, self-defeating. And that will worsen the Postal Service's budget situation.

Rather, Democrats should look for other sources of revenue to help the Postal Service balance its budget, long-term. These include: 1) raising the cost of first-class mail to 60 cents by 2024 and 70 cents by 2028, 2) changing rural mail delivery rates for first-class mail: too many rural areas are at the far outreaches of the nation – they must be charged higher rates to offset their higher delivery and pickup costs; these rural routes have been subsidized for too long, 3) substantially decreasing the number of first-class delivery days to rural areas: six-day delivery is absurd; reduce it to twice per week, which is more than an adequate frequency to deliver and receive rural mail; 4) eliminate sparsely-used rural post offices – cut them by at least 10 percent by 2024 and then another 10 percent by 2028.

The aforementioned changes, combined with productivity improvements, and another idea (described below) should enable the USPS to reduce, then eliminate its 12-month operating deficit, provided first-class mail returns to near-normal levels, after the 2020 coronavirus pandemic ends. (As of October 2020, U.S. first-class mail volume had declined substantially.)

USPS E-mail Program: Next, place this in the *"Why didn't they think of it earlier?"* category. And - credit yours truly with the idea: the USPS should start an e-mail system on a grand scale that offers a discount for all classes of hard-copy mail, including first-class and package postage. The Postal Service can also sell advertisements/display ads around its e-mail web pages, similar to other services. There is no reason why the Postal Service should not benefit from the long-term trend to digital mail/online services. A program like this is long, long overdue. Why should the Postal Service have surrendered the digital mail realm, beginning in 1995? To be sure, it had and still has – as the strongest-performing provider – an advantage in the hard copy/paper mail delivery realm. But the U.S. Government, via the Defense Advanced Research Projects Agency (DARPA), was instrumental in the internet's inception. The analysis forwarded here argues the Postal Service should have ridden close behind DARPA and established an e-mail service from the internet's start – and that was before e-mail templates became revenue cash-cows with all sorts of add-ons, in addition to the staple display advertisement revenue! The USPS had a built-in national network of stores/service centers (post offices), an established, trusted brand, and enduring relationships with loyal customers: it was a natural for an e-mail network. All it needed was servers. Therefore, moving forward, the Postal Service must make up for lost time and establish a free, universal e-mail service for all U.S. citizens and naturalized residents (including Green Card holders and DACA/DREAM individuals). Annual e-mail revenue estimate: $5 to $7 billion. Annual revenue probably will be considerably larger than that at the start. [And it could take the form of natural, literal-logical e-mail address, such as: john.citizen@postoffice.com or jane.citizen@postalservice.com.]

USPS Truck Advertising Program: Another, potential revenue source for the Postal Service concerns truck/vehicle advertising. Again, like the e-mail advertising program, it has to be administered tactfully, prudently so that only appropriate ads are sold. That said, there is no reason why U.S. Postal Service trucks, vans and other vehicles cannot sell advertisements for local businesses such as: groceries stores, universities/colleges, health clubs, civic/arts events, and leisure centers (such as skating rinks, aquatics centers, ski resorts, tennis clubs, golf course), and local dentists/doctors, among other businesses. As long as the activity is wholesome, constructive and serves the common good – the U.S. Postal Service should consider it. Annual truck/vehicle display advertising revenue estimate: $1 to 2 billion. Again, actual, initial annual revenue will probably be higher.

Amtrak

It's been said so often it's a cliché, but there's more than an ounce of truth to it: *"Each year (or decade), Amtrak receives just enough money from Congress to survive, but not enough to thrive."*

In the decade ahead, 2020-2029, that must change: the U.S. Congress must either fund Amtrak adequately, or find some other operational format that can provide full, long-distance and regional train service. Amtrak's F2020 budget was $3.018 billion and its F2021 request is $3.000 billion. The analysis forwarded here argues Amtrak's budget should be increased. Here's why:

When the 2020 coronavirus pandemic hit, quarantines and state shutdowns, and later social distancing requirements, reduced Amtrak ridership by more than 85 percent. Other transportation modes – air, bus, regional rail, commuter rail, subways – experienced similar plunges. Some dropped more than 90 percent. Further, as of late-2020, most have recovered only a portion of their pre-pandemic service, and the outlook for future demand increases looks uncertain/bumpy, at best, at least regarding the first half of 2021. Moreover, absent a vaccine, it is hard to see droves of citizens returning to trains, planes, hotels, theatres, stadiums, concerts, and other mass-participation activities. As a result, Amtrak's revenue will likely remain depressed through F2021, which started Oct 1, 2020, and into F2022. And that means Congress has to act to - at minimum - let Amtrak officials know what their revenue status is.

At this book's publishing time (fall 2020), Amtrak was carrying about 6,000 passengers a day, compared to its normal, pre-pandemic load of 90,000 a day. Prior to the pandemic, Amtrak, among other service cuts, reduced its long-distance service to three times per week, down from daily service. Its Silver Star also operates three times per week; the Silver Meteor, four days; and the Auto Train, daily. All told, and when combined with Northeast Corridor service, most stations on the national network have just one train departure per day. So far, Amtrak's reduced service has not jeopardized its daily slots on the nation's Class 1 host railroads, but that could change. All of the above suggests the obvious: absent a sudden improvement in public health conditions – such as a 90 percent U.S. vaccine rate – Amtrak's passenger demand outlook looks weak, at best. And that's why Congress must step up and create a sound financial foundation so that Amtrak can at least weather the traffic drought period that has affected so many transit, hospitality, restaurant, museum, art gallery, and theatre operations – until customer demand improves in late 2021/early 2022.

Ideally, what Congress should do, and what progressives and Democrats should push for in the new Biden Administration, is a comprehensive expansion and rebuilding of Amtrak. In other words, as with the Northeast Corridor's Acela service, where density allows, make Amtrak train service a true, fair alternative to flying or driving. The United States' mostly rural landscape has hindered regional Amtrak service, even as it has boosted long-distance service. Hence, that means any Democratic effort to expand Amtrak (and refurbish existing track) in a big way will be "a heavy lift" i.e. hard task, politically. Given that reality, and other more-pressing progressive priorities mentioned in this book, Democrats should tactfully and artfully allocate fund increases to Amtrak – lobby for modest increases in F2021 and F2022, then larger increases in F2023-F2030.

***

And full disclosure: yours truly is biased in favor of the rail, which is a fancy way of saying he likes trains. Ever since he was a kid growing up in a diverse, small town in the northeast United States between New York and Boston - a town that, ironically, had two freight train lines dissecting it, but not a passenger or commuter rail line, (the closest Amtrak station was 6 miles away) - he's loved trains. Later, in his many trips to New York City to see relatives, especially in the summer, he would take Amtrak to Pennsylvania Station, or Metro-North's commuter rail to Grand Central Terminal: the trips and stays in Manhattan only heightened his interest in trains and rail transport. There is something unique about train transport. Perhaps it's the fact that people are traveling together on a journey, as opposed to individually in the dominant mode of transportation in the United States - the car - that generates the special feeling? Or perhaps it's because one can observe more as a passenger in a train than as a driver in a car? Perhaps, for yours truly at least, it is due to the fact that trains, save a delay at the station or severe weather, generally run unimpeded, whereas vehicles - at least vehicles in the northeast U.S. where the author grew up – faced daily rush-hour periods when traffic jammed, or slowed to a crawl. The late, great comedian Alan King's line about New York is true: *"Why do they call it rush hour in New York...when nothing moves?"* Trains seemed to always make progress, get where they needed to go; for car travel, the answer was, "That depends on the time of day." As a kid growing up, yours truly always marveled at how New York City thrived with its commuter rail (and in the city, with its subway) systems, while many, other U.S. cities chose to abandon their rail systems, light-rail systems, and trolleys, once highways were built, to their detriment; some cities have added them back, and if yours truly had a say, most would. From a commuter standpoint, the analysis forwarded here argues that tearing up the rails was a mistake; regarding inter-city transport, some of these cities and towns fought to retain their stations and rail line links; others did not – another mistake. The latter was so prevalent that Amtrak took over just a shadow of the United States' once vast rail system: bad decisions by these towns/cities and Congress led to the U.S.'s skimpy national rail network. It's hard to believe, but in the 1920s nearly all inter-city passenger travel in the U.S. was by rail.

Was the inter-city rail network meant to decline? Technology and geography certainly played a big part. Once the interstate highway system was built - a needed change and one, as noted earlier in this book, the U.S. Government initiated – trains immediately had a major and an unprecedented competitor in cars, buses, and later, trucks. Moreover, it's important to note that this new transportation system – the highway – was subsidized on a massive scale by federal and state governments; most existing railway lines were not. Then, in the late 1950s/early 1960s, when air travel began to take off (pun intended) with the jet age, passenger rail travel plummeted even more. Those factors, plus work rules that hindered technology-driven change, resulted in many passenger railroad companies ending operation or filing for bankruptcy. The loss of most of the U.S. Postal Service's business to trucks and airplanes by 1966 reduced railroad revenue even more. By 1969, the end of a national, passenger rail network was imminent. Most Americans loved the new freedom and speed of travel the tech changes ushered in with cars and airplanes, but at the same time many felt bad about the possible loss of train travel. The mood in the country was progress-oriented, change-favoring, but few also wanted the simultaneous extinction of the railroad system.

The U.S. Congress felt the same way, and in 1970 it passed and President Richard Nixon signed into law the Rail Passenger Service Act which formed the National Railroad Passenger Corporation, doing business as Amtrak. By May 1971, Amtrak had encompassed 20 of 26 major railroads in operation at the time. Since 1971, the phrase that best characterizes Amtrak's condition is "status quo" or "little change." Despite the addition of the lucrative Boston-to-Washington Northeast Corridor in 1976, on which the

Acela high-speed train runs – something that has helped Amtrak generate significant revenue – the nation has not established a full, national, inter-city rail network. As noted, Congress's stance toward Amtrak has been to provide just enough funds for it to survive, but not enough for it to thrive. Hence, as the decade continues, Democrats should attempt to fully-fund Amtrak, while also not disrupting other priorities, especially ending the pandemic and getting the U.S. economy growing again.

Public Broadcasting Service and National Public Radio

Ask Americans what they think of "television" in the United States and you're almost certain to get dozens of adjectives and opinions thrown your way. What amounts to good/important t.v. to one person, may be tepid t.v. to a second, and downright boring/uninteresting to a third. Without question, there is a subjective element to television viewing preferences, based on education, interests, and entertainment options, among other factors.

That said, Americans tend to agree on two dimensions of both network television (CBS, NBC, ABC, Fox) and cable t.v. channels: 1) there's too much sex and violence and 2) not enough programming is educational: a considerable amount of programming is banal, base, and at times appears to appeal to the lowest-common-denominator of viewers. Moreover, sometimes you think network executives are intentionally trying to insult the intelligence of the American people. Intentional or not, a lot of American t.v. is, to put it diplomatically, sub-par. In other words, it's bad – hardly the shows/content you want young people watching (or even not-so-young people watching). Has it always been this way? That is a subject and debate for another time. Briefly, here: television always had content that was strong/high-quality, and even more shows that appealed to the lowest-common-denominator, i.e. it featured "cheap thrill" shows. Further, while one can debate, as the saying goes, "until the cows come," whether American t.v. in the last 30 years has deteriorated/maintained the same quality level, one fact is beyond dispute: despite the advent of cable t.v., and the increase in channels available with satellite t.v. systems such as DirecTV, “Much of American television is a vast wasteland,” to cite the late Roman Catholic Priest Father Thomas Dubay.

Cord-cutting galore: In other words, there’s a reason why so many Americans are “cutting the cable cord.” With an abundance of streaming services - such as Netflix, YouTube TV, Disney+, Apple TV+, Hulu, AT&T TV NOW, and Sling TV - young people especially, those ages 21-39, are cutting the cable cord, or not signing up for cable t.v. service when they join the workforce – something that has cable t.v. executives concerned. To be sure, some of this shunning of cable t.v. represents a generational, tech-driven, behavior change – young adults are choosing internet t.v. and streaming video, including movie services, for their video viewing needs. Or as one young college student remarked in a survey for this book, “Why should I pay $80 per month for cable t.v. with 150 channels, when 130 of those channels are useless for me? Most of what cable t.v. offers, I’m not interested in, so it’s a waste of money.” Still, while some of the cord-cutting is from millennials and Gen Zers, some of it is not: some it is other people who no longer want to pay for dozens of poor-quality, non-educational shows that proliferate on cable t.v. systems.

An option - PBS and NPR: Is there a relatively inexpensive option? Certainly. Cutting the cord, then using the aforementioned streaming services, and other streaming options, for your viewing needs, is one. The offerings available on the internet increase each year, and connectivity/streaming technology is improving, as well. The internet may not have as many situation comedies available (called “sitcoms”), but people are finding out they didn’t really miss that sitcom that promos said they should watch. Moreover, these viewers are finding out that the $80 or $90 monthly fee wasn’t worth it, either, after living without cable t.v. for a few months.

Another option is public television, and to a lesser extent - because it's in a different medium, radio - National Public Radio. Congress started two public broadcast systems under the non-profit Corporation for Public Broadcasting: television's Public Broadcasting Service (PBS) in 1967 and National Public Radio (NPR) in 1970. Stations on each network are funded by the U.S. Government, by non-private foundations, private corporations and by viewers / listeners.

PBS is the largest provider of content on the PBS network of 354 stations, but not the sole provider. It's produced such critically-acclaimed series as "Sesame Street," "PBS NewsHour," "Masterpiece," "Frontline," "Washington Week," "Antiques Roadshow," "Nova," "Nature," "This Old House," "American Experience," and "Great Performances."

Time and space do not permit a full description and analysis of the contributions these fine shows have made to American society and culture, but know that more than one adolescent after watching "Nova" has been inspired to pursue a career in chemistry or biology or medicine; more than one after watching a special on the Golden Gate Bridge has been inspired to pursue a career in engineering; similarly with "Masterpiece," "Great Performances," and the arts etc.

Ditto for NPR: It produces radio news, commentary, analysis and culture shows that represent the highest standards of broadcast journalism. It also offers in-depth coverage and discussion of issues facing the United States, and international issues.

NPR produces a morning and afternoon news program, called "Morning Edition," and "All Things Considered," respectively. NPR also distributes selected programs produced by affiliated NPR stations.

The true value of public broadcasting: Ratings for PBS and NPR programs vary by show, topic, and a range of other factors. Some shows are very popular, others less-so, but two points are essential: 1) each has a core audience that welcomes high-quality programming, and 2) public broadcasting offers options and programming generally not available from private t.v. networks and stations.

To be sure, with technology making hundreds of stations on cable/satellite television available, viewers certainly have more options, but don't forget that most channels require cable/satellite subscription. PBS and NPR do not: if you have a television that can receive a digital signal or a radio over terrestrial airwaves, or a smartphone with a radio app, the programming is available to you.

In other words, PBS and NPR provide near-universal access to high-quality t.v. and radio shows, for free. Viewers/listeners can donate to each broadcast operation, as is their option with any non-profit organization, should they choose to do so, but it is not required.

Quality programming. Free over-the-air access. PBS and NPR are two more examples of your federal government at work – additional examples of the good the United States Government does.

Given the above, progressives and Democrats – long-time supporters of public broadcasting – should maintain or enhance that support in the decade ahead.

Scenario: This policy change would likely draw from scenarios 1 and 2. The existing institutions are more than adequate to achieve progressive goals, including with increased funds and program reforms.

****

American Ethos: NASA And A Return Trip To The Moon By 2025

The United States has "an important errand to do," of sorts, but it's an errand that's not close by: it's a quarter of a million miles away, on the Moon. (Or 228,900 miles or 384,472 kilometers from Earth, to be exact.)

You see, when Apollo 11 landed on the Moon in July 1969, with Lunar Module Commander/Astronaut Neil Armstrong becoming the first human to walk on the moon, fellow Lunar Module Astronaut Buzz Aldrin becoming the second, the two planted the American flag, along with a plaque. (Astronaut Michael Collins piloted the Command Module that orbited the Moon while Armstrong and Aldrin spent about 21 hours on the Moon, collected samples and performed other tasks.) However, when the Lunar Module blasted off from the Moon to re-dock with the Command Module for the return trip to Earth, its jets created thrust that, unfortunately, tipped over the American flag. However, readers should know this: with President Joe Biden's election, the American flag on the Moon will be re-positioned upright, as the United States will likely return to the Moon. The United States has an important errand to do, and the analysis forwarded here argues the nation could return to the Moon as early as 2025.

One Giant Leap For Mankind

When Armstrong stepped onto the Moon, (saying "One small step for [a] man, one giant leap for mankind") and the trio later returned successfully to the Earth, the United States had fulfilled the objective/goal set in 1961 by the late President John F. Kennedy, who proposed it in a session before Congress: *"I believe that this nation should commit itself to achieving the goal, before this decade is out, of landing a man on the Moon and returning him safely to the Earth."* The completed mission also ended the Space Race, the 20th century competition between the communist world's Soviet Union and the democratic world's United States

Aldrin on Moon. (Credit: NASA.)

for supremacy in space. Although space flight technology was hardly the sole factor in evaluating a government system's economic, technological and military capability, let alone its record supporting human rights, in practice the Space Race became the "Cold War in space." Each side was expected to cite and use a successful flight as proof of their system's ideological superiority. Moreover, although the Soviets had (and Russia today has) many breakthroughs and achievements in space flight/travel, the race to the Moon was won incontrovertibly by the United States.

Further, for a boy growing up in an All-American, industrial, middle-class / working-class town, the Apollo 11 mission meant many things. Concerning immediate goals, it gave him a chance to talk about the mission in his 2nd-grade class in elementary school, including describing in a basic way each astronaut's work. More generally, it gave him his first impression of NASA – the National Aeronautic and Space Administration, including a chance to learn about its many roles. Later, he would learn about how a nation marshals resources for a job as big as space flight, and other endeavors; it inspired in him a respect and admiration for a government – his United States Government – that could do such impressive things.

His 2nd-grade teacher, recapping the mission that fall 1969, recited the words inscribed on a plaque the Apollo 11 astronauts left on the Moon: *"Here men from the planet Earth first set foot upon the Moon July 1969, A.D. We came in peace for all mankind."* They came in peace – as it should have been, should be, and will be in the future. Further, a future Moon mission holds the prospect of setting the stage for additional Moon missions to build a space station in lunar orbit – the Lunar Gateway / Artemis Program, which will serve as a staging point for lunar exploration and for the Deep Space Transport (DST) concept for transport to Mars. DST, also called the Mars Transit

Apollo 11 Astronauts Neil Armstrong, Michael Collins and Buzz Aldrin, 1969. (Credit: NASA.)

Vehicle, is a crewed interplanetary spacecraft concept by NASA to support science exploration missions to Mars of up to 1,000 days.

The Moon mission was an impressive thing. Hence, it goes without saying that a return trip to the Moon would be an impressive thing. And know this: during the Biden presidency, the United States will return to the Moon, and there's a good chance the nation will be the first to land a woman and a man on the moon, by 2025.

(President Lyndon B. Johnson signs the U.S. Civil Rights Act of 1964 as Rev. Martin Luther King, Jr., and other officials look on, on 2 July 1964. Photo credit: U.S. National Archives.)

Chapter 22: U.S. Department of Minority Affairs and Diversity

"The arc of the moral universe is long, but it bends toward justice." - Rev. Martin Luther King, Jr.

This next issue would have been one of the initial chapters in the book, due to its importance, but because so many real-time events were (and are) occurring relating to the issue, its composition was delayed until late-2020. Further, it's an issue progressives and Democrats have the stronger philosophical argument on and should lobby for in the new Biden Administration.

The issue: U.S. civil rights and the establishment of a new department and cabinet-level secretary in the federal government: a U.S. Department of Minority Affairs and Diversity (DMAD).

The death of George Floyd in Minneapolis, Minnesota on May 25, 2020 after allegedly passing a counterfeit $20 bill at a grocery store sparked protests against police brutality in the United States, and against racial discrimination. For many, Floyd's death symbolized and was representative of the brutality against and general mistreatment of African American males by police. Floyd died after Minneapolis Police Officer Derek Chauvin, a white police officer, pressed his knee on Floyd's neck for more than eight minutes, as Floyd was handcuffed face-down on the street, while two other officers further restrained Floyd, and a fourth officer prevented onlookers from intervening. As noted, Floyd's death sparked protests and demonstrations across the United States, and globally, increased public support for U.S. police reforms, and increased support for the U.S.-based Black Lives Matter civil rights movement. Chauvin has been charged with second-degree murder, third-degree murder and second-degree manslaughter. The three other officers present during the incident, Tou Thao, J. Alexander Kueng, and Thomas Lane, were charged with aiding and abetting a crime. All officers were fired from the Minneapolis Police Department and await a trial expected to begin in March 2021.

Further, Floyd's death was another in a long history of police excessive force incidents that led to African American deaths. Others included: Eric Garner, 17 July 2014; Michael Brown, 9 August 2014; Tamir Rice, 22 November 2014; Walter Scott, 4 April 2015; Alton Sterling, 5 July 2016; Philando Castile, 6 July 2016; Stephon Clark, 18 March 2018; Breonna Taylor, 13 March 2020, and George Floyd, 25 May 2020.

In addition, Floyd's death has prompted a U.S. reckoning – a review by private and public organizations of: 1) anti-discrimination policies, 2) efforts to hire/promote African Americans and other people of color, 3) overall treatment of minorities in organizations, 4) investigations of pervasive racism (also called systemic racism), and 5) a review of policing policies/public safety laws.

Comprehensive reform: The analysis forwarded here argues that progressives / Democrats and the new Biden Administration should push for a comprehensive reform policy in U.S. civil rights in five steps: 1) a new cabinet-level department called the U.S. Department of Minority Affairs and Diversity, 2) police reform, 3) public safety reform, 4) U.S. voting rights enforcement, and 5) reparations.

U.S. Department of Minority Affairs and Diversity (DMAD): This new department would be empowered to work with the U.S. civil rights division of the U.S. Department of Justice (DOJ) to partner with corporate and non-profit organization human resource professionals, recruiters, and managers to encourage the hiring of more minority job applicants – all minority applicants, African American, Hispanic-American, Asian-American, Islamic-American, Indian (East Asian)-Americans, etc., with the goal of having their employment in these organizations reflect their representation in: 1) their local communities and 2) the U.S. population at large. The diversity division of the department would do the same for the LGBTQ community, and any other community/group the department deems appropriate for inclusion, consistent with existing federal law.

Police reform: Reforms in four areas would be undertaken - 1) change the "reasonable force" doctrine to "necessary force" doctrine; 2) set up a national database for police officer code of conduct violations, searchable by all jurisdictions, and the public at large, to prevent the re-hiring of poor-performing and racist police officers; 3) establish, with the assistance of the U.S. Department of Health and Human Services (HHS) and the Federal Bureau of Investigation (FBI) a Uniform Law Enforcement Psychological and Personality Test with a minimum passing score, to allow only psychologically-healthy, emotionally-stable, respectful individuals to apply for law enforcement positions; 4) require all states to establish civilian review boards for excessive force and other police regulation/code of conduct violations, if the state does not have a board already. Each board will have 7 members, 5 of whom are citizens, and are appointed jointly by the state House majority party leader and state House minority party leader of each state's legislature, 1 will be a local police department member, chosen by that state's attorney general, and 1 will be a police department member appointed by the governor. These boards would be able to access the national database for police officer conduct and be able to remove officers and recommend both criminal and civil action. (For the 5 board members appointed by the legislative majority leader and minority party leader, both must agree to a member's appointment for that person to serve on the civilian review committee.)

Public safety reform: The DMAD will also make recommendations to all jurisdictions on a DMAD-initiated basis or a jurisdiction-initiated basis concerning efforts to reimagine public safety, in order to reduce crime, enhance community development and, equally significant, to enhance the socio-economic development of all citizens in an examined jurisdiction / community. As part of this process, DMAD will help communities evaluate whether shifting funds from classic police operations to social service operations will achieve the aforementioned objectives. (Social services include: physical/mental health professionals, social workers, guidance counselors, educators, after-school personnel, career service professionals, childcare/day care personnel, nutrition specialists, case workers, and related personnel.)

U.S. voting rights enforcement: The DMAD will also have the power to investigate every instance or potential instance of voter suppression or voting prevention, and to impose immediate changes. Example investigation areas: extra voter identification requirements, reduced or changed polling stations, reduced or changed voting times, other burdensome voting registration requirements or voting action requirements, including burdensome mailing requirements, signatures or fees. The DMAD also would have the authority to expand a voting time window and/or set a voting time/window for any jurisdiction. The goal would be a 3-month voting period, with early voting, mail-in-ballot voting, and absentee ballot voting. Under no circumstance should a voting window be less than 14 days.

Further, with the above in mind, and in order to achieve the above, the U.S. Congress, aided by the new Democratic Party majority in the House and Senate that took effect in January 2021, should pass a new U.S. Voting Rights Act – call it the U.S Voting Rights Act of 2021 / John Lewis Voting Rights Act. It is fitting that the act be named in honor of Civil Rights Leader Lewis, who was a member of the Big Six civil rights leaders: Rev. Martin Luther King, Jr., James Farmer, John Lewis, A. Philip Randolph Roy Wilkins and Whitney Young. The six were instrumental in the March on Washington for Jobs and Freedom in 1963, at the height of the U.S. Civil Rights Movement. In 1965, Lewis, along with many other activists, during the Selma to Montgomery March across the Edmund Pettus Bridge, was attacked and beaten by state troopers, an incident that became known as "Bloody Sunday" – March 7, 1965. Lewis went on to serve as an Atlanta city councilman and then as U.S. Representative from Georgia's 5th District for 23 years, from 1987 until this death in 2020. Lewis played an important role in the passage of many rights laws and social justice programs, as well as many of other public policies, and served as Senior Chief Deputy Whip; he received many honorary degrees and awards, including the Presidential Medal of Freedom.

The John Lewis Voting Rights Act should contain the following components - in addition to the 3-month voting window, (September 1 through December 1 for the November election, other 3-month periods for elections that occur outside November), the bill should contain: 1) automatic registration at age 18, 2) free mail-in ballots for any voter requesting one, 3) a quadrupling of poll locations, all funded by the federal government, 4) extended voting hours on all election days: 6 a.m. to 9 p.m., 5) voting monitors, who can report any attempt to suppress, intimidate, discourage or otherwise interfere with a voter's right to vote, 6) the power to eliminate all burdensome voting requirements, beyond a simple identification requirement, that can suppress voting, 7) the power to arrest state, county and town officials who are suspected of having violated a voting rights law, with information forwarded to the U.S. Justice Department for prosecution, and 8) grades 6-8 reading materials to teach public school and private school students the importance of voting.

The goal of the 2021 U.S. Voting Rights Act / John Lewis Voting Rights Act would be to ban and eliminate all barriers - particularly those imposed by conservatives / Republican Party – that suppressed turnout and/or that had the effect of reduce turnout among lower-income Americans and members of disadvantaged minority groups. Democracy, at its first step, means protecting everyone's right to vote, and every citizen must work to achieve this goal.

Reparations: The DMAD would also establish a Reparations Czar who will have a 10-year authority, which may be extended 5 years jointly by the U.S. president and the Speaker of the U.S. House, to establish a minimum of 5 origination committees (one for each time zone, and one for U.S. territories), to begin the process of determining financial awards for African Americans, due to slavery, Jim Crow, segregation, and acts of discrimination up through January 20, 2021 at 12 noon EST. The eight-member origination committees would be selected jointly by the U.S. president and the Speaker of the House. The origination committees, where a majority rules, would submit their findings and estimates to a 6-member executive committee headed by the Reparations Czar; a 5-3 vote advances a file to the executive committee; 4-4 or less does not. The 6-member executive committee would be chosen (five members, one each) by the U.S. Senate and U.S. House leadership. (U.S. Senate Majority Leader, Senate Minority Leader, U.S. House Speaker, House Majority Leader and the House Minority Leader.) Appointed by the U.S. president, and subject to the consent of a simple majority in the U.S. Senate, the Reparations Czar would be the sixth member of the executive committee. [Further, the analysis forwarded here argues that a qualified, experienced candidate for

Reparations Czar would be mediation and alternative dispute resolution specialist Kenneth Feinberg. (See Profile: Kenneth Feinberg.) Feinberg was appointed Special Master of the U.S. Government's September 11th Victim Compensation Fund and served as the Special Master for TARP Executive Compensation. Additionally, Feinberg served as the government-appointed administrator of the BP Deepwater Horizon Disaster Victim Compensation Fund.] To be clear: by charter, the reparations executive committee will contain at least 2 African American citizens, and three other adults deemed most likely to represent the public at large. The Reparations Czar would serve as the sixth vote on the 6-member executive committee, but due to his experience in compensation, he/she would have the power to point out an item overlooked, and can ask the executive committee to re-evaluate a given compensation amount, or an aspect of a compensation file that may have been overlooked. Other executive committee members can bring attention to these items, as well, but only the Reparations Czar can refer the point back to the origination committee for further review. Otherwise, the Reparations Czar counts as 1 vote on the executive committee and for reparation final decisions, the majority rules. In other words, a 4-2 vote in favor of a reparations amount by the executive committee for File Y approves that reparations amount.

The First Step

The five reform areas represent the first step in a long-overdue review of public sector and private sector policies regarding racial discrimination, the status of minorities, and diversity. Racism and discrimination are real, and they are pervasive in the United States. Further, the analysis forwarded here argues that in some jurisdictions and in some organizations, racism and discrimination is systemic. A more-prevalent condition in the United States is pervasive racism and discrimination. These five reforms are designed to begin the process of consciousness raising, policy change and actual monetary damage awards. Having a cabinet-level position will ensure that both the U.S. president and Congress keep minority affairs and diversity more front-and-center in their decision-making process: in addition, these two issues will finally receive the top-priority status they have always deserved and should have had decades ago. (Indeed, as of late-2020 it appears some states have done a better job at prioritizing the interests of minority groups and diversity, than other states.) Police reform will begin to create a system where police officers are more-accountable to the community and to society, via civilian review boards, via the necessary force doctrine and via recruiting and hiring only most healthy, adjusted, conscientious adults for law enforcement positions via a Uniform Law Enforcement Psychological and Personality Test. Further, U.S. voting rights reform will help create a system – finally – in which voting is easy, not time-pressured, and free from voter suppression. Simply, the goal is a system where everyone can vote, easily. Finally, the Reparations Czar with his committees and staff will begin the process of determining fair compensation for all African Americans affected by slavery, Jim Crow, segregation, and acts of discrimination up through Jan. 20, 2021 at 12 noon EST.

To be sure, the above are not simple nor easy tasks, but they are tasks that progressives and Democrats should lobby for strongly in the new Biden Administration. They are at the foundation of that more perfect union.

Scenario: This policy change would likely draw from scenarios 1 thru 3. The most important new institution in this public policy area will be the DMAD, but progressives and Democrats will also have much work to do reforming police safety regulations, especially regarding the use of force by police (a change from the "reasonable force" to "necessary force" doctrine), as well as work with the FBI, DOJ and DHS to develop a Uniform Law Enforcement Psychological and Personality Test for all potential candidates for law enforcement personnel positions.

2015 – The Year Of Equal Rights For LGBTQ Americans

One could make the case that one of the quickest and unexpected advances in U.S. civil rights / social policy occurred in 2015 when the U.S. Supreme Court, in Obergefell v. Hodges (576 U.S. 2015), ruled 5-4 that the fundamental right to marry is guaranteed to same-sex couples by both the due process clause and the equal protection clause of the 14th Amendment of the U.S. Constitution.

Of course, many would disagree, and argue that the achievement of same-sex marriage rights, and the rights of the lesbian, gay, bisexual and transgender community (LGBTQ) more-generally, has been anything but quick in the United States. The Stonewall Inn demonstration that, arguably, marked the beginning of the gay liberation movement and modern fight for LGBTQ rights, occurred in 1969. Harvey Milk, a member of the San Francisco board of supervisors and a gay rights activist, was assassinated in 1978. (Milk was posthumously awarded the Presidential Medal of Freedom by President Barack Obama in 2009.) In other words, nearly 50 years in any era is hardly a short period of time or a rapid social advance.

The Times, They Are A Changin'

Still, compared to where the

LGBT Flag. (Credit: WikiCommons, public domain.)

United States was in, for example, 1996 – 25 years ago – the change appears quick, or at least quicker than many expected. Consider: In 1996 most Americans opposed same-sex marriage, only 27 percent favored it, according to a Gallup Poll. In 2019, most Americans – 63 percent favored it, according to a Gallup Poll taken before the Supreme Court's Obergefell decision. And according to Pew Research, millennials, Americans age 18-36, overwhelmingly supported it: 74 percent. Moreover, prior to the June 2015 Supreme Court Obergefell decision, 36 states, and the District of Columbia and Guam, had already issued marriage licenses to same-sex couples. The Commonwealth of Puerto Rico started issuing same-sex licenses in July 2015. Hence, despite opposition from many conservative groups, considerable social change was occurring in the land from 1996 through 2015, therefore it's not as if the high court's decision did not reflect the views of at least a plurality of Americans: it did, and most likely, a clear majority. And, as a result of the 2015 Supreme Court decision, same-sex couples now enjoy the same legal rights as married heterosexual couples and are recognized on official documents, such as birth and death certificates. No state – short of a new amendment to the U.S. Constitution – something that's extremely hard to achieve – can rescind that right.

The Arc Of History

Further, the analysis forwarded here argues that the social change represents a civilization and social advance. Since antiquity, probably longer, gays and lesbians have lived and contributed in every sector of the economy, in every dimension of society. Members of the LGBTQ community are doctors, lawyers, armed forces troops, artisans, police officers, architects, chefs, fashion designers, construction workers, athletes, CEOs, soldiers, pilots, nurses, car mechanics, teachers, diplomats, public officials, secretaries, musicians and much more. They were subject to horrific persecution – a chapter that, in the interpretation of this author – still requires some public monetary restitution and reparation. That reparation may be a few years off, but at least as a result of the Supreme Court's landmark decision, members of the LGBTQ community are today what they always should have been: citizens with equal rights in these United States.

The late New York Gov. Mario Cuomo, D-New York, who served as governor from 1983 to 1994, was once asked why, despite all of the rancor, divisiveness, backbiting, corrosive comments, and problems, he chose to run for and serve in public office?

"Because, young man," Cuomo responded, "every once in a while, you get a chance to move the stone."

Know that in 2015 the United States moved the stone.

TRIVIA TEST 9: U.S. Public Policy, Economy

(Answers in Appendix, Page 354.)

1. After the Great Depression intensified in 1930 with rising U.S. unemployment, President Herbert Hoover did which of the following?
a) He called for fiscal stimulus
b) He called for federal infrastructure projects financed by public debt.
c) He called for states to hire unemployed workers
d) He did almost nothing

2. Which of the following is true?
a) President Hoover was born in Canada
b) President Hoover had the same economic philosophy as President Franklin D. Roosevelt
c) President Hoover believed war with Australia was inevitable
d) President Hoover believed the private sector / free market left to its own would reduce U.S. unemployment quickly

3. According to most historians, President Hoover:
a) Was the best U.S. president
b) Was a trailblazing thinker who liked to get out ahead of problems and solve them before they grew
c) Was the president most likely to agree with President Barack Obama's Affordable Care Act health insurance program
d) Was not a top 15 U.S. president

Then Gov. Reagan, Nancy Reagan, First Lady Pat Nixon, President Nixon, 1970. (Credit: U.S. National Archives.)

4. Hoover's economic policies are most similar to which president's?
a) President Ronald Reagan b) FDR c) LBJ d) President Harry Truman

5. Hoover, like many, thought the 1920s prosperity would continue, but he failed to recognize which economic problems?
a) a persistent farm crisis
b) a saturation of consumer goods, like vehicles
c) income inequality
d) all of the above

6. The founder of the Republican Party was?
a) Jefferson
b) Lincoln
c) Hamilton
d) John Adams

President Abraham Lincoln, 1863. (Credit: U.S. National Archives.)

7. Which former vice president has played a major role in publicizing the problem of climate change / global warming caused by humans?
a) Dan Quayle
b) Harry Truman
c) Al Gore
d) Hubert Humphrey

8. Which president said, “Every gun that is made, every warship launched, every rocket fired signifies, in the final sense, a theft from those who hunger and are not fed, those who are cold and are not clothed.” ?
a) President Eisenhower
b) President Nixon
c) President Reagan
d) President Franklin D. Roosevelt

9. Which presidential candidate did not run for office in the 1968 election?
a) Nixon
b) Humphrey
c) Wallace
d) Gary Johnson

10) Which section of the United States used to be dominated by the Democratic Party, but now elects mostly Republican U.S. senators and U.S. representatives?
a) The Northeast
b) The South
c) The Pacific West
d) The Midwest

(The U.S. Centers for Disease Control and Prevention, Atlanta, Georgia. Credit: U.S. Department of Health and Human Services.)

Chapter 23: The Coronavirus Pandemic

"You don't determine the timing of lockdowns and openings in a pandemic. The virus determines the schedule. -National Institutes of Health, Infectious Disease Director Dr. Anthony Fauci

Another issue where progressives and Democrats have the philosophically stronger argument and a better solution is the 2020 coronavirus pandemic, COVID-19. Simply, Democrats wanted a national lockdown, as well as a medical supply and testing program which would have contained the coronavirus and saved tens of thousands of lives, if not hundreds of thousands of lives. The Trump Administration and U.S. Senate/House Republicans did not.

Further, another reason the above is an accurate statement is obvious enough (and it is a very sad reality, a very sad state of affairs for the United States): as of the start of January 2021, the coronavirus - despite a heroic, successful lockdown, social distancing and quarantine effort by New York, New Jersey and other northeast U.S. states – was not under control in

Florida, Texas, and Arizona – three major population centers. And infections were rising in more than a 10 other states. The Florida, Texas and Arizona outbreaks occurred largely due to one reason: Republican governors refused to lockdown their states early – when New York did in March – then they re-opened too soon, obeying President Donald Trump's deeply flawed advice. Their mistake has led to a horrific public health outcome: instead of containing the coronavirus's first-wave by early summer - as did France, Germany and many other European nations - virus cases rose in July and August. The United States had more than 182,645 deaths and 5.9 million cases as of Aug. 25, 2020, and health care systems and resources were coming under strain in the three states mentioned, and in others. Moreover, there was concern that infected adults traveling from the outbreak states would jeopardize containment efforts in the northeast, hence New York and New Jersey and other states had implemented quarantines for people from the outbreak states. (As of 24 January 2021, the United States had 429,288 deaths and 25,867,573 cases.)

Further, if all of the above looks like a major public policy failure by the Trump Administration and other Republicans in Congress and in the states who supported him, that would not be a stretch. Simply, Trump's policy to try to keep the economy open and not implement an immediate, national lockdown in March 2020 was an enormous mistake – colossally wrong – and, as noted, it has caused tens of thousands of needless, preventable deaths and injuries from infection. Moreover, the analysis forwarded here argues it will go down as one of the major policy failures by an American president in the modern era. And, reiterating – instead of containing the virus by early summer – containment is nowhere in sight as of January 2021, with the nation in the midst of its second wave – the winter 2021 wave: local hospitals are doing their best to make sure they have adequate PPE, as well as medical staff for the colder months, during which doctors and epidemiologists say the second wave will peak. Further, the U.S. health care system also is deploying resources for the normal, annual flu season, which also starts in the fall. As the above suggests, the United States in January 2021 remains in a health care emergency, with an uncertain outcome – and this crisis was largely preventable: Trump's repeated mistakes caused the virus to expand – with dozens of preventable, avoidable infection zones created. What a task the nation faces in the fall 2020/spring 2021! Once again, as in the winter/spring 2020, it's going to take a heroic effort just to contain the virus in the next six months, and to prevent the U.S. health care system from becoming severely strained, to the detriment of patients.

Here's a summary of the Trump Administration's mistakes and misguided policies that have magnified the pandemic in the United States:

China first reported a cluster of pneumonia in the city of Wuhan on December 31, 2019. On January 7, 2020, Chinese health officials confirmed that this cluster was caused by a novel coronavirus, COVID-19.

The U.S. Intelligence Community informed the U.S. Centers for Disease Control and Prevention (CDC) and the Trump Administration of an almost certain pandemic spread to the United States on January 7, 2020. CDC provide its first warning on the coronavirus on January 8, 2020.

Trump did "almost nothing," according to one source, *in the next eight weeks,* to cope with the impending pandemic. "He should have placed the nation in lockdown on that day," [January 8] the source said.

During that period, Trump held campaign rallies on: January 9, 14, 28, 30, February 10, 19, 20, 21 & 28.

During that period Trump played golf on: January 18, 19, February 1, 15, March 7 and 8.

Analysis: Trump's inaction during that eight-week period substantially worsened the pandemic - a pandemic that could have been neutralized. His inaction has literally resulted in tens of thousands of needless, preventable deaths - and probably hundreds of thousands of deaths. [Moreover, the injuries of COVID-19 survivors could ultimately total in the hundreds of thousands of individuals, with varying internal organ damage and other injuries. The virus is not exclusive to the lungs - it can and has damaged numerous other organs and body functions, and the story of the needless, preventable injuries and other ailments these individuals suffered, due to Trump's enormous mistakes and bad decisions, is worthy of research and increased public awareness about, but that is a subject for another time.]

The earliest confirmed case of the coronavirus in the United States occurred on February 6, 2020 in Santa Clara County, California.

Further, Trump's subsequent decisions read like a case study in mistakes, incompetency and wrong decisions in a public health crisis. Consider:

-Trump failed to implement a national lockdown. National Institute of Health Allergy and Infectious Diseases Director Dr. Anthony Fauci repeatedly said a national lockdown, if implemented early (in March or April), although economically costly, would have contained the coronavirus and best-positioned the United States for the inevitable second wave in the fall 2020. Simply, that national lockdown would have saved tens of thousands of lives. Trump repeatedly refused to implement a national lockdown.

-Failure to mobilize U.S. factories: Trump failed to immediately mobilize the U.S. manufacturing sector to produce personal protection equipment (PPE) on a national, grand scale under the Defense Production Act (DPA) to prevent PPE shortages. Along with the shortage of ventilators and other equipment, the PPE shortage cost lives in New York, New Jersey and in other states. And, in August 2020, PPE shortages were also being reported in Arizona, Florida and Texas – a second batch of preventable, avoidable risk, due to Trump's failure to mobilize the U.S. factory sector. Trump's decision in this area was and remains inexcusable. Conversely, one of President Biden's first decisions after taking office in January 2021 was to invoke the DPA via executive order to substantially increase the supply of all PPE – and other health care supplies, such as vials need for vaccines. President Biden followed-up that executive other actions will more than 35 other executive orders, many to check the pandemic.

-The PPE shortage also led to another reprehensible and totally-preventable practice: States were forced *to bid against each other (!!),* in a kind of survival-of-the-fittest nightmare that pitted rich states against poor, and large states and small. (Trump's decision that led to this is a disgrace! The analysis forwarded here also argues that it may have been criminal, but we'll save that discussion for another time.)

-National testing program: As of October 2020, the Trump Administration has failed to start a national testing program. Again: unacceptable! Trump expected the states to easily manage their testing programs. But states aren't set up to do mass-testing and to cope with a pandemic: it is the job of the federal government to prevent and deal with pandemics! As a result, states have scrambled to start and manage testing programs, with some (New York, New Jersey) faring better than others. Reiterating – this is another, basic policy failure by Trump – one that has cost lives. Conversely, once again, upon entering office President Biden deployed resources via an executive order to implement a national testing plan to enable the CDC and NIH officials determine where the coronavirus is spreading and help public health officials contain it.

-U.S. health care personnel: Trump failed – repeatedly – to mobilize the full resources of the U.S. Department of Health and Human Services (HHS), to establish a national deployment center for health care personnel. Again, inexcusable! And it's another decision that cost lives – both in the civilian population and among health care professionals and other first responders. Further, a national deployment center and personnel database would have recruited, screened/vetted, rostered and then deployed on an as-needed and emergency-team basis - nurses, doctors, support personnel, and clinicians to every area of the country and hospital that needed them. The Trump Administration failed to do it, emergency room team and hospital staffs in hot-spot zones/outbreak areas soon became overwhelmed, and patient deaths and other tragedies ensued. And the same crisis almost happened in Florida, Texas and Arizona in mid-summer, as outbreaks intensified in those states in August 2020. Reiterating, this mistake by

Trump was inexcusable and costly: it is much easier and healthier for the federal government to build a roster of experienced, reliable medical talent, pay them and tell them to be prepared to de deployed/stationed on a moment's notice. Instead, individual states had to set up their own rosters – a fragmented, inefficient, time-consuming process that cost lives.

-Masks/face coverings: Another inexcusable – and counter-productive and irrational – mistake by the Trump Administration and by Trump, personally. Dr. Fauci and then Coronavirus Task Force Coordinator Dr. Deborah Birx, among many other medical professionals, have repeatedly stated that masks/face coverings substantially decrease the spread of the coronavirus. Clinical and controlled studies overwhelming confirm how masks, when worn properly, help prevent the spread of the virus and help contain it. Masks primarily protect other people from you, but they do provide some protection for the wearer. But, from day 1 through July 2020 of the virus on U.S. soil, Trump not only refused to implement a mandatory mask wearing requirement - he did not advocate wearing a mask. Again, that was inexcusable. How many lives has this decision cost? The author will leave it to Fauci, Birx and other medical professionals to determine that precise total, but it has to be in the thousands, perhaps tens of thousands. Further, all health care officials agree that masks, combined with social distancing, frequent hand washing and reduced interactions/no congregating, is the quickest way to reduce the spread of the virus, and to contain it, prior to a vaccine. In addition, Trump's failure to at least set an example by regularly wearing a mask no-doubt encouraged many of his supporters to not wear one in public, either – enhancing the virus's spread. In sum, Trump's failure to issue an executive order mandating mask wearing cost thousands of lives – most likely many more – and his personal example to not wear one until a July 11 visit to Walter Reed National Military Medical Center in Bethesda, Maryland threw more gasoline on a virus fire that did not need extra accelerant. Trump's mask decision was counter-productive and irrational – and it set back containment efforts. It represents another intrinsic failure by the Trump Administration that has substantially damaged the public health of the United States. And again,

President Biden's executive order in early January 2021 required mask wearing on selected modes of U.S. transportation, and he also asked all Americans to wear a mask for 100 days.

An avoidable, preventable U.S. health care catastrophe

A failure to implement a national lockdown. A failure to mobilize U.S. factories for PPE production. No national testing program. No U.S. health care personnel database. No mask/face covering executive order. A failure by the president to even advocate mask/face cover wearing as a practice vital to contain the virus. Add it up and what one has is an avoidable U.S. health care catastrophe caused by the Trump Administration and the equally-complicit Republican Party in Congress: they own this failure. It is a colossal failure – it ranks with the worst public policy decisions in U.S. history. As noted, as of January 2021, the coronavirus still has not been contained in much of the United States, largely due to Trump Administration's mistakes and red Republican state failures: there is no end in sight, regarding the virus's spread.

Given Trump's and the Republican Party's colossal failure to contain the coronavirus, what should be progressives' and Democrats' response?

Progressives and Democrats should proceed with their comprehensive U.S. health care policy – a policy to address the coronavirus pandemic "on all fronts." That means, as described in Chapters 1, 2 and 11, progressives / Democrats, united with the new Biden Administration, should make major investments in the U.S. public health care system, including building and expanding public hospitals, increasing PPE manufacturing in the United States, substantially increase funding to the states for the same, as well as increasing funds to make public schools virus-free; that effort should also include increased funds for comprehensive testing and tracing of the virus, extended unemployment benefits and day care/childcare aid, and a major increase in infrastructure spending - at least $750 billion in infrastructure projects, and probably closer to $1 trillion – to return the U.S. economy to a sustainable growth track, and reduce the output gap, among other programs.

Some may assert that the infrastructure component is too large: nothing could be further from the truth. The U.S. GDP/output hole and personal income hole due to layoffs is so large that, absent fiscal stimulus and infrastructure spending, the U.S. economy is on-track to contract by more than 20 percent - in other words on track for its worst depression since the Great Depression. (In mid-2020, the Democratic Party-led U.S. House passed the $3.7 trillion HEROES act, which serves as the fifth stimulus bill, designed to fill the aforementioned GDP/output and personal income hole; unfortunately, the Republican Party-led U.S. Senate did not act, and some coronavirus pandemic assistance programs expired in late July 2020, creating more economic hardship for the American people.) In short, the Democrats and the new Biden Administration must do what Trump and the Republican Party has failed to do: it must put the people and U.S. public health first (!!) – not personal or political goals.

**

If there was any doubt about the need for the continuance of a New Progressive Era, and its many economic and social reforms, by progressives/Democrats and the new Biden Administration, the Trump Administration's failure to contain the 2020 coronavirus pandemic sealed it. All the Trump Administration had to do was contain the coronavirus in March and April 2020, and U.S. public health would have vectored higher and the U.S. economic expansion would have continued. Trump's policy mistakes, incompetence, disinterest, and narcissism prevented that: he failed, colossally. The Trump Administration's mistakes and misguided policies have disheartened the nation. As a consequence, an economic crisis has ensued, and social unrest has increased. Now, as the nation starts 2021, the United States under President Biden has taken actions to address the three crises at once: the coronavirus pandemic, an economic recession with a more than 10 percent unemployment rate, and a social crisis. In addition to the executive orders, President Biden has sent Congress a $1.9 trillion to contain the virus. That action will be followed by an additional infrastructure bill to create millions of new jobs – in many sectors. As of publication of this book, the Democratic-led U.S. House and U.S. Senate were about to start debating the $1.9 trillion pandemic bill, with Democratic leadership signaling they wanted to pass the bill in two weeks, to get urgently-needed aid to unemployed adults, families, idled business and to support public health operations in every state, among other programs. Democratic majorities in the U.S. House and U.S. Senate and the new Biden Administration will make the correct choices and end these three crises that threaten the nation and our wellbeing. As President Biden said, "Help is on the way." Biden and the Democrats are already making up for lost time.

Further, as of January 2021, the U.S. FDA had approved two vaccines: Pfizer's and Moderna's, which each require two doses, with a Johnson & Johnson 1-dose vaccine expected to receive approval by mid-February. (A fourth vaccine, by a two-dose vaccine by AstraZeneca/Oxford, probably will not be approved for use in the United States until April 2021. The Trump Administration's vaccine distribution plan has been poor, to put it diplomatically: Trump left vaccine distribution entirely up to the states, and with many having little experience coordinating such a massive logistics effort – the results have been predictable: only about 6 percent of the U.S. population had been vaccinated by late January 2021, with officials vaccinating front-line workers (health care professionals, police / fire / EMT personnel) first. Conversely, upon taking office President Biden implemented a national vaccine distribution plan – including the setting up of 100 Federal Emergency Management Centers (FEMA) in the 50 states solely to administer vaccine shots, among many other initiatives. The Biden Administration's goal is to administer at least 100 million doses in its first 100 days.

Scenario: This policy change would likely draw from scenarios 1 thru 3. Progressives/Democrats will need to add funds to existing institutions, such as HHS, create new agencies, particularly for PPE production and perhaps for vaccines, and revise regulations.

American Ethos: Vaccine Test Volunteers – The Best Of These United States

The late Gov. Mario Cuomo, D-New York, would cite a life lesson often at public policy events and on the campaign trail. Gov. Cuomo would tell the story from his childhood, while growing up, about this fascinating event he would often see before his eyes: men, dressed in heavy coats and carrying a large hose with water, rushing toward a burning building.

"It was really quite extraordinary," Gov. Cuomo would say. "Men [and now men and women] rushing toward this multi-story building, flames shooting out of the side, temperatures exceeding 1,000 F degrees. Again, they were running TOWARD the fire. Well, now I don't know about you – but when I was a child growing up my grandmother would yell and tell me, *'Mario, stay away from the fire!! Stay back!! Stay back, Mario! The fire will burn you!! The fire and smoke will kill you!!'* And yet, here again on this street on that day, there were these men running TOWARD the fire. They WANTED to go WHERE THE FIRE WAS. It was really quite extraordinary. They didn't care that the fire could sear their face, that the smoke could blind them, that the heat could burn

US Centers for Disease Control and Prevention. (Credit: U.S. HHS.)

them beyond recognition – there was someone in the building, perhaps several people, who had to be saved. Again, it was really quite extraordinary."

Among other goals, this book has tried to tell the story of at least some of the heroes in these United States – people who put the national interest and the common good above self-interest – and surely, like the firefighters Gov. Cuomo described, within that august membership are vaccine volunteers.

At times, the nation in 2020, facing several economic, political and social issues, seems like it's never been more divided, but a review of the 1860s will reveal that is not the case. Further, amid the polarization, Americans can agree on this: the United States must find an effective, safe COVID-19 vaccine, and efforts that speed that are a blessing. Place vaccine volunteers in the category of speeding that goal: they are taking time from other pursuits and taking other risks – in order to help researchers determine quicker which vaccine works and is safe. Moreover, given COVID-19's contagiousness and lethalness, researchers are trying to accomplish in months what usually takes years. The results, so far? The volunteers are making a difference: as of November 2020 there were two promising vaccine candidates, with human trials well underway. Along with the work by research labs, much of that progress is due to vaccine volunteers' courage.

How To Become A Vaccine Volunteer

Also, the federal government launched a website in July 2020 for those interested in becoming volunteers:

Coronaviruspreventionnetwork.org

It's possible that HHS will have enough volunteers by the time of this book's publishing: but the only way to determine that is to visit the site. What are researchers looking for in volunteers? Some questions address how likely you'll contract the virus, including questions on your race, occupation, and how many people you interact with daily. If you're diligent in wearing a mask while outside, don't leave home much, work remotely and don't interact with many people in a day, you would not make the best volunteer. The reason? The point of the vaccine study is to see if it protects people who get sick with COVID-19, and if you stay home it's hard to tell if the vaccine kept you healthy or if staying home kept you healthy. Vaccine researchers will also be looking for volunteers who are over age 65, with underlying conditions, such as hypertension, lung disease, diabetes and morbid obesity, since these individuals are more likely to become ill with COVID-19.

The time volunteers will save is much-needed, particularly in the United States, which lost roughly 8 weeks by not fully mobilizing the federal government in February 2020, by not implementing a national lockdown immediately, and by failing to invoke the Defense Production Act to manufacture personal protection equipment (PPE). Simply, those decisions led to preventable, needless deaths. The nation wasted valuable time, and now it has to make up for that lost time by substantially shrinking the vaccine development time: vaccine volunteers are a big factor in that time-save/task. They are the virus world's firefighters. Gov. Mario Cuomo would be very proud.

(President Herbert Hoover with White House Press Secretary Ted Joslin in 1932. Photo credit: U.S. National Archives.)

Chapter 24: A Note On Conservatism

"Ayn Rand, her ideology was near-perfect in its immorality." - Author Gore Vidal

And now a note on conservatism, and this issue - obviously - is an issue where progressives/Democrats have the philosophically stronger argument. No discussion of progressivism and issues/problems facing the nation is complete without touching on conservatism. But, really, a more-pressing question today is – what remains of conservatism? What does it stand for? And who is a conservative? And does conservatism have any utility at all?

Historically, liberalism differed from conservatism on three points: 1) human nature, 2) outlook on life and 3) role of government. Historically, progressives had: 1) a positive view of human nature – that human beings are basically good, 2) regarding life, they were idealists and 3) regarding the role of government, they viewed it as "an activator" – an institution that can achieve tremendous good, and called for a larger government role, in addition to its regulatory role. (Recall Chapter 18: *etatism* - the theory of the positive state.)

Conversely, historically, conservativism had: 1) a negative view of human nature – that human beings are basically bad, 2) regarding life, they were realists and 3) regarding the role of government, they viewed it as largely "a regulator," and called for a very limited government role.

But what has happened to conservatism, as we enter the 21st century's third decade? What do conservatives believe now, after they nominated Trump? And after his policies were implemented? Trump, the N.Y. real estate developer, shredded conservatism and made it almost as obsolete and discredited as the Republican Party itself. Some background is in order:

Since 1981, the Republican Party has boasted a large conservative constituency: it was its base. It no longer is. Conservatism has been cast aside. And, as anyone who has been following U.S politics, public policy and foreign policy since 2016 knows – the Republican Party, itself, has been cast aside. The Republican Party or Grand Old Party (GOP) no longer exists. It is the party of Trumpism, and little else. The Republican Party's core planks of: 1) pro-immigration/free markets, 2) balanced budgets/fiscal responsibility and 3) a strong defense/national security have been replaced with: 1) protectionism/nativism, 2) massive fiscal deficits and 3) isolationism, and with, some would argue, a surrender to a Russian-led world, with wide discretion for China – or, at minimum, a large retreat by the United States from the international stage – the end of the United States's period as the hegemon, or an era of hegemonic stability - with negative consequences for its allies. In other words, in 2020 the Republican Party is a shadow of its former self – it is unrecognizable - with its only defining / determining characteristic beginning what Trump supports and opposes. The Republican Party has capitulated almost 100 percent to Trump. It is a cult of Trump, basically. And with that cult, conservatism was swept away.

What's more, traditionally, conservatives believed in the rule of law, the separation of powers and the U.S. Constitution's checks and balances. Under Trump, Republicans sold their soul again – capitulated – they sold their soul, compromised their ethics, their conscience and, really, went against common sense by failing to remove Trump in the 2020 U.S. impeachment trial for: 1) abusing his power with regard to Ukraine by withholding defense aid and trying to coerce Ukraine into launching a baseless investigation of the Democrats, 2) collaborating with the Russians in the 2016 U.S. presidential election, and 3) abusing the powers of the office of the presidency in other ways – from holding political / campaign rallies on the White House lawn, to failing to ask foreign dignitaries to NOT stay at his Washington, D.C. hotel, and other properties, creating a conflict of interest, and for granting presidential pardons for political supporters, as well as for cronies who failed to fully cooperate with U.S. Special Counsel Mueller's investigation. Trump has repeatedly violated the rule of law, abused his power, violated the U.S. Constitution AND obstructed justice (at least 10 times, according to the Mueller Report) – but Republicans, save U.S. Sen. Mitt Romney's vote to convict him in the impeachment trial – did nothing. Hence, no conservatives exist in today's Republican Party: not on Capitol Hill, anyway. If they did, they would not have violated the core conservative tenets this paragraph just discussed.

Therefore, what's left of today's craven, corrupt, unethical, hypocritical, incoherent conservatism? Well, there are tax cuts for upper income groups/the top 10 percent of U.S. income filers. There! That still exists! Tax cuts for people and groups who don't need them!! In 2017, the Republican Party, led by Trump, passed a huge tax cut for millionaires and billionaires – one that the working-class and the middle-class barely noticed in their paychecks because their tax cut was so small. At the same time, the top 10 percent reaped millions and billions! And it will cost U.S. taxpayers at least $1.9 trillion (!!) over 10 years, according to the Congressional Budget Office. (Side note: those millionaires and billionaires favored by the Trump tax cut continue to reap money to this day, even after the coronavirus pandemic-induced recession that has caused U.S. unemployment to soar.) Further, the tax cut was a fraud! Repeat: Trump's. Tax. Cut. Was. A. Fraud. Republicans and conservatives asserted it would stimulate GDP growth substantially and create millions of new jobs. It did neither! The U.S. economy did not grow that much faster, as measured by GDP and few new jobs were created, compared to the economy's pre-tax cut growth rate. President Obama in his first three years created more jobs than Trump, whom the author sometimes refers to as the N.Y. real estate developer. (Yours truly refers to him as that because that's all he is – that's where his primary skill set resides: he's a real estate developer.) Trump's tax cut was and is a sham and another false promise to those he claimed he would help – and it's something progressives/Democrats must immediately reverse in the new Biden Administration. And not only is Trump's tax cut a sham, it also ballooned the U.S. budget deficit: when the Obama Administration ended, the annual U.S. budget deficit was about $295 billion a year and trending lower. After Trump's conservative tax cut, the budget deficit quickly surged to more than $650 billion per year, then to $850 billion per year, and now CBO is projecting nearly $1 trillion annual budget deficits for as far as the eye can see. (!!) Hence, while conservatives may still promote tax cuts for the wealthy, their ideology has been discredited economically and fiscally: conservative economics is a dead end, a bad bargain, a waste of time; it's empty, useless and does not serve the nation. Moreover, if the tax cut is not reversed, the U.S. will run massive, $1 trillion deficits for as far as the eye can see, and it will affect the nation's credit rating, jeopardizing both the U.S. economy and the global economy in the process. Underscoring, Democrats and the new Biden Administration must place the United States on a sound, sustainable fiscal track – one where the nation pays its bills - by reversing in 2021 or 2022 the regressive, counter-productive and ultimately economic recovery-jeopardizing 2017 Trump tax cut for millionaires and billionaires.

Tax cuts discredited, what else remains of conservatism? Well, Republican conservatives will still back indiscriminate regulation cuts and favor conservative judges. Each is not in the national interest. Each is proving with Trump in the Oval Office that they are leading to policies that don't serve the public interest, let alone the common good, and the national interest. Progressives/Democrats, united with the new Biden Administration, should reverse most regulation changes implemented by Trump – regulations related to the environment, health care, education, and labor, among other areas - and also of course seek liberal/judicial activist judges for the courts, especially for the U.S. Supreme Court.

Another conservatism flaw: it is individual-centric – it asserts that every goal, challenge, concern or problem is driven by the individual. (Some call this individual determinism.) And, by extension, if you can't solve the problem by yourself, you must be flawed, deficient, inferior. Really, it is a crude, simplistic, flippant, dismissive, inaccurate and unjust way of looking at problems. Why do conservatives continue to trot-out this trope, this canard that slanders individuals even more than it insults them, and that implants wrong ideas? One reason - it's a rationalization that they use to absolve themselves of responsibility to the community or common good, really. It is very convenient trope for conservatives' ideology and rhetoric: the poor, the working poor, the vulnerable, the marginalized are in poverty or have a problem? *Why, it's their own fault!* We conservatives are not responsible, and neither are our policies, and we don't have to help! And the system or structural factors did not play a role in the problem, so don't try to reform the system! Don't place any demands on us conservatives. Needless to say, conservativism's individual-centric causation assertion is tidy/simplistic and flawed, at best, and is injurious, cruel, irresponsible and destructive at worst. It is tidy - and hence not predictive - because it doesn't consider the myriad of other factors that could have, for example, led to a person's impoverished state. These include: 1) a broken home, 2) a lack of parental role models, 3) a poor school or underperforming school system, 4) a crime-ridden neighborhood, 5) gang activity while growing up, 6) regular violence, 7) a prolonged economic recession, 8) a sector displaced by international production, 9) prejudiced neighbors or a prejudiced town, 10) pervasive racism / discrimination, systemic racism/discrimination, 11) a lack of support for college prep programs, 12) no vocational schools nearby, 13) a practice of legal-but-segregated institutions, or 14) a natural calamity, among other factors. Conservatism's individual-centric causation is injurious, cruel and destructive because it wrongfully asserts that poverty or a person's plight is always due to the individual's own failing, period - and nothing else. To listen to conservatives, it is either a person's alleged lack of intelligence, laziness, poor decision making, poor life choices, ineptitude, or poor performance led to their condition. (Needless to add, the author argues the aforementioned is a harsh and slanderous conclusion.) But, again, it's a convenient myth for conservatives to propagandize because it rationalizes their choice to not reform the system, it rationalizes their irresponsibility - to not implement macroeconomic reforms - and political reforms - when the problem is systemic or flawed at a macroeconomic level, i.e., at a structural or system level. And why do conservatives fail to reform the system? Why are they reluctant to act? Because it preserves their wealth, and in some cases, wealth stolen from workers/employees via wage theft in an unjust system; at minimum, it preserves the status quo - the rules as they are - which are often regressive, exploitative and poverty-creating. In sum, readers and U.S. citizens should not swallow the lie of conservatism: to be sure, some individual problems are individual in root. As my favorite nun taught yours truly: *In life, you must continually make good choices and also deploy common sense, but not all problems are individual-based.* Further, the analysis forwarded here argues that many problems are not individual-based: many are systemic, macro, structural! Hence, progressives and Democrats must keep macro-factors forefront as they address the nation's economic and social problems.

Another problem with conservatism - one that is an extension of its individual-centric focus: it advocates/promotes a hyper-individualism, a logical but deeply problematic tenet. Problematic because it ignores many of the errors individuals commit, and the destructiveness of those individual actions. Conservatives and Republicans, it seems, will protect anything in the name of individual choices, and a very wide zone of action, which they call 'autonomy.' Consider: Conservatives opposed seat belt use laws in the United States because, they claimed, the laws reduced personal liberty. Seriously? Seat belt use is an affront to liberty? Yup, conservatives once argued this. (Some would even ban mandatory U.S. seat belt use laws today.) Most others view the laws as saving tens of thousands of lives in vehicle crashes/accidents. Conservatives also favored corporate polluting of rivers and lakes because environmental laws and regulations restricted business freedom, or the freedom of commerce. They also opposed laws that prevent younger adults – an impressionable segment of the population -

from smoking, because they restrict lifestyle freedom (even if it causes cancer). And conservatives are the first to oppose a progressive income tax, even for individuals with gross incomes over $5 million per year, asserting it reduces their consumption / investing freedom. And then there's perhaps the granddaddy of them all: conservatives / Republicans opposed the ACA / Obamacare because, they alleged (falsely) that it reduced citizens' health care insurance freedom. (Yours truly has not met one individual who could not afford health care insurance before the ACA, who, after obtaining health care insurance under the ACA, said they felt 'less free.' All individuals yours truly spoke with said they were glad they were receiving regular health care services – with some receiving regular check-ups for the first time in their lives.) The list of actions conservatives oppose for what is in fact hyper-individualism reasons is endless. The truth? None of the above reduced anyone's freedom in a tangible way: they did lead to better societal outcomes, however. Accordingly, toss conservatives' / Republicans' hyper-individualism in the waste basket: it is a flawed, counter-productive, inappropriate idea. And, as others have noted, including University of British Columbia Anthropologist Wade Davis, that conservative emphasis on hyper-individualism has hurt the United States' ability to form a community, let alone a society. Canada offers a much more effective social compact than the United States - one with cheaper health care insurance plans, better schools for all citizens, and living wages for all workers - but Canadians don't feel any 'less free' than Americans. That in and of itself says a lot about the impact and the destructiveness of conservatives' hyper-individualism.

But beyond the above, beyond the warping of conservatism and the destruction of the Republican Party and the creation of a frightening, cult of personality-esque Trumpism under Trump, beyond the deceptive over-emphasis on individual utility, what else is harmful about this twisted conservatism? Clearly, its hypocrisy. And that hypocrisy is not mild, it reeks! Senate and House Republicans are hypocrites: they preach capitalism, but practice socialism for their constituencies. Example: Republicans routinely vote against the SNAP/food stamp program for the poor, yet are fine with approving more than $52 billion in federal aid – welfare – for farmers, large and small. Another example: They allow small royalty fees for public lands for oil and natural gas drillers, but they will vote against an increase in the Earned Income Tax Credit for the poor/working poor and they'll vote against tax credits for day care. Hypocrites! Another: They oppose student loan subsidies and college federal aid/Pell Grants, but they have no problem subsidizing – for more than 100 years (!!) – rural U.S. Postal Service delivery to far, remote towns and villages. It costs a lot more to mail a letter from Oklahoma to Idaho than it does to mail a letter from White Plains, N.Y. to Yonkers, N.Y. Democrats, liberals (and others) are thus subsidizing and have been subsidizing for decades rural Republicans' mail service: and this subsidy runs into the billions of dollars per year. Again, conservative and Republican hypocrisy! Still another example: In early August 2020, Republicans favored a 100 percent tax write-off for executive lunches, but opposed a $600 per week Pandemic Unemployment Assistance (PUA) extension for Americans who lost their job through no fault of their own. (!) How dare those Americans lose their job, due to a lethal, highly-contagious virus. (!) The above are examples of double-standards of the very worst sort. Don't ever let anyone tell you today's conservatives favor capitalism. When a public policy favors progressives / Democrats, conservatives call it socialism; but when it favors conservatives / Republicans, they call it 'a necessary, essential government service or program.' Hypocrites! Just one more, and it is a glaring hypocrisy: U.S. Sen. Ted Cruz, R-Texas, one of the poorest excuses for a U.S. Senator since the establishment of the United States, an individual who repeatedly lambasts 'excessive government spending' and argues for budget cuts, even for programs that benefit the poorest Americans, nevertheless wants the new U.S. Space Force Command headquarters built where? Where? Wait for it….*Texas.* Imagine that? Talk about rank hypocrisy. Dear old Ted Cruz, you have to love him. (Not!) Cruz is a poster child for Republican hypocrisy and conservative hypocrisy: sorry Ted, you can't have it both ways – if you're against government spending, then we won't burden your state, Texas, with the additional 1,400 or 1,500 federal jobs, possibly more, that the headquarters is expected to require in the state that's ultimately chosen. (And the above jobs total does not include new, lateral jobs created in the state by the headquarters.) Further, in general conservatives / Republicans favor federal programs that provide benefits to their constituencies (imagine that?); what they don't like are federal programs that benefit Democrats. Double standard? Yup. Hypocritical? Yup. Craven? Yup. Biased? Yup. Are these policies that progressives and Democrats need to reverse – or at least see to it that a uniform standard is applied, starting in 2021? Yup.

Another fault/liability of conservatism/Republicans: their decades-long and near-metaphysical-certitude belief in the correctness of free markets/private sector, and its so-called inability to make a mistake. Conservatives *want every decision in your life based on market forces in the private sector, basically.* And, according to them, the market cannot make a mistake. Well, as noted earlier, the free market/the private sector offers many benefits, including entrepreneurship, innovation, ingenuity, dynamism, reward for work, risk taking, wealth building, and a more-efficient deployment of resources, among other benefits; but…free markets also produce "winners" and "losers" and if the floor isn't high enough, that leads to poverty for the losers, and as history has demonstrated many times, destitution. And worse. (See: the French Revolution, 1789-1799, and the Soviet Russian Bolshevik Revolution of 1917, among others.) Another way of thinking about this is that capitalism, like other economic systems, ranks tasks, lower-paid to higher-paid: someone will be lower-paid. And if that lower-paid segment does not earn a living wage, poverty and destitution will ensue. Further, if an individual cannot learn skills to move up, one can see how this can lead to a long-term or lifelong permanent, impoverished state. That's why, among many other reasons, progressives/Democrats strongly support a living wage for all jobs. Conservatives/Republicans argue, "People will ascend." That is true: many do, but some do not, which provides philosophical support for a living wage. In other words, free markets/the private sector, absent a legitimate social safety net / social welfare state, are harsh, and inhuman. Think, conservatives: there's a reason capitalist Germany in 2020 has a generous social welfare state. Think! There's a reason France in 2020 has an equally-generous support system, too. Think! Were there any unfavorable events in human history that caused them to end certain policies? Which were those? And what were the economic and social reforms? Research! Think! Analyze! Reach an informed conclusion! Point: the United States needs to be wise and enlightened about *the upside AND the downside to markets* and implement a legitimate social safety net: we must avoid the mistakes of France, Germany, the United Kingdom and many other formerly too-capitalist, too-free market economies.

Still another fault of conservatism is its denialism. Conservatism can look at objective, needless, preventable human suffering and pain, and say, *"Problem? Is there a problem here? We conservatives don't see anything wrong."* How cruel. How harsh. How callous. How indifferent. And, some would argue, how spiteful. Further, conservatism exists from year-to-year blithely and cavalierly asserting that the U.S. economic system – corporate capitalism – is not harsh, with citations of only its virtues/benefits and none of it faults/liabilities. But few other scholars, economists, analysts, even officers at the Central Intelligence Agency, not brainwashed by conservative propaganda and rhetoric, would deny the harshness of the U.S.'s current economic system - corporate capitalism. To be sure, the American economic system, as noted, has many benefits, the chief among these, again, being: entrepreneurship, innovation, ingenuity, dynamism, reward for work, risk taking, wealth building, a more-efficient deployment of resources, and the primacy of science-led commerce. But to deny the harshness of the American economic system - a system that's much more harsh than many Western European economic systems – is to refuse to accept a matter of incontrovertible fact. And, monstrously and ridiculously, one conservative theorist, Ayn Rand, asserted that the harshness that does exist is *something that should exist* – i.e., the state is not capable of reducing suffering and should not be permitted to do so – and if the individual/corporations/free market do not reduce suffering, so be it. Ayn Rand's worldview is the antithesis of what a humane, enlightened, democratic, civilized nation does:

it is the antithesis of the public interest, let alone the common good or the national interest. Conservatives' and Rand's society is a harsh society. And it is appalling! The late, great author Gore Vidal perhaps best characterized Ayn Rand's conservative ideology/worldview when he said it was, "Near perfect in its immorality."

Another flaw in conservatism: the myth of the self-made individual or 'self-made man.' This trope has been promoted for decades, but it was discredited in the 1930s, if not sooner. Here's one example: a small business owner in the eastern United States has claimed – for at least 10 years – that he is a 'self-made man, who has never been dependent on the government.' However, the evidence belies that, but we'll leave it to readers to decide. Here's his story:

'Self-made man' - whom we'll call MM, was born in a classic, all-American, industrial, working-class/middle-class town. The street where his home resided on was paved with town funds (subsidy for MM), the separate municipal water and sewer systems were installed with town funds (subsidy), and the street's light fixtures were paid for with town and state funds (subsidy). He attended public schools in grades kindergarten through grade 12, graduating from high school, paid for by town, state and federal funds (subsidy). The area he lives in also contains state highways that he regularly uses for work and leisure, paid for by state and federal funds (subsidy). He enjoys fresh water and seashore pursuits and leisure activities, with environmental, maintenance, waste removal tasks paid for with local, state and federal funds (subsidy). He'll fly on a commercial flight, occasionally, using an area airport paid for by state and federal funds (subsidy). The air traffic control system that keeps the sky he flies in safe is paid for by federal funds (subsidy). We've described a portion of his life, but by no means his entire life – and we've already noted at least 8 taxpayer subsidies. And there are many, many more, relating to health, safety and national defense: in other words, his life has been heavily subsidized, and he is dependent on the government in a big way. 'Self-made man' is, in fact, "U.S. society-made man." And yet, he touts, he's a 'self-made man' who hasn't been dependent on the government. Seriously? If the aforementioned is 'self-made man' he's got a bright future as a court jester in one of Shakespeare's plays because he's either joking, not stating the truth or is a fool, because his life has been subsidized and he's been dependent on local, state and the federal government since day 1. The point here is obvious enough: whenever a conservative, a Republican or someone else tells you he/she is a 'self-made individual,' a bell should go off in your head: nothing could be further from the truth. Conservatives routinely trot-out this trope/gaslighting technique to imply that they aren't costing the government money, that they are achievers, and others are 'moochers.' Simply, that is false, and a slander of their fellow Americans. Here's the truth, the facts, the reality: we are ALL dependent on the government in our nation, and we all contribute to its achievements and strength.

Still another fault/liability of conservatism/Republicans: they believe the only people who have a claim to a middle-class, dignified, humane life – basically the American dream – are the wealthy, executives, upper-income adults, business owners/merchants, entrepreneurs, and other white-collar professionals. *Conversely, progressives and Democrats argue that EVERY person – every citizen – has the right to a dignified, humane life – and to all of the benefits offered to the middle-class.* To repeat: Democrats believe everyone in society has a right to a dignified life – blue-collar workers, gig workers, artists, for-contract workers, delivery workers, babysitters/nannies, service sector employees – everyone! And Democrats will implement policies to achieve that goal – to create a more perfect union. As one might sense, this is a major philosophical difference between conservatives and progressives: Republicans, for the most part, will not use policies to ensure human dignity. Democrats will deploy them all the time, and the new Biden Administration in 2021 will work to achieve that goal, including: adequate, living wages for all adults, adequate housing, affordable health care insurance, a superior education/vocational skills to meet 21st century demands, a variety of leisure opportunities, as well opportunities to explore the arts. Conservatives and Republicans see the middle-class life as kind of an elite, exclusive fraternity, where they, at worst, try to keep people out, and, at best, make it very hard to let people in/help them ascend. Progressives/Democrats see the middle-class life - "the good life," as the legendary, late, great Washington Post Managing Editor Ben Bradley called it - as a right for all, and they work to eliminate barriers – chief among these being sub-standard wages and inadequate education/job training – so that the middle-class sphere is always expanding. In other words, progressives/Democrats want an economy and society where all members live a dignified life, fulfill their potential and have a say in their democracy – an economy and society in which all can flourish. (That's a major reason Democrats favor unions and collective bargaining, as well as many other protections for the workforce.) Don't ever let a conservative slide by with the old lie, the rhetoric that "You can't have what middle-income citizens have." That is a lie told by flawed, supply side-distorted conservatives: *Every person, by virtue of his or her birth, is worthy of a middle-income life, or better.* Every job has worth and should be paid a living wage. Every person has a claim to the American dream, and progressives/Democrats must ensure that our nation's laws and institutions support these goals.

But beyond the above, another glaring - and incontrovertible - indictment of conservatism is its ineffectualness. As the saying goes, "The proof of the pudding is in the eating" and in the final analysis conservatism is indicted because it does not solve most economic and social problems. To repeat, for the conservative readers who did not have time to write that down: Conservatism. Does. Not. Solve. Most. Economic. And. Social. Problems. After 40 years of conservative supply side economics (1981-2008) – massive income tax cuts for the rich and upper income groups, inordinate deregulation and cutbacks to the United States' social safety net - what has resulted? We now have massive inequalities in income and wealth, the persistence of poverty, and too many Americans not earning a living wage. Meanwhile, a host of other economic and social problems have persisted, or worsened, including the too-high cost of a college education and health care insurance and too many Americans entering retirement age with no private pension and little savings. The conservatives' response? There is none – beyond more tax cuts for the wealthy, and false blaming individuals for their status. (Underscoring: conservative Art Laffer's supply-side income tax cuts for the rich and upper income groups was wrong on Day 1, and it is wrong today. Laffer's top-brackets-favoring tax cut did not lead to massive GDP growth, it did not create more jobs than Keynesian economics, and it did not balance the federal budget. In fact, Laffer's tax cut for upper income groups was tried at the local level, again, most recently in Kansas, and it nearly bankrupted the state: it robbed the state of funds for essential public programs and services, especially for public education. At a basic level, Laffer's theory does not heed Keynesian economic theory, nor does it offer evidence, either theoretically or in real-world practical models, that it can generate massive GDP growth and job growth while simultaneously balancing a fiscal budget. Laffer's tax cut for the rich is good at one thing: decreasing the amount of money the rich and upper income groups pay in income taxes.) Repeat: conservatives offer very little to solve these economic and social problems. Most conservative pundits don't even try – a main tactic by this faction is to not talk about issues – because they know they don't have the philosophically or morally stronger argument. Hence, silence is their preference. (Axiom: "The power to keep issues off the table is real power.") But those that do talk or write, spout mostly nonsense: really, it is more of a psychological protest than a practical governance philosophy or governance plan. Many conservatives are perfectly comfortable with "the status quo" and doing nothing: the problem is – the economic and social problems are real, they are tangible. The problems (stagnant wages, unemployment, underemployment, unaffordable health care insurance, high-cost housing, inadequate support for education, a lack of quality day care, climate change, the increase in adults who are marginalized from the economy and society, etc.) are placing real stress on society. There is no debate: the U.S. economy and society contain stresses that must be addressed. And if/when these stresses combine with declining earnings growth for America's major corporations, the stress will metastasize into a crisis: and the United States in 2021 is certainly experiencing one now. Hence, 'doing nothing' is not an option and conservatism must be abandoned for intrinsic reasons: it is ineffectual, and the American people, now more than ever, need a pro-active, practical governance philosophy that is progressivism, led by the Democratic Party, to solve the economic and social problems that conservatism has failed to do and let fester for 40 years. Further, if you, the reader and citizen, remember little else from this book, know this: the American people want problems solved, and they will reward the party and/or coalition that solves them.

Further, that conservative/Republican ineffectualness has its most-visible and public interest-damaging expression in current Congressional Republicans - the Congressional Republicans of 2017-2020. It's as if Senate and House Republicans have never been through a major recession (hello? one occurred in 2008-2009) or another crisis. All Senate and House Republicans do in the current Congress is strike a partisan chord/stance: as noted above, the answer they utter is the same to every problem - it's always tax cuts for upper-income groups and business, deregulation, 100 percent opposition to counter-ideas and blame the opposition. That barely works when the U.S. economy is growing at a low rate, as it was in 2019 before the year ended, (thru December 2019, Trump had created fewer jobs per year than Obama did), but when the coronavirus pandemic hit in early 2020, conservatives' / Republicans' discredited and bankrupt stance was laid bare and it became a case study of the GOP's utter ineffectualness. (In fact, today's Trumpism/conservatism is a miasma - a truly toxic brew: it is nativist, racist, prone to despotism, ignorant, and filled with contempt and crackpot theories. Time and space prevent a thorough discussion here of the damage each fault does to the U.S. economy and society; they will have to wait for yours truly's second book, Book 2.) Had conservatives / Republicans featured a practical, governing philosophy like progressives/Democrats do under Keynesian economics, in 2019 they perhaps would have seen and been attentive to the weak domestic demand, structural inequalities in income and wealth, the persistent poverty - much of it caused by low wages in selected job segments - the stagnant earnings, longstanding trade imbalances, deteriorating voter rights and rising, needless human suffering, and last but not least the problem of climate change, and recommended needed economic and social reforms. But conservatism in the Republican Party - and we use both terms loosely - is a gong, a noisy cymbal, a lot of sound and fury signifying very little, to paraphrase Shakespeare. (And Shakespeare probably would have indicted them as much.) As a result, conservatism's economic ineffectualness and moral and social bankruptcy were exposed first by the 2020 coronavirus pandemic, which Republicans failed to contain, and then by the recession, which occurred because a national lockdown was not imposed immediately in March 2020 with federal fiscal stimulus bridge-money, allowing the coronavirus to plague states across the country for months/quarters longer than it should have, with awful consequences for U.S. families, businesses and the economy, in general. It is not an overstatement to argue conservativism/Republicanism as the new decade begins is: "1) feed your base and 2) tax cuts and tax preferences for your cronies." That sham of a plan may have worked slightly, when the U.S. economy was growing a little in 2019, but that's not nearly enough to solve the nation's problems, let alone govern, during a crisis (or a triple crisis: a pandemic, recession, and social problems).

But the worst fault of conservatism, and this certainly applies for conservatives and Republicans today, is that they have little or no interest in using the state to reduce and eliminate needless human suffering and pain. Conservatives/Republicans either don't recognize the problem, of if they do, they just don't care, or even if they recognize the problem and do care, they don't want or believe the state – including the federal government – should do anything to eliminate the suffering and pain. Yours truly doesn't know which is worse: either conservatives and Republicans are inept or they are ignorant, callous, cruel, and primitive. Perhaps, at times, they are a combination. The bottom line is this: that response is wrong! Flat out wrong! Very wrong! And it is unacceptable for an enlightened democracy and humanitarian civilization. (If their stance borders on spite, it's beyond wrong, it's evil, but this analysis will assume they are not spiteful, and keep it in the category of wrong.) As noted, progressives and Democrats believe in the "positive state" – that the state can and should be used to eliminate needless, preventable human suffering and pain. Accordingly, Democrats and the Biden Administration in 2021 must get right to work and immediately pass legislation - and implement executive orders - to not only reverse the many mistakes of the Trump Administration, they must also take actions to reduce and then eliminate needless, preventable human suffering and pain. And right now, in the United States, with the triple crises of the coronavirus pandemic, a recession, and social unrest, there is a lot of needless, preventable human suffering and pain.

Having read the above, the reader might conclude, is conservatism/the Republican Party, inherently or intrinsically cruel? It's almost always uncomfortable to state a harsh truth, but the reality is, sadly, today's Republican Party, which is comprised largely of this brand or distorted version of conservativism, is inherently cruel. Examples and evidence abound, and time and space limitations do not permit a thorough elaboration here, but consider: 1) Republican efforts to deny Medicaid - basic medical care for the poor / working poor - in more than a dozen red Republican states; 2) repeated legislation in the states to reduce unemployment compensation; 3) efforts at the national level to not extend $600 per week Pandemic Unemployment Assistance (PUA) to adults who lost employment through no fault of their own in 2020; in August 2020, about 20 Senate Republicans said they would not vote for any PUA extension, after it expired on July 31, 2020; 4) countless efforts to disenfranchise voters and suppress the vote; and 5) numerous votes to deny basic health care to immigrants who are refugees - including children. And there are dozens of other cruel and counter-productive actions - actions that represent the worst of these United States. To be sure, the Republican Party of 30, 40, 50 years ago had uncaring, cruel members, but it also had caring moderates, as well as conservatives who would not undertake the above actions. The Republican Party of 2020 appears to have few such members and/or is dominated by conservatives who are cruel. There's no other way to put it accurately. It's as simple as that.

Earlier we noted conservatism's individual-centric focus to a fault, or its hyper-individualism – an ideology that, if carried to its logical extension leads to a survival-of-the-fittest economic and social Darwinism – a very harsh, cruel society in which the poor, the vulnerable, the weak, and the less-fortunate are left to fend for themselves, and if needless human suffering and pain occur, so be it, says the conservative. Under that stance, the conservative has little obligation to society, let alone an interest in forming a community. Pope Francis has called this hyper-individualism "the virus of radical individualism." During his Christmas message delivered 25 December 2020 Pope Francis said: "Nor can we let the virus of radical individualism win us over and make us indifferent to the suffering of other brothers and sisters. I cannot put myself before others, putting the laws of the market and invention patents above the laws of love and the health of the community." Pope Francis also asked national leaders, businesses, and international organizations to seek solutions for all, and vaccines for all, especially the most vulnerable and needy, in all regions of the world. In fact, the coronavirus pandemic is showing us the flaws and destructiveness of hyper-individualism. According to the conservative stance, a vaccine would only go to those who can pay for it. As noted, an economic system as conservative as that would lead to untold, preventable, avoidable deaths and human suffering – just from the coronavirus, which would not be contained as quick, due to people not having enough money to purchase the vaccine. That stance would lead to a human catastrophe beyond what the United States and the world are currently trying to check – which is all the more reason to abandon the ill-conceived, harmful hyper-individualism advocated by many conservatives. A "Wild, Wild West" organization of society was absurd when it occurred in the United States from 1869-1890; it would be catastrophic today.

Some may counter that the United States has boasted a *rugged individualism* culture since its inception. Fair enough: one can be a "rugged individualist," just don't take it to the extreme. Don't become a *radical individualist* – someone who believes U.S. corporate capitalism without an adequate social safety net / social welfare state is enough for a modern / postmodern society. (And, as this book has described, the U.S.'s current social safety is not adequate. It is a band-aid that needs many boosts and reforms, as outlined.) Unlike many Western European economic systems, corporate capitalism in the United States is harsh, and without an adequate social safety net / social welfare state it is social Darwinism, or “radical individualism” – a practice and trend that would ultimately undermine our economy, society and nation. Hence, be rugged *but not radical.* Society leading to community counts, too, not merely the individual.

Further, as noted, the conservative response - one has to call it a response, because it certainly isn’t an answer - to every problem…is either another income tax cut for millionaires and billionaires, a capital gains tax cut or a reduction in regulations. (!) In other words, they don’t have many responses and they certainly don’t have many answers. Not ones that lead to public policies that eliminate human suffering and pain, anyway. The analysis forwarded here argues that this strikes yours truly as a callous or indifferent stance by conservatives, it is wrong, and it cannot be the policy of the United States Government. Conservatives’ indifference or ignorance must be cast aside, along with their metaphysical belief in the free market/private sector. The progressive/Democratic march and motto should be: we will have free markets with a legitimate social safety net / social welfare state – not a band aid – to counter the harshness, arbitrariness and capriciousness of the free market.

In sum, conservatism, always weak regarding a public policy response to an economic or social problem, is even more callous, indifferent, and ineffectual under Trumpism. In fact, in many ways today’s so called ‘conservatism,’ is malignant – quite destructive and damaging. The American people can’t rely on or wait for the market - the ‘metaphysical market’ or other response from the private sector - to solve problems that have lingered for 40 years and that conservatives through supply-side economics help perpetuate and worsen. The American people want action now! Further, as discussed earlier, it was the piling up or the aggregation of economic-problem-after-economic-problem, social-problem-after-social-problem, over 40 years - under largely conservative/Republican rule and their system, supply-side economics (low taxes for upper income groups, few regulations, little support for education, health care, housing and the environment) - that convinced yours truly to conclude that the answers/solutions to problems had to be found elsewhere and that the United States was overdue for a New Progressive Era. Hence, the sooner Americans abandon conservatism and more-fully commit to progressivism and the Democrats, the sooner the nation will re-invest in health care, in higher education, in job training, in housing, in renewable energy, in the environment, in voting rights and in dozens of other public assets and public needs, as we build that more perfect union. Or as President Biden calls it – as we "build back better." And it goes without saying that, the author believes the American people deserve those investments, and more.

Scenario: The reforms recommended above will require scenarios 1 thru 4, and perhaps some of 5. In other words, progressives/Democrats united with the new Biden Administration, will need and should use every tool in their tool kit to solve economic and social problems, and build that more perfect union. As noted, President Biden calls it "build back better." Yours truly likes the sound of that, as it has the goal in sight, which is:

"Every person, by virtue of his or her birth, is worthy of a middle-income life, or better. Every job has worth and should be paid a living wage. Every person has a claim to the American dream, and progressives/Democrats must ensure that our nation's laws and institutions support these goals."

They Said It: Presidential Humor 3

President Lyndon B. Johnson, often referred to LBJ, had a unique sense of humor that spanned many subjects and styles. During one departure from the White House, LBJ walked toward the wrong helicopter transport. There were two helicopters, the first for the president, known as "Marine One," and the second for the press and some staff.

The U.S. Marine on duty saluted LBJ and said, "Excuse me, Mr. President, but that helicopter over there, to the left, that's your helicopter, sir, not this one."

LBJ, did not change his path, kept walking, glanced back at the Marine and said, "Son, they's all my helicopters."

**

LBJ was also experienced in marriage. And he sometimes gave marital advice.

"I have learned the secret to a happy marriage," President Johnson said. "Let your wife think she's getting her way. Then…let her have her way."

President Johnson official portrait, 1967
(Credit: U.S. National Archives.)

**

At a White House meeting after a report on a federal program that President Johnson favored, a young U.S. representative at the meeting then presented in painstaking and methodical fashion a counter-argument – i.e., why the program should be eliminated from the budget.

After the Congressman finished his report, LBJ put his glasses on, looked at the Congressman, looked down at his notes, then looked up again at the Congressman and said, "Son, do you know who you're talking to?"

**

LBJ, as protests and civil unrest started to increase against the controversial and unsuccessful Vietnam War, encountered more hecklers and protestors during his speeches, particularly on university campuses.

During one speech, the chanting got so loud and pointed, President Johnson paused while reading his speech, and shouted into the microphone, "I'm the only president you ha-aavve!"

**

In 1963, President John F. Kennedy, who had chronic back problems, at a news conference was asked by a reporter, "What was the condition of the president's back?"

President Kennedy, paused for a moment, then as he pointed to the next questioner, said, "Oh, it depends on the weather - political and otherwise."

**

Without question, President Lyndon B. Johnson was frank, sometimes too frank. But during his "structured frank" moments, he often uttered statements that were illuminating insights:

LBJ: "You say you dislike politics, but you're a politician about something important in your life, isn't that so? Tell the truth."

TRIVIA TEST 10: U.S. All-Encompassing

(Answers in Appendix, Page 354.)

1. True or False: The 2020 Democratic Party presidential nominee Joe Biden has served in elected office more than 40 years
a) True b) False

2. The 2020 Democratic Party vice presidential nominee Kamala Harris attended which college as an undergraduate?
a) Yale b) University of Connecticut c) Brown d) Howard University

3. Joe Biden's was born in which state?
a) Alaska b) New York c) New Jersey d) Pennsylvania

William Penn (Credit: U.S. National Archives.)

4. Vice President Kamala Harris was born in which state?
a) New Jersey b) Ohio c) Virginia d) California

5. The last time the same party won 3 presidential elections in a row was what year? Which election marked the third victory?
a) 1952 b) 1956 c) 1988 d) 1976

6. True or False: H. Ross Perot was a presidential candidate.
a) True b) False

7. Which of the following is true?
In presidential elections since 1992, the Republican Party usually wins:
a) Connecticut b) Texas c) California d) Massachusetts

8. Which of the following is true?
In presidential elections since 1992, the Democratic Party usually wins: a) Oklahoma b) Nebraska c) New York d) Montana

9. Which presidential candidate received the most votes in the 1992 election?
a) Clinton b) Bush c) Perot d) Jones

10) The last year the Democratic Party controlled the U.S. presidency, House and Senate was?
a) 1953 b) 1973 c) 1981 d) 2010

BONUS QUESTIONS: Worth 2 points (or 2 correct answers) each:

BONUS Q1: The only woman nominated to be vice president by the Republican Party was:

a) Abagail Adams b) Betsy Ross c) Sarah Palin d) Nancy Reagan

BONUS Q2: Counting the Democratic Party and the Republican Party, how many women have been nominated to be either president or vice president?

a) 1 b) 2 c) 4 d) 3

BONUS Q3: The first African American woman elected to the U.S. Congress was:

a) Shirley Chisholm b) Harriet Tubman c) Eleanor Holmes Norton d) Angela Davis

BONUS Q4: Speaker Nancy Pelosi's father was:

a) Mayor of Chicago b) Mayor of Boston c) Governor of Arizona d) Mayor of Baltimore

Congratulations! You have completed the Trivia Test. Answers to all 100 questions and the four Bonus Questions can be found in the Appendix on Page 354.

President Nixon's Resignation - Was Watergate About Watergate?

The details of the case are well known. That is, as the analysis below will seek to demonstrate, at least the public record of what happened is well known.

In August 1974, President Richard Nixon resigned after evidence revealed he had known about, if not guided, the cover-up of the illegal break-in at the Watergate office complex in Washington, D.C. in June 1972 that hosted the Democratic National Committee headquarters. Rather than face impeachment, and a probable conviction in the U.S. Senate, Nixon resigned.

But the lingering mystery of Watergate concerns the to-date uninvestigated role of the Central Intelligence Agency (CIA). It is well known that five of the seven Watergate burglars had worked for the CIA, including E. Howard Hunt and James McCord. What's more, four were Cuban-Americans from Miami who were involved in the disastrous 1961 Bay of Pigs operation when misguided anti-Castro rebels tried to overthrow a much larger Cuba military and communist government - a government that had widespread support of Cuba's people. Hunt and McCord and had been personally

Former CIA Director Richard Helms. (Credit: U.S. National Archives.)

close to CIA Director Richard Helms for more than a decade.

Helms Denies CIA Involvement

Helms, in U.S. Senate testimony in August 1973, denied any and all CIA involvement in the Watergate break-in. "The agency had nothing to do with the Watergate break-in," Helms said, while testifying. "And I hope all the newsmen in the room hear me clearly now."

The Nixon / Helms relationship started reasonably well, but the record shows that Helms was always concerned about Hunt's role as a White House consultant. Hunt had classified information on numerous, past CIA operations. Conversely, Hunt thought his CIA work would push Nixon to help him mount a criminal defense against the Watergate charges, or at minimum get the charges reduced. Nixon felt the same way: "You open that scab and there's a hell of a lot of things," Nixon said, "and we just feel that it would be very detrimental to have things go any further. This involves these Cubans, Hunt and a lot of hanky-panky that we have nothing to do with ourselves." What's more, Nixon felt the common interest both CIA and his White House had in not having sensitive - and potentially institution-damaging - information revealed would prompt the CIA to try to block the Federal Bureau of Investigation's (FBI) Watergate investigation. Nixon indicated as much to aide H.R. Haldeman, who said to Helms it might expose "that whole Bay of Pigs thing," which Haldeman and aide John Ehrlichman came to interpret as information *not* about the Bay of Pigs, but about the *November 22, 1963 assassination of President John F. Kennedy.*

'Nothing to do with Bay of Pigs'

But Helms, a shrewd, experienced bureaucratic operator, declined. Nixon had calculated incorrectly. Helms gave strong signals he would not help Nixon by screaming at Haldeman during a meeting at which he cited the Hunt exposure risk, that "This has nothing to do with the Bay of Pigs!! This has nothing to do with the Bay of Pigs!!"

Equally puzzling is the fact that despite evidence of CIA fingerprints on the Watergate matter, the press, led by The Washington Post, focused their investigation solely on Nixon and his administration's staff.

Helms later pled guilty to lying to Congress about a CIA assassination conspiracy in Chile. Nixon, of course, resigned. Hunt, Haldeman and Ehrlichman went to prison. But the CIA's role in Watergate remains unclear, as does the reason why The Washington Post focused like a laser on Nixon, when the facts suggested much wider guilt.

(Adults state the Oath of Allegiance to become U.S. citizens at a naturalization ceremony in Grand Canyon National Park, Arizona, United States in September 2010. Credit: National Park Service.)

Chapter: 25: U.S. Immigration Policy

"Give me your tired, your poor,
Your huddled masses yearning to breathe free,
The wretched refuse of your teeming shore.
Send these, the homeless, tempest-tost to me,
I lift my lamp beside the golden door!"

-From: "The New Colossus," by Poet Emma Lazarus, inscribed on a plaque on the Statue of Liberty, 1903, New York, N.Y.

U.S. immigration is another issue where progressives and Democrats have the philosophically stronger argument. And how. Moreover, although the issue contains many facets, progressives/Democrats united with the new Biden Administration should be guided by one theme in 2021: ending the

Trump Administration's inhumane and brutal immigration detention and related policies. Trump's policies – including separating children from mothers and fathers, and putting children in cages – go against everything the United States stands for. They are abhorrent. Period.

Executive orders: Given his November 2020 election win, President Biden's first order of business should be several executive orders to end the horrific family separation policy and also immediately deploy funds to re-unite families and begin building temporary housing for the thousands of children and families in detention centers. Many if not most immigrants are refugees, including mothers with children, fleeing violence and drug gangs in Central America, and related social problems. The notion that the United States would separate children from families and "lock them up" – and place children in cages – is not only inhumane, it defies common sense and goes against America's fundamental values. Detention should only be a last resort, and under no circumstance should children be placed in cages.

Rather, progressives/Democrats using funds allocated by an executive order, and legislation, after President Biden immigration bill has been passed, should have the United States Government build small villages where families can remain, until U.S. immigration courts and public officials can evaluate their refugee/asylum petition. Families should be kept together unless U.S. Immigration and Customs Enforcement (ICE) officials determine there is the threat of violence or other psychological or behavior problems (including substance abuse) that require a family member(s) to be separated from the family. Also, these should be full-service villages with adequate health care, education and modest recreation facilities.

Hearings in court: Second, Democrats should lobby to end ICE removal tactics without a trial, for all but known criminals and violent offenders. Each refugee must be given a fair court hearing: doing anything less would violate the U.S. Constitution's due process, equal protection and unreasonable search and seizure guarantees.

U.S. citizenship: Democrats must work to clarify the process / road to U.S. citizenship. Many immigrants are fleeing poverty or simply seeking a means to support their family with them and/or loved ones back home. Democrats must also establish policies that protect the rights of workers vulnerable to abuse, including for-contract and temporary workers, guest workers and unauthorized workers; and they must also ban racial profiling.

Detention, deportation and due process: Simply, no immigrant, refugee or asylum seeker should be in detention or deported without a hearing, and during that hearing the U.S. Government bears the burden of showing that detention or deportation is necessary. (For known criminals, violent offenders and/or individuals with other behavioral problems, including substance abuse, isolation must occur, before that case can be assessed.) In short, a court and ICE officials must determine if that an individual(s) is a danger to the community, including the constructed U.S. immigration villages.

State and local laws: Democrats must lobby to pass legislation to maintain the supremacy of federal law over state and local laws. They must work to overturn any immigration law that invites or leads to racial profiling against Latinos, Asian-Americans or others presumed to be "foreign" based on their appearance or language.

Deferred Action for Childhood Arrivals (DACA): In June 2020, the U.S. Supreme Court, in a 5-4 decision, ruled that the Trump Administration did not take the proper steps to end the DACA program, also called "Dreamers," and the court rejected arguments that the program is illegal, and that court also rejected the assertion that the courts have no role to play in reviewing the decision to end it. The decision covers the 650,000 people who have been in the United States since they were children and are in the country illegally.

How should Democrats follow-up regarding the above? First, the new Biden Administration should issue an executive order on day 1 making all 650,000 DACA members U.S. citizens. Period. The Biden Administration should then immediately follow-up and make all DACA protections permanent. A U.S. Congress/Obama Administration impasse led to the DACA program in 2012. A Republican-led U.S. House failed to pass comprehensive U.S. immigration reform, hence President Obama formally protected people from deportation while also allowing them to work and study in the United States. The Trump Administration challenged that plan in court; hence, with the U.S. Supreme Court's June 2020 ruling, Democrats should confidently charge forward to not only codify DACA protections, but to ease DACA members' transition to the United States, and ensure that future DACA members immediately receive the same rights, i.e., ensure that regulatory actions by a Republican president do not reverse or limit that U.S. citizenship right.

Further, as one of his initial acts as president in his first week, President Biden introduced a sweeping plan to revise U.S. immigration – including a path to U.S. citizenship for the estimated 11 million undocumented immigrants living in the United States.

The nation of immigrants: No matter what conservatives, Republicans and others may assert, the United States is a nation of immigrants. It is "the nation of nations." As such, it has a special role in international relations. And most certainly, the United States must always be the last refuge for those seeking asylum. (More will be said about that special role in this book's conclusion, and then a thorough discussion in Book 2.) For now, know that the United States would not have become the successful, diverse nation it is today, without immigrants. Immigrants literally built this country – to be sure, with the help of others, as well, including descendants from the 13 original colonies – and it is a feat that's unparalleled in world history. Boosted the incalculable contributions from immigrants, the United States ascended from typical nation status to superpower status in the modern era, especially during the Cold War, to become the world's preeminent democracy. Our U.S. Bill of Rights, rule of law, civil service system, independent judiciary, and (largely) merit-based economy remain a model for all nations and societies. And within that has been the creed: that the

United States is a nation not based on a people from one race, ethnicity or religion, but *based on an idea:* democracy, and majority rule with respect to minority rights, and equal justice under law. That idea holds that every person, once naturalized here or attaining citizenship – no matter who they are, or where they came from, or what line of work they do, or how they worship (or don't worship), is an American. No other nation on Earth has welcomed as many people and nationalities as citizens as the United States. In that sense, immigration is intrinsic to the United States: it is a defining characteristic of the nation. Immigration literally renews, re-energizes and enrichens the United States: each assimilation adds to the nation's tapestry. And it goes without saying, that the analysis forwarded here argues that the assimilation must continue. The United States must always remain the home for the tempest tossed, in Emma Lazarus's words, the asylum for refugees, the golden door. The United States must always remain a sanctuary for the persecuted, the marginalized, the vulnerable, and the excluded. As such, progressives and Democrats must do everything they can, starting in 2021, to restore adequate, robust immigration to these United States.

Scenario: This policy change would likely draw from scenarios 1 thru 3. Many U.S. immigration reforms can be implemented by executive order and by regulation reforms. Some will require new institutions, such as the building of immigration villages to enable refugees/those seeking asylum to live a dignified, humane life before their U.S. immigration court hearing. Needless to add, progressives and Democrats, united with President Biden, should "exert every muscle" to promptly end the Trump Administration's barbaric and inhumane policy, and replace it with a U.S. immigration system that is humane, that respects the infinite worth of each person, and that enables each person to live a full, dignified life - in other words, to flourish.

(Apollo 11 Astronaut Edwin "Buzz" Aldrin prepares to salute the American flag on the Moon, July 1969. Credit: NASA Astronaut Neil Armstrong.)

Conclusion

"You give the United States Government the benefit of the doubt. Period." -Joseph S. Lazzaro, "Kid Lightning," God rest his soul, U.S. Army veteran (Korean War, 1952-1954), and father of the author.

As noted in the Preface, this book is designed to show the correct path the American people and the United States Government should take: led by President Biden and a Democratic Party-led Congress, it should implement progressive policies in a New Progressive Era to solve the many economic and social problems facing the nation - problems largely caused by the incorrect conservative policies implemented from 1981-2008, a period that will, arguably, be known as the New Gilded Age. The book's goal is to show that, propelled by a progressive majority, a New Progressive Era can produce a more-humane, more-just society – the more perfect union Americans seek. It argued that while many of the solutions to our nation's economic and social problems can be found in the private sector/the free market, many cannot and will need an activist public sector to solve them. In doing so, the book argues and relies heavily on the effective, dependable philosophy of etatism - the positive state - the theory that the state - at all levels in the United States – town/city, county, state, federal - can solve economic and social problems, and in doing so advance the U.S. economy, society and civilization. Further, in the particular case of the United States, the book calls for elected officials to actively and frequently deploy federal government solutions, where other levels are not the most-effective or practical option, and/or where the local/state governments do not have the resources to address a problem. In short, progressives/Democrats believe the state, in addition to the private sector, can solve economic and social problems and achieve a more perfect union.

What does that more perfect union look like? It has policies that achieve the common good, that are in the national interest and the public interest and that, in the words of Pope Francis, "*Enable all citizens to flourish.*" In other words, it enables each person to live a humane, dignified, middle-class life. I.E., that means the middle-class life is available not merely for the wealthy, upper classes, executives, college-educated professionals, merchants and businesses - but for everyone; it enables each person to fulfill his/her potential and destiny. *At minimum,* that more perfect union is one that uses all institutions (private, public, non-profit) to eliminate needless human suffering and pain.

Further, as noted, historically Congress and the U.S. president respond to a crisis or problem in a classic reform-within-the-system way, but it's useful and educational/illuminating to note that there are four other response types, called scenarios. Again, they are:

1-reform within the system (Typical reforms after a crisis in U.S. corporate capitalism.)

2-Reforms within the system with structural changes (One example: guaranteed minimum income or Social Security.)

3-New system (One example: Democratic socialism, or a variant thereof.)

4-Change even beyond a new system (The slow, incremental de-activation of life/the world as we used to know it.)

5-The not likely (but still possible) scenario.

- -

Further, it will become clearer to the reader in Book 2 - and certainly in Book 3 - why yours truly listed the scenarios for economic and social reform. (I.E., "the method to his madness" - why Lazzaro included these 5 scenarios.)

Book 1 also discussed 25 issues facing the United States, and presented evidence arguing why progressives/Democrats have the superior public policy response or answer – the stronger philosophical argument – for most economic and social problems facing the United States.

25 Issues/policy areas: Just to review, those 25 issues/policy areas are: 1) public health care investment, 2) Medicare expansion to age 55, 3) $15 per hour minimum wage/living wage, 4) improve Social Security / the Super Pension, 5) rebuild U.S. infrastructure, 6) higher education/vocational school investment, 7) universal broadband (including wifi), 8) U.S. housing investment, 9) renewable energy program, 10) new manufacturing era, 11) personal time off, 12) improved work conditions and universal worker benefits, 13) the environment - re-thinking our relationship with nature, 14) U.S. Department of Defense/defense policy, 15) social media in the United

States and the U.S. Cyber Warfare Force, 16) technology and the U.S. workforce, 17) U.S. National Service Program, 18) etatism - the positive state, 19) U.S. Intelligence Community, 20) 51st and 52nd states: Washington Douglass Commonwealth and Puerto Rico, 21) NASA, U.S. Postal Service, Amtrak and PBS & NPR, 22) U.S. Department of Minority Affairs and Diversity, 23) the coronavirus pandemic, 24) a note on conservatism, and 25) U.S. immigration policy.

Below is a recap / summary of each:

In Chapter 1, we noted that the U.S.'s private sector-dominated health care system, while possessing many virtues, did not have nearly the resources and capacity needed to quickly contain the 2020 coronavirus pandemic outbreak. That inadequacy, combined with the Trump Administration's eight-week delay in responding to the outbreak, cost at least tens of thousands of lives – it led to tens of thousands of preventable, avoidable, needless deaths (and probably many more) - and countless injuries. Progressives and Democrats must end the U.S.'s fragmented public / private health care system by: 1) establishing a public option and/or universal health insurance, and 2) investing in hospitals and supplies - which are among the nation's most vital public goods. To help achieve the above, the United States must establish 200 U.S. hospitals, operated by the federal government.

In Chapter 2, Medicare's strong performance meant that it is a logical choice for expansion to age 55 to help reduce and then eliminate the number of older Americans who lose health insurance after a job layoff or corporate downsizing. Progressives/Democrats should also push to reduce insurance co-pays, enhance risk pools and lower premiums in the Affordable Care Act / Obamacare to help reduce the number of Americans who are uninsured. The goal should be zero (0) Americans uninsured by mid-2029.

Next, Chapter 3 discussed the longstanding problem in the United States of inadequate wages in many job segments. Progressives/Democrats should push for a $15 per hour minimum wage in 2021, with some float down/up for lower-cost/higher-cost town, cities and regions. Democrats should also work to strengthen collective bargaining/support for unions at the state and federal levels, and allocate funds for education and job training. Progressives and Democrats should also seek to cut public school class sizes in half and lobby for a $60,000 per year minimum teacher salary. Job bank: Given the large amount of job dislocation that's likely to occur due to globalization, the United States must also move toward some form of federal job bank. If an adult could not find a suitable, formal training-related position, and if retraining under federal/state job re-training programs was not possible, that person would be awarded a job by the U.S. Government for up to 3 years.

In Chapter 4, strategies to improve Social Security, the U.S.'s primary pension plan for retirees, were outlined. The goals: 1) no individual living in poverty, 2) more individuals who are leading dignified, middle-income lives, and 3) the disabled/vulnerable are adequately cared for. Progressives and Democrats should work ardently with the new Biden Administration to: 1) increase the minimum monthly benefit to $1,750 per month, 2) raise the minimum disability benefit to $1,200 per month, 3) lower the full retirement age to 65 in 2024 and to 62 in 2028, and lower the early retirement age to 60 in 2024 and to 57 in 2028, and 4) create a Super Pension for a $1,000 per month pension benefit for any person who does not qualify for the above programs, funded by a 1 percent wealth tax - a one-time tax that will serve as an endowment for the program. Ideally, that tax will yield an endowment of about $1 trillion.

In Chapter 5, the state of the U.S.'s infrastructure was evaluated. To be sure, there are some "bright stars" and green shoots, but overall, the grade for the nation's infrastructure is abysmal. According to the American Society of Civil Engineers (ASCE), the organization's 2017 grade for the U.S. infrastructure was: D+. Progressives/Democrats must lobby hard with the new Biden Administration to implement a comprehensive infrastructure rebuilding plan, which will total in the trillions of dollars. Due to the scope of the rebuilding task, every funding mechanism must be considered: public, private-public, private-built-with-a-public-lease, cooperative, worker-owned, naming-rights funded, and more. In the process, millions of good-paying jobs will be created - something that will also boost U.S. GDP.

Next, Chapter 6 addressed higher education and vocational skills training. Simply, the U.S. must create a new "GI Bill for displaced workers" - in part to address the likely job dislocation caused by globalization and automation. The comprehensive education revitalization program is as follows: education building renovations, $750 billion; vocational schools' capital plant, $100 billion; displaced workers fund, $100 billion; 21st century education fund for innovative/strategic-edge sectors, $100 billion; 21st century cultural fund, $50 billion; student loan forgiveness programs, $500 billion. Total education program cost: $1.6 trillion. In other words, as long as the federal government remains committed to higher education and vocational skills training, the United States' workforce will be prepared for the 21st century economy.

In Chapter 7, the vitalness of universal broadband (including wifi) was outlined. The 2020 coronavirus pandemic in the United States made clear that universal broadband is not merely a luxury, it is a necessity. It's vital - for health care/public health, home-office function, remote education/classroom education, and business/commerce/the economy. Progressives/Democrats must fund a new U.S. Broadband Center to create a reliable broadband network, accessible everywhere in the United States, for a subscription cost of no more than $10 per month. On a means-tested, sliding-scale basis, the broadband service should be offered for an even lower fee or for free, to the poor/working poor. An alternative plan would have the federal government establish broadband cooperatives in each state, or regionally (northeast, midwest, south, mountain, and west).

Chapter 8 addressed U.S. housing. One of the values or staples/essential components of the "American dream" is home ownership, and progressives and Democrats should lobby for a new federal housing program, with the following components: starter home construction - at least 100,000 units per year; expanded mortgage eligibility; $50 billion to revitalize public housing;

$20 billion for rental assistance to the poor/working poor, and low-income U.S. Veterans who are not covered by other federal housing programs; and $10 billion per year for 10 years to house the homeless. While U.S. Sen. Sanders' goal of 10 million housing units may be slightly high, his line of thinking and intent is on-the-mark: the United States must build houses and apartments where other organizations do not, to ensure that no one is homeless. Ever. Period.

In Chapter 9, the renewable energy sector, and its enormous potential to make the U.S. fossil fuel-free and energy independent was addressed. Progressives/Democrats should commit to an "all of the above" energy program - supporting hydro, wind, solar, geothermal, biomass, and tidal. The United States should have as its goal generating at least 50 percent of its electricity from renewable sources by 2030. Further, in addition to major tax credits, a new institution - such as the United States Renewable Energy Authority - will be needed to jump-start both the sector and the renewable energy era.

Next, Chapter 10 called for a new U.S. manufacturing era. The 2020 coronavirus pandemic has caused more than 1 million factory job layoffs and also exposed other national vulnerabilities. To address the above, the United States should bring home, for domestic production, health care goods production (including PPE - personal protective equipment), all defense production, most manufactured goods (in general), and also ban most cheap, low-quality, imported goods. In short, progressives/Democrats must prioritize the home-sourcing of manufactured goods and commit to a program that adds 500,000 factory jobs per year, for 10 years. Simply, the United States must become manufacturing self-sufficient – and never again have to rely on any other nation for vital goods.

The issue of personal time off (PTO) was addressed in Chapter 11. The United States does not have a minimum vacation requirement for full-time employees. Not even one week! Progressives/Democrats must commit themselves to placing U.S. PTO on a par with Western Europe nations. To achieve the above and more, the following actions were proposed: 1) federal vacation law (two weeks); 2) paid sick time; 3) childcare/day care - a $2,000 tax credit for each qualifying child; 4) maternal leave, up to 24 weeks of unpaid leave; and 5) paid homemaking - a $1,000 to $1,200 per month stipend, income-based. Paid homemaking will likely be the most controversial, trailblazing program, as it has garnered little support in the United States, despite being common in Europe. All PTO programs are worthy of implementation, however.

In Chapter 12, improved work conditions and universal worker benefits were discussed. As with broadband tech, the 2020 coronavirus pandemic laid bare the unhealthy, poor working conditions in several U.S. sectors, especially meat packing/meat processing. Progressives/Democrats in Congress should sponsor and lobby for legislation that increases social distance spaces and implement other public health equipment measures at these plants. A workers injury fund also should be established. Finally, a benefits bank should be established so that every adult in the United States has access to fringe benefits, such as health care insurance, dental insurance, a 401K/403B plan, transit benefit, vision care, and medical savings accounts, among other benefits. The benefits bank, by creating benefits portability, will help eliminate "job lock" in the United States - unlocking value and creativity, which will boost U.S. GDP, lead to more, value-added skills being deployed, and thus increase U.S. wealth.

Chapter 13 proposed a re-thinking of the United States' relationship with nature/the environment. In addition to programs that reduce fossil fuel use, major changes were recommended in manufacturing, consumption, and residences, with the goal of increasing use of recyclable materials, and other real estate development and quality-of-life changes that reduce waste. The possibilities for reform are almost limitless. The key is to implement progressive ideas that achieve sustainable communities, that enhance the quality of life of all, while reducing, then eliminating pollution and waste; in other words, policies that achieve the common good. Through the actions of progressives/Democrats, the United States must re-think and re-envision our relationship with nature: there must be a change in humanity's relationship with nature. Being a steward is inadequate, and as we saw in the previous 120 years, it led to terrible environment mistakes. In the 21st century, the United States, like the rest of the world, must live more in-harmony with nature.

Next, in Chapter 14, U.S. defense policy was addressed. Simply, progressives/Democrats must restore the good word of the United States internationally, with all democratic allies: repair NATO, repair relations with our Pacific allies, resume North Korea denuclearization talks, re-commit to a two-state solution in the Middle East (Israel, Palestinian Authority), and secure the border with Mexico and help Mexico enable all refugees to live humane, dignified lives. Major increases were also proposed for all branches of the U.S. Department of Defense, for F2022. U.S. Army, $230 billion; U.S. Navy, $240 billion; U.S. Air Force, $230 billion; U.S. Coast Guard, $15 billion; U.S. Marines, Navy Seals, Army Green Berets and other Special Operations Forces: $80 billion. Progressives/Democrats must also re-commit the nation to the strategic arms reduction talks (START) to reduce nuclear warheads to 3,000 each for the United States and Russia, by 2024.

In Chapter 15, the vitalness of establishing a U.S. Cyber Warfare Force was outlined. Simply, social media in the United States will change because it has to change: there are too many bad actors. Chief among these bad actors: the Russians, but also China, Iran and North Korea. The United States Intelligence Community (USIC), in its 2017 assessment, concluded that Russia interfered in the 2016 U.S. presidential election, Russia helped Republican Party nominee Donald Trump, hurt Democratic Party nominee Hillary Clinton, swayed voters to vote for Trump and discouraged other voters - largely Democrats and Independent/Unaffiliated voters - from voting for Clinton, resulting in a slight electoral college win for the Republican nominee. Clinton won the popular vote by a large margin, nearly 3 million votes: 65,853,514 to 62,984,828 and should have become the 45th president of the United States, but because Trump eeked-out wins in Pennsylvania, Michigan and Wisconsin, he entered the Oval Office. Simply, this foreign interference in a U.S. election that affected its outcome must never happen again. To achieve this goal, progressives/Democrats must lobby for the establishment of a U.S. Cyber Warfare Force and department in the U.S. Department of Defense. In addition, social media companies and social news aggregation sites must establish monitoring committees to self-monitor, discern, and reject content that's disinformation, hate-speech, that incites violence/insurrection, represents extremism and/or is content from a bad actor.

Chapter 16 addressed technology and its impact on the U.S. workforce. Technology – artificial intelligence (AI), machine learning, data analytics, robotics, automated systems, self-driving vehicles and drones, as well as other technologies not deployed yet and/or not pervasively used yet – will cause substantial job cuts and job consolidations, in many sectors. The job losses have only just begun, and concerning sectors, perhaps a better statement is – name a sector that won't be affected by technology and incur job losses in the decade ahead? Along with comprehensive worker retraining programs (discussed in Chapter 6), progressives/Democrats should lobby for creative and unique solutions to worker dislocation, including a guaranteed minimum income (GMI). Another option, paid homemaking, would be a major step for the United States. These and other ideas should all be a part of progressives' / Democrats' policy palette for the U.S. workforce in the new Biden Administration, while also remaining decidedly in the pro-technology camp. In other words, ignoring technological change and automation won't make them disappear: better to shape them, to create a "technology with a human face" as the nation ventures further into the uber-competitive 21st century economy.

In Chapter 17, the U.S. National Service Program (USNSP) was discussed. The United States must implement a national service program, which is primarily for its younger adults, but also for selected others who are suitable for and can benefit from the program. For too long, national service has been neglected. It's time to reverse that incorrect, counter-productive trend. Progressives and Democrats should support and promote the new, positive, constructive standard: national service. Required service: Initially, the top-end age limit will be 30, with lotteries for ages 23-30 so that they comprise 1/5 of the that year's class of 25,000 adults (5,000), and ages 18-22 comprising 4/5 of the adults (20,000). Adults ages 18-22 will have an open-enrollment period: if the 20,000-adult minimum is not met, a lottery will occur for that age group, as well. Adults ages 18-22 can delay their service for up to 4 years. The exceptions to the lottery entry requirement would be if the adult enters U.S. military service, has a legally-defined disability or if an extreme family hardship exists. (There will also be selected personal hardship exemptions granted, including for health: a young adult who has recently recovered from cancer, or another serious illness, such as the coronavirus/COVID-19, will be granted exemptions, if USNSP medical personnel determine that it is not in the interest of the adult's health or safety to continue with national service.) With the above, all corners of society will share in the costs and responsibilities of building and maintaining democracy in the United States.

Chapter 18 discussed etatism - the positive state, the theoretical foundation and practical goal of this book. Progressives / Democrats believe that the state (especially the federal government) can and should be used to solve economic and social problems, and to eliminate needless human suffering and pain. Accordingly, progressives/Democrats, thru both educational and program means, should do everything within their power to promote this outlook, as the sooner most Americans adopt it, the sooner the nation will support public policy solutions to address longstanding problems and pass them into law.

Next, the U.S. intelligence community (USIC) was addressed in Chapter 19. As former CIA Western Hemisphere Director David Atlee Phillips outlined, a secret organization is a risk in any society - that's incontrovertible. But what's also incontrovertible is the need to develop a capacity to know what the enemies and adversaries - current and potential - of the United States are doing. After four disastrous years of the Trump Administration, in which, it seemed, every American value was violated and every American interest undermined, progressives/Democrats must re-establish the national norm that went absent 2017-2020: emphasize the close, daily dialogue between the White House/Congress and the USIC, led by the Central Intelligence Agency (CIA).

Chapter 20 discussed the proposed creation of the 51st and 52nd states in Washington Douglass Commonwealth (currently Washington, D.C.) and Puerto Rico (currently U.S. territory Puerto Rico). Residents of both states deserve statehood, and, in the case of Douglass Commonwealth, it will end "taxation without representation." Progressives and Democrats, united with the new Biden Administration, should move forward with statehoods for Washington, D.C. and Puerto Rico. Statehood will give the citizens of these new states a government based on the consent of the governed, local control/home rule, and equal representation in the U.S. Congress.

In Chapter 21, the National Aeronautics and Space Administration (NASA), the U.S. Postal Service, Amtrak, the Public Broadcasting Service (PBS) and National Public Radio (NPR) were discussed. Progressives / Democrats should recommit NASA to both a manned Moon mission, and a Mars mission; recommend new revenue streams for the U.S. Postal Service (e-mail service, display advertising, among other revenue streams); appropriate a budget increase that will enable Amtrak to thrive, and not merely to survive, and to fully fund both PBS and NPR. Each is a public asset of inestimable worth.

In Chapter 22, the establishment of a U.S. Department of Minority Affairs and Diversity (DMAD) - including a cabinet-level secretary - was discussed. Progressives/Democrats should lobby for its creation to address five civil rights areas: 1) diversity training and methods to increase diversity in all companies, public agencies and organizations, 2) police recruitment and performance evaluation reform, 3) public safety reform, 4) U.S. voting rights enforcement, and 5) reparations. The DMAD would also establish a Reparations Czar who will have a 10-year authority, which may be extended 5 years jointly by the U.S. president and the Speaker of the U.S. House, to establish a minimum of 5 origination committees (one for each time zone, and one for U.S. territories), to begin the process of determining reparations awards for African Americans, due to slavery, Jim Crow, segregation, and acts of discrimination up through Jan. 20, 2021 at 12 noon EST.

Next, in Chapter 23, the 2020 coronavirus pandemic was discussed. The analysis forwarded here argues the coronavirus outbreak in the United States was a largely preventable, avoidable catastrophe. Due to the incompetence, mistakes and benign neglect of the Trump Administration, tens of thousands of needless, preventable deaths occurred, as well as injuries and infections. And as of November 2020, those mistakes meant the coronavirus was not under control – when, with competent, pro-active measures – including a national lockdown – it could have been contained if not eradicated, by mid-2020. In response, progressives/Democrats should proceed with their comprehensive U.S. health care policy – a policy to address the coronavirus pandemic "on all fronts." That means, as described in Chapters 1, 2 and 11, Democrats, united with the new Biden Administration, should make major investments in the U.S. public health care system, including building and expanding public hospitals, increasing PPE manufacturing in the United States, and substantially increasing funding to the states for the same, as well as to make public schools virus-free; that effort should also include extended unemployment benefits and day care/childcare aid, and a major increase in infrastructure spending – at least $750 billion in infrastructure projects, and probably closer to $1 trillion, among other programs, to help the U.S. economy emerge from a deep recession and achieve sustainable, balanced GDP growth with shared prosperity.

Chapter 24 addressed conservatism, its flawed premises, discredited ideas, dubious goals and other major philosophical errors. Conservatism - always weak regarding a public policy response to an economic or social problem - is even more callous, indifferent, and ineffectual under Trumpism. In fact, in many ways today's so called 'conservatism' is malignant – quite destructive, damaging - and it has almost no answers to today's economic and social problems. Today's Trumpism/conservatism is a miasma - a truly toxic brew: it is nativist, racist, prone to despotism, ignorant, receptive to authoritarians who do not believe in democracy, and filled with contempt and crackpot theories. Time and space prevent a thorough discussion here of the damage each fault does to the U.S. economy and society; they will have to wait for yours truly's second book, Book 2. Simply, conservatism in its current form is a carcass that must be discarded, so that the United States can strength its democracy and solve problems in a New Progressive Era.

Finally, in Chapter 25, U.S. immigration policy was discussed. Via executive orders and legislation, progressives/Democrats must end horrific family separations at the border, deploy funds to reunite families, clarify the process for U.S. citizenship, establish a pathway to U.S. citizenship to all Deferred Action for Childhood Arrival (DACA) members, and secure all borders. In addition, the United States must recommit itself to being the asylum for refugees. The United States must always remain a sanctuary for the persecuted, the marginalized and the vulnerable. Progressives/Democrats should "exert every muscle" to promptly end the Trump Administration's barbaric immigration policy, and replace it with a U.S. immigration system that is humane, that respects the infinite worth of each person, and that enables each person to live a full, dignified life.

***

In that sense, with the 25 issues/policy areas, this book is a practical guide, a road map for the New Progressive Era - and a practical guide to economic and social reform. And: it is a call to action! Conversely, the hardened of heart, or conservatives/Republicans, and/or others without an open mind will rarely, if ever, accept federal intervention. (Frequently, they even oppose state/local intervention.) This book was not written for them. But for progressives, Democrats, Independents, moderates, the unaffiliated, those getting involved in politics and/or public policy for the first time, for new arrivals to the country, for those who seek a democratic way of life, for those who share the perspective of this book, and for others who simply believe, hope and know that a better economy and society is possible, they

KNOW that implementing at least some of the public policy changes discussed here will improve the U.S. economy and society, advance civilization and create a more perfect union. This book was written for all of you.

Further, does yours truly expect all 25 economic and social policy reforms to be completed during the Biden Administration's first term, or with a second term, in eight years? Of course not - but achieving at least some will continue the New Progressive Era the author argues was started, as noted, with the election of President Obama in 2008, and continued with his re-election in 2012. Hopefully, reforms for 12 or 15 issues/policies can be implemented in a potential Biden two-term administration over eight years, 2021-2028. What's more, it will be up to the next, elected Democratic president, after that, in 2028, to continue to work on the agenda, to work on the remaining issues/policies of the 25, to continue the work of the New Progressive Era. And - equally significant, if not even more important - in the years 2028-2036 that next Democratic president has to work *to implement even more progressive change.*

What? You say - *"There are even more issues/policy areas to be addressed, where progressives will seek to implement economic and social reforms?"*

Yes, there are, and that's the subject of Book 2.

Book 2 discusses more progressive changes, more populist reforms, and how to achieve a truly democratic economy and truly democratic political institutions that serve all, especially and as a prerequisite: the typical person.

But there's much more in Book 2. Book 2, called **"The United States Government - transforming the liberal-conservative consensus,"** discusses what changes must occur - and how the nation can achieve those changes - for the United States to become a more perfect union and to fulfill what the author argues is its historical and eternal destiny.

In other words, as Book 2 will describe, implementing progressive changes, populist reforms, achieving a truly democratic economy and truly democratic political institutions - as great and as quality-of-life-impacting as those achievements are - are not enough. Far from it. That's because, literally and eternally, regarding the United States, read Luke 12:48 - "To whom much is given, much is expected." We must also transform the liberal-conservative consensus.

But what is *transforming the liberal-conservative consensus?* Well, obviously, much more will be said about what transforming the liberal-conservative consensus is and how to achieve it, in Book 2. (It comprises the bulk of the subject of Book 2.) Here is an introduction:

For now, know that the United States has always had an outsized role in human history and human civilization. At least, that's a major premise in Book 2. i.e., "the analysis forwarded here argues the United States has had a special, outside role." Further, the Biblical New Testament passage (Luke 12:48), "To whom much is given, much is expected," applies to the 1,000th degree to the United States. To understand this, consider:

You have to pull the lens back. Way back and up high. Really high. Pull the lens back to a point where you are 50,000 miles above the Earth, and viewing the Earth from space, or perhaps, from an even higher vantage point. If Heaven exists (and yours truly believes it does), and if you were in Heaven, and were with the angels, and observed things going on in the world today, and you had a chance to converse with the angels, how would you respond to the following question:

"The angels, looking at how the United States has affected humanity, human civilization, the environment, and this one natural home we call Earth, in general, during the past 245 years, do you think the angels are generally pleased with the United States or generally disappointed?"

Book 2 will discuss the response of the angels and the changes the United States *must make* - changes that will transform the liberal-conservative consensus.

Epilogue

"The answer for the problems of democracy is......more democracy."

-N.Y. Gov. Al Smith

"Beyond the life of the individual, beyond the life of the corporation, is the life of the nation."

"In the United States, economics structures the debate."

The 2020 U.S. presidential election, which Vice President Biden said was "a battle for the soul of our nation," turned out to be exactly that – and yours truly is happy – no, delighted is the better word – to report that Biden, Harris and the Democrats won, President Biden became the 46th president of the United States on January 20, 2021, and Vice President Harris became vice president of the United States. Harris's election win is also historic: Harris becomes the first woman, first African American woman and first Asian-American woman to be elected vice president. Awesome and amazing! (And long overdue.)

Further, although others may falsely assert and baselessly claim otherwise, Biden's victory margin was substantial. In November 2020, 81,268,867 adults voted for Biden, and 74,216,747 voted for Trump.

Biden 81,268,757
Trump 74,216,722

The electoral vote total was even more impressive:

Biden 306
Trump 232

Biden won all blue states and also 4 of the 6 swing states: Pennsylvania, Michigan, Wisconsin, and Arizona, while also flipping/winning red state Georgia. Trump won only 2 swing states: Florida and North Carolina.

However, although Biden won by more than 7 million votes – a very large victory – down-ballot Democrats in the U.S. House and U.S. Senate did not fare as well. Overall, the Democratic Party underperformed expectations for each chamber. The reasons for the Democrat down-ballot underperformance vary and are complex – and time and space does not permit a thorough elaboration of them here: in some races, it appears Democrats were falsely tagged/labelled with certain characteristics, and that may have played a role. (Much more will be said about the 2020 election in Book 2.) In the U.S. House, analysts had expected Democrats to gain about 9 to 11 seats; they ended up losing 11 seats, which deceased the Democratic Party's majority from 233-195 to 222-212.

In the U.S. Senate, analysts had expected Democrats to gain 4 to 5 seats; they three, including the 2 Georgia Senate seats still to be determined in Georgia Run-off Election on Jan. 5, 2021, placing the Senate at 50-50, but with Vice President Harris as the tie-breaker vote, the Democrats regained Majority Control of the Senate, 51-50. U.S. Senate Charles Schumer, D-New York, became Majority Leader, swapping places, with U.S. Sen. Mitch McConnell, R-Kentucky, who became Minority Leader.

Hence, from a distribution of power standpoint, as a result of the Democrats' Georgia Run-off Election win, the United States Government is united under the Democratic Party. To be sure, the Democrats' majority in the Senate is as slim as it can be, 51-50, and Republicans will have considerable via the filibuster, however if Schumer and McConnell cannot reach an agreement on an organizing resolution, Senate Democrats will likely expand use of reconciliation to pass their legislative agenda, and they may vote to eliminate the filibuster entirely.

New Progressive Era, 2008-

Therefore, as a result of President Biden's and Congressional Democrats' victory, can one conclude that the United States had entered a

New Progressive Era in 2008? The Democrats' Georgia Run-off race wins make a case for it: the Democratic Party double-win in the red Republican state suggests that voters want change by uniting the government – but what one can definitively say, based solely on the 7-million-vote Biden-Harris election victory, is that voters wanted something else other than the Trump Administration's four years of incompetency, corruption, ludicrous decisions and outright cruelty, along with continual insults and disrespect by Trump for almost everyone who disagreed with him. Further, in addition to acts of disloyalty and abuse of power by Trump, 2017-2020 was a period when our federal government was absent, and it showed. It was an interregnum. At least 10 economic and social indicators regressed, not the least of which was income inequality. Further, Trump had one chance to demonstrate leadership – the pandemic: he failed. As a result of Trump's failure to contain the 2020 coronavirus pandemic, more than 400,000 Americans had lost their lives to COVID-19 as of January 2021 – with at least tens of thousands of those deaths being preventable: as noted, it is a disgrace, perhaps the worst U.S. public policy failure in the modern era. Moreover, that failure to contain the coronavirus plunged the U.S. economy into a recession – a recession that continued in January 2021, as Biden and Harris took office. As of December 2020, the nation was short a staggering 10 million full-time jobs, with unemployment above 8 percent in many states, and above 6.5 percent nationally. It is an enormous jobs, income and GDP output deficit – one that will take years to recover from. Further, the two crises Trump failed to address worsened a third: inequality / social conditions. There is no way one can sugarcoat it: what a horrible performance by the Republican Party and an awful legacy by Trump! Trump will go down in history as one the United States' worst presidents. He is certainly the worst president since President Nixon (1968-1974) and probably since President Andrew Johnson (1865-1869). And as a result, the Biden Administration faces years of hard tasks, or "heavy lifts" as they are called in public policy circles – tasks that will require many progressive economic and social reforms. But does President Biden have a progressive mandate and are the American people prepared to support Biden, Harris and the Democrats, based on the 2020 U.S. presidential election outcome? The analysis forwarded argues that while the House / Senate election results do not incontrovertibly indicate that the nation entered a New Progressive Era beginning in 2008, in the popular vote, the last four presidential elections have been won by the Democratic Party (2008, 2012, 2016, 2020), and were it not for Russian interference and a quirk in the electoral college in 2016, we would have been in the midst of an uninterrupted Democratic presidency since 2008. That would make 16 consecutive years of Democratic presidencies, 2008-2024. That suggests, that while we may not have entered a New Progressive Era in 2008, the American people want progressive / Democratic Party-based economic reforms because the Republican Party hasn't implemented ideas that work. In fact, many Republicans don't even acknowledge that the problems exist! What's more, aside from the ACA/Obamacare and some improved environmental regulations, the entire 2008-2020 period can be characterized as an era when the United States – largely due to the Republican Party – failed to implement long-overdue economic and social reforms. Moreover, conservatives and Republicans tout their legislative achievements and assert they've addressed economic and social concerns, but after they've been voted out of office, the problems are still there. Doubt this? As the late, great Gov. Al Smith, D-New York, would say, "Let's look at the record." Health care? U.S. uninsured rates rose under Trump. Jobs? 10 million U.S. jobs lost and an unemployment rate *about double* what it was when Trump entered office. Consider this ignominious achievement by Trump: Trump is the first president in the modern / postmodern era to not create jobs during his presidency - there are fewer jobs now in the nation than when he started. Living wage / higher minimum wage: the Republican Party, once again, blocked all Democratic Party efforts to increase the federal minimum wage, which at $7.25 per hour is not only ridiculously low, it is embarrassing and inhumane. Higher education? Fewer students are able to afford college. Student loans? No major federal plan to help students restructure student loan debt, let alone eliminate it. Climate change? No progress by Trump to reduce both global warming and fossil fuel use – in fact, the exact opposite occurred: Trump abandoned the Kyoto Protocol; President-elect Biden, led by Climate Czar John Kerry, rejoined the protocol during the Biden Administration initial weeks. In sum, while as a result of the 2020 U.S. presidential election we cannot definitively conclude that the United States had entered a New Progressive Era in 2008, we can say that the economic and social problems that progressive reforms can solve remain, the Republican Party has not offered effective solutions, and the voters - time and again - have voted Republicans out of office and said, "We want action. We want economic and social reforms. Fix the problems."

Now, which issues to start with? Well, this book has outlined the top 25 issues, but it obviously defers to President Biden and Vice President Harris, in consultation with Congressional Democrats, who have prioritized appropriately and have the interest of every American at heart.

President Biden's issue priorities:

1-Contain the coronavirus

2-Economic recovery and simultaneously build back better

3-Heal our nation / advance racial equity

On to the above, the author would add:

4-U.S. immigration reform / refugee and asylum restoration

A note on each:

1-Contain the coronavirus - Biden, by listening to the science, our doctors and other public health professionals, and by deploying the assets of the CDC, HHS, NIH and FDA, will implement an urgent, robust, professional national response to the growing public health and economic crisis caused by the 2020 coronavirus pandemic.

Expect nearly every U.S. health care system weakness to be addressed, especially regarding PPE, virus testing and contact tracing, and health care personnel supplementation. The Biden Administration will also likely add /

shift funds so that more vaccine doses can be administered to the American people sooner. As of December 2020, two vaccines – by Pfizer and Moderna – have been approved by the FDA. A third, by Johnson & Johnson, is expected in April. The Biden Administration has already promised to vaccinate 100 million Americans in the first 100 days: the analysis forwarded here argues look for assets to be deployed to exceed that total, so that more than 50 percent of the nation has been vaccinated by June 1.

Yours truly would add, by a Biden executive order, a public health option and, by legislation, a network of 200 federally-owned U.S. health care hospitals – called the United States Health Care Service (USHCS), as discussed in Chapter 1. As noted, these would be strategically located and allocated, based on population and health care service needs. Further, along with the federal government recruiting a new corps of doctors and nurses for these facilities, local doctors and nurses also can provide services at these hospitals. The goal would be to create a federal public health care system that's robust – one that can withstand the surge in patients caused by a pandemic or other national emergency – and that, at minimum, can ensure that every citizen, regardless of insurance plan, has access to adequate health care services and facilities.

2-Economic recovery - Biden, Harris and the Democrats want an economy that works for everyone – not just upper-income groups, large corporations and professionals. Both correctly note that the economic crisis / jobs crisis cannot be solved until we solve the public health crisis, and with the U.S. trending toward 95 percent vaccination and a safe, virus-free environment by improved public sector and private sector disinfecting / sanitizing practices, most sectors of the economy will reopen, by late 2021. That fact, combined with Biden's plan to build back better, invest in green tech, and invest in higher education / vocational skills training, and efforts to make it easier for workers to organize unions and collectively bargain, will add the millions of new, good-paying jobs – many in manufacturing – that American workers seek and need. Biden, Harris and the Democrats will announce more programs and policies designed to create good-paying jobs, and jump-start job growth – including a plan to rebuild the U.S.'s infrastructure - in the administration's initial months.

On top of the above, the author would add a legislative push to increase the minimum wage to $15 per hour, with a regional cost adjustment.

Further, as noted, obviously a major component of Biden-Harris's building back better will include infrastructure rebuilding, discussed in Chapter 5. Post-2020 U.S. election, yours truly is even more convinced of the need to make it a legislative priority in the Biden Administration, as it is win-win-win and urgently needed. Individuals benefit from the good-paying jobs towns/counties/states benefit and it also boosts U.S. GDP. Moreover, those jobs are particularly needed/important, given that the U.S. economy was at least 10 million full-time jobs short, as of December 2020 – there is a huge jobs deficit. And, as noted, according to the American Society of Civil Engineers (ASCE), the organization's 2017 grade for the U.S. infrastructure was: D+. Progressives/Democrats must lobby hard with the new Biden Administration to implement a comprehensive infrastructure rebuilding plan. Also, now is the time, from an interest/financing cost standpoint, for the United States Government to rebuild: interest rates are very low – in some cases they are as low as they've been in 40 years. (As noted, the list of public goods, facilities, assets to upgrade is voluminous. Every state has multiple projects – everything from public transit systems, to airports, to water systems, to sewage treatment plants, to roads, bridges, highways, public parks, schools, universities, hospitals, clinics, libraries, the electric grid, performing arts centers, theatres, and more: it will certainly take more than one 8-year administration to complete, but the work has to begin now if the United States hopes to remain a strong competitor in the globalized 21st century economy.) Hence, the federal government can borrow at very low rates – substantially reducing the interest payment/debt service cost for capital improvement bonds. U.S. Sen. Sanders summed up the infrastructure argument very well: "Millions are unemployed and our roads and bridges are falling apart....We can spend $1 trillion to put Americans to work fixing our nation's crumbling infrastructure. Let's rebuild America and create jobs." Sen. Sanders said. The author could not agree more.

3-Heal our nation - Biden, Harris and the Democrats will address pervasive/systemic racism, and the growing economic inequality in our nation by uplifting Black and Brown communities via building an economy where every American receives a fair return for their work, and has an equal chance to ascend and flourish.

Specifically, the Biden-Harris administration will:

*Spur public-private investment through a new small business opportunity plan.

*Reform opportunity zones to fulfill their promise.

*Make a historic commitment to equalizing federal procurement.

*Ensure the Biden-Harris housing plan makes bold investments in homeownership and access to affordable housing for Black, Brown and Native American Families.

*Achieve equity in management, training, and higher education opportunities connected to the jobs of the future.

*Boost retirement security and financial wealth for Black, Brown, and Native American Families.

*Ensure workers of color are compensated fairly and treated with dignity.

*Ensure equity in Biden's bold infrastructure and clean energy investments.

*Support second chances for economic success.

*Strengthen the U.S. Federal Reserve's focus on racial economic gaps.

*Promote diversity and accountability in leadership across key positions in all federal agencies.

*Build a 21st century care infrastructure.

*Address longstanding inequities in agriculture.

4-U.S. immigration reform / refugee and asylum restoration - As noted, the Biden Administration has not placed this issue in its top 3; yours truly would add it to the priority list.

Simply, via executive orders and legislation, Biden, Harris and the Democrats must end horrific family separations at the border, deploy funds to reunite families, clarify the process for U.S. citizenship, grant citizenship to all Deferred Action for Childhood Arrival (DACA) members, and secure all borders. Reiterating – the horrific policy of putting children in cages must end! And restitution must be made to those who have been affected by this awful practice by the Trump Administration. In addition, the United States must recommit itself to being the asylum for refugees. The United States must always remain a sanctuary for the persecuted, the marginalized and the vulnerable. Progressives/Democrats should exert every muscle to promptly end the Trump Administration's barbaric immigration policy, and replace it with a U.S. immigration system that is humane, that respects the infinite worth of each person, and that enables each person to live a full, dignified life.

2021 - After the top 4 issues

How many more issues discussed in this book may be addressed in 2021 and 2022? Well, President Biden may set the record for executive orders issued in year 1. Trump pushed the envelope, to say the least, regarding executive orders – pushed by his Attorney General William Barr, a proponent of expansive executive power. In fact, Barr advocated, in many ways, a view of almost unlimited, unchecked executive power. What's more, although Barr's boundary-pushing stance was criticized by judicial scholars, almost nothing was done to check Trump's executive orders, hence at least some public policy practitioners argue that a new, expansive era of presidential executive order power exists. Therefore, if Republicans retain control of the Senate, look for the Biden Administration to use the executive order power extensively – or liberally (pun intended) – to match Trump's power and to undo the very harmful and destructive actions Trump undertook while in the Oval Office. Of course, the Biden Administration will deploy other tools – including department/agency regulations and rules – and Republicans on Capitol Hill may protest – but it won't matter: Trump via Barr expanded executive power, and if it exists for a Republican president, it most certainly exists for any and all Democratic presidents. Anything less would be a double-standard of the very worst sort. Further, the analysis forwarded here argues readers should look for many, important executive orders, especially in 2021 and 2022. Reiterating, those executive orders have the potential to reverse/stop many misguided decisions by Trump, and substantially improve life in the United States – including addressing several of the 25 issues discussed in his book.

Biden Cabinet: Ample, experienced, willing talent pool

Another refreshing and distinguishing feature of the transition has been the number and breadth of experienced, Washington-savvy, versatile professionals eager to join the Biden Administration – including many who have experience with the levers of power in Washington and how to use them to enact policy. To be sure, there are always talented professionals willing to enter public policy, but the sense is that after the Trump Administration's countless mistakes, destructive decisions and outright damage to institutions as well as public policies, more Democrats are determined and eager to join the Biden Administration – to reverse the damage inflicted by Trump. And, if the level of talent, experience and quality of the talent pool is any indicator, Democrats and those who believe in the public interest and common good want the mistakes corrected in a hurry, and they dearly want a functioning, attentive, caring and professional United States Government restored. As of December 2020, President-elect Biden has recruited to his team:

Kamala Harris, Vice President

Antony Blinken, Secretary of State

Lloyd Austin, Secretary of Defense

Avril Haines, Director of National Intelligence

Merrick Garland, Attorney General

Janet Yellen, Secretary of the Treasury

Neera Tandem, Director of the Office of Management and Budget

Cecilia Rouse, Chair of the Council of Economic Advisors

Linda Thomas-Greenfield, U.S. Ambassador to the United Nations

John Kerry, Special Presidential Envoy for Climate

Dr. Marcella Nunez-Smith, COVID-19 Equity Task Force Chair

Xavier Becerra, Secretary of Health and Human Services

Michael Regan, Secretary of the Environmental Protection Agency

Deb Haaland, Secretary of the Interior

Jennifer Granholm, Secretary of Energy

Alejandro Mayorkas, Director of Homeland Security

Denis McDonough, Secretary of Veterans Affairs

Dr. Vivek Murthy, Surgeon General

Dr. Rochelle Walensky, Director of the Centers for Disease Control and Prevention

Dr. Anthony Fauci, NIH, Chief Medical Advisor

Pete Buttigieg, Secretary of Transportation

Miguel Cardona, Secretary of Education

Tom Vilsack, Secretary of Agriculture

Gina Raimondo, Secretary of Commerce

Marty Walsh, Secretary of Labor

Marcia Fudge, Secretary of Housing and Urban Development

TBD, Director of the Office of Management and Budget

Katherine Tai, U.S. Trade Representative

Cecilia Rouse, Chair of the Council of Economic Advisors

Eric Lander, Science Advisor, Director of the Office of Science and Technology Policy

Jen Psaki, White House Press Secretary

Ron Klain, Chief of Staff

Without question, the above is an impressive list of talent. The candidates are almost all experienced, savvy Washington public policy professionals, who understand how policy is formulated and implemented to solve problems. And all appear to share the same objective: to reverse the damage done by the Trump Administration, solve problems, restore faith in the U.S. Government at home and internationally, and prove how the federal government can solve economic and social problems, and in doing so make life better for all Americans.

Biden-Harris and the New Manufacturing Era

After the top 4 issues, the Biden Administration, as noted in Chapter 10, must focus on manufacturing, and in doing it will achieve a number of goals/objectives. The Biden Administration must create a New Manufacturing Era in the United States. The 2020 coronavirus pandemic caused more than 1 million factory job layoffs and also exposed other national vulnerabilities, and as of November 2020, the United States was still down a staggering 590,000 manufacturing jobs (!!) and about 10 million full-time jobs, overall. As noted earlier, to address the above, the

United States should bring home, for domestic production, health care goods production (including PPE - personal protective equipment), all defense production, most manufactured goods (in general), and also ban most cheap, low-quality, imported goods. In short, progressives/Democrats must prioritize *the home-sourcing of manufactured goods* and commit to a program that adds 500,000 factory jobs per year, for 10 years. Simply, the United States must become manufacturing self-sufficient – and never again have to rely on any other nation for vital goods.

That 500,000 per year manufacturing jobs goal may seem high / overly ambitious, but it's not, for the reasons stated below, and "it will yield much productive fruit," as the author's grandfather used to say. First, it will create millions of good-paying jobs that don't require a college degree; some won't even require additional vocational skills training. Second, it will help heal our nation: many non-college-educated adults, often after a job loss or other trauma/setback in life, adopted right-wing extremist viewpoints, with some joining far right groups. To be sure, some individuals are hard-core racists and bigots who will not change their views nor petition the government for a peaceful resolution of issues/conflicts. To be clear - they must be monitored and imprisoned if/when they violate the law. However, the analysis forwarded here argues that most non-college educated adults who adopted right-wing extremist views or joined right-wing extremist groups don't want to continue that worldview / way of life: *most are in a crisis, they have a problem and they want it solved.* A New Manufacturing Era in the Biden Administration would solve that problem – it would provide rewarding, living-wage work for millions, restoring a stake in the American economic system to people who feel they've lost it. In doing so, yours truly argues it will end much of the right-wing extremism we see in our nation today: it would help create a shared-prosperity economy in which industrial workers and everyone else can flourish. Third, in the process, it could also create 25 million to 30 million new and/or returning members of the Democratic Party; a major effort by the Democratic Party to recruit more working-class members to its ranks, particularly in rural America, as well as to recruit ideologically moderate voters, is long overdue. Fourth, the New Manufacturing Era would also reduce, to a certain degree, the enormous economic and social inequalities that exist in the nation. Indeed, a New Manufacturing Era has the potential to "yield much productive fruit" – be part of the solution to create a more-fair economy, build back better, and heal our nation. In sum, it has the capacity to help create that new, vibrant, 21st century economy that the United States requires for everyone to achieve the American dream.

Public option / ACA improvement and U.S. health care workforce expansion

Next, as soon as possible in January/February/March 2021 in the Biden Administration, Biden, Harris and the Democrats must tackle two health care issues in need of urgent attention.

First, drawing on ideas from Sen. Sanders, President-elect Biden must improve the ACA/Obamacare to reduce the number of uninsured Americans / the ranks of the uninsured. One long-term fix, as noted in Chapter 2, is Medicare expansion to age 55. Further, Biden-Harris have already called for Medicare expansion to age 60. Assuming Biden cannot lower Medicare eligibility to age 60 by executive order, Biden should use his power as president to craft a temporary public option for those who currently do not have health care insurance, through existing ACA power. Simultaneously, the Biden Administration should work with Congressional Democrats to craft a permanent public option, for the same bloc of citizens. (Other actions to improve the ACA/Obamacare can be forwarded at a later date.) The public option change is vital because still too many Americans do not have health care insurance, and the ranks of the uninsured have been substantially swelled by layoffs caused by the 2020 coronavirus pandemic's recession. Having one American without health care insurance is an unacceptable condition.

Second, in addition to the network of 200 federally-owned U.S. health care hospitals – called the United States Health Care Service (USHCS) - to address health care service deficiencies revealed by the coronavirus – Biden, Harris and Congressional Democrats must create a federal "surge and flex" system for nurses, doctors and other health care personnel. And the reason is obvious enough: at the state level, hospital staffs are hitting capacity and becoming overwhelmed - burnout, and triaging of patients is occurring – and those conditions should never exist – not with the United States' resources. The federal "surge and flex" network would establish a pool of available talent that can be deployed as patient demand requires, locally. The federal government would also add funds for moving expenses and housing support for up to six months. Further, this network should be expanded to include ambulance personnel – many regions of which are seeing their ambulance services utilized to the max. New York State ingeniously implemented a highly-effective "surge and flex" network for the state – and federal officials can adopt its best practices and learn what worked and what didn't. The goal would be to prevent the U.S. health care system from collapsing during the coronavirus pandemic.

Schedule F repeal and universal broadband implementation

Next, Schedule F: Yours truly is happy to report, President Biden repealed Schedule F in his first two weeks in office. Basically, Schedule F took civil service positions with a policy impact and shifts them to political-appointee status – removing all their civil service protections. In a summary, it would have politicized a huge portion of civil service positions, ruining the impartial, fair-mind, merit-based nature of these civil service policy positions. Trump implemented it as a power grab to try to increase the number civil service positions he can control via political appointments so that he could stock them with his political hacks, Republican partisans and cronies. Simply, President Biden's reversal of Schedule F, by executive order– has restored the invaluable independence of these talented civil service professionals. President Biden should also rehire anyone fired under Schedule F.

Also: Another shoutout for Universal Broadband

Next, universal broadband, outlined in Chapter 7, must be implemented by the Biden Administration, as soon as possible.

As noted, the 2020 coronavirus pandemic in the United States made clear that universal broadband is not merely a luxury, it is a necessity. It's vital - for health care/public health, home-office function, education, and business/commerce/the economy. Further, the lack of broadband internet access for poor/low-income citizens, as well as coverage gaps in rural America and elsewhere, laid bare how the lack of this vital service worsens economic inequality. Hence, in the short-term, and perhaps by executive order, the Biden Administration should take immediately steps to lower / eliminate broadband cost.

What's more, the 2020 U.S. presidential election, with the increased use of the mailed-in ballot, underscores the need for universal broadband. Consider: broadband access makes it easy for the poor and rural areas to request a mailed-in ballot. Without broadband access, do many of these citizens even attempt to request a mailed-in ballot? Probably not, and that only underscores the need for universal broadband: it will help ensure that each voter's franchise is protected.

Long-term, as noted in Chapter 7, progressives/Democrats must fund a new U.S. Broadband Center to create a reliable broadband network, accessible everywhere in the United States, for a subscription cost of no more than $10 per month. On a means-tested basis, the broadband service should be offered for an even lower fee or for free, to the poor/working poor. An alternative plan would have the federal government establish broadband cooperatives in each state, or regionally (northeast, midwest, south, mountain, and west). Universal broadband is vital is so many ways, including helping achieve a level economic playing field for all Americans.

The more perfect union

As noted in the Preface, this book is designed to show the correct path the American people and the United States Government should take: led by U.S. President Biden, a Democrat, and a Democratic Party-led Congress, it should implement progressive policies in a New Progressive Era to solve the many economic and social problems facing the nation - problems largely caused by incorrect conservative policies implemented from 1981-2008, a period that will, arguably, be known as the New Gilded Age. As of January 6, 2021, we now know that the Democrats will control the executive branch, the U.S. House and the U.S. Senate; Democrats Jon Ossoff and Rev. Raphael Warnock defeated incumbent Republican Senators David Perdue and Kelly Loeffler on January 5 in the 2 Georgia Run-off Elections. As a result, although Senate seats are tied 50-50, Vice President Kamala Harris's tie-breaker 51st vote means the Democratic Party controls the Senate, and with it – control of the United States Government. It is a huge win for the Democratic Party, both in terms of winning 2 Senate seats in the formerly red state of Georgia (which now looks much more purple, or at least less-red), and in terms of the legislative outlook: the Georgia win substantially helps Democrats' ability to implement progressive (and some centrist) economic and social reforms. President Biden, Vice President Harris and Congressional Democrats now know they can soldier-on and – while the Senate filibuster can still prevent much legislation – the Democrats know they control the legislative calendar, ALL committees, and if Biden and Majority Leader U.S. Sen. Charles Schumer, D-New York and House Speaker Nancy Pelosi, D-California, choose to expand the use of reconciliation, they will be able to implement many progressive economic and social reforms, among others, as this book has outlined. In addition, while the dual-seat win in Georgia does not confirm that the United States entered a New Progressive Era in 2008, the data points are adding up that suggest an era of progressive economic and social reform supported by a majority of Americans is ahead. Consider: President Obama wins election in 2008, and implements the nation's first universal health care insurance system – the ACA/Obamacare; President Obama wins re-election in 2012; Madam Secretary Hillary Clinton wins the popular vote for president in 2016, and should have entered the White House, but Russian interference involving massive disinformation dissemination on social media resulted in an electoral college loss; the Democrats regain majority control of the U.S. House in 2018; the Democrats win the presidency and regain majority control of the U.S. Senate in 2020; Democrats have now won the popular vote for U.S. president in *7 out of the last 8 elections!* (1992, 1996, 2000,

2008, 2012, 2016, 2020.) In sum, the January 5 dual-seat Senate win is a huge victory for the Democratic Party, and for the goal of a more perfect union: we are a nation that looks like - while it may not have entered a New Progressive Era as pronounced as it did in 1896 - is on the cusp of implementing major, progressive economic and social reforms. Indeed, the evidence is piling up that the New Gilded Age ended in 2008. (Moreover, as noted, this book is a roadmap, a guide to 25 issues that need to be addressed, but it is hardly a comprehensive list. Further, it goes without saying, but bears repeating: the Biden Administration's legislative agenda will vary, based on a number of factors, not the least of which is what President Biden and Majority Leader Schumer / Speaker Pelosi believe is the best economic and social reform track for the nation.)

**

As noted, the 25 issues represent by no means a comprehensive list. Further, the twin-crises of the coronavirus pandemic and the deep recession it caused – with the nation still short more than 10 million jobs as of January 2021 - will chart the likely initial two major legislative steps for the Biden Administration: 1) contain the virus and 2) jump start sustainable economic growth via building back better. Biden-Harris and the Democrats must exert every muscle to contain the coronavirus, end the economic recession, reduce inequality and heal our nation. Biden-Harris and the Democrats will work in any environment to achieve policies in the common good, the national interest and the public interest. They will do this because they believe in *the promise of democracy and the economy* – and they know that economic and social reforms will continue the reforms implemented by President Obama, and that would have been implemented, had Madam Secretary Hillary Clinton entered the Oval Office in 2017; they will continue the struggle to achieve that more-humane, more-just society – the more perfect union the American people seek. President Biden and Vice President Harris were inaugurated on January 20, 2021. The work continues.

Acknowledgements

"My mother thanks you, my father thanks you, my sister thanks you. And most certainly of all, I thank you."

-traditional closing by Broadway Producer/Entertainer George M. Cohan

There are those who claim to be a "self-made man" or "a self-made person" etc. Yours truly is not one of them. My life, and by extension, this book, and Book 2 and Book 3 in this 3-book series, is the result of contributions from many friends and mentors, and of course, from my family. Or, as I say, so much grace and love has been invested in me, my primary goal is to pay back that investment with a healthy rate of return / interest rate. Humbly and sincerely, that is the least I can do. This book, Book 1, is one small payment - one small installment in that repayment plan. Book 2 and Book 3 will be additional payments.

Further, in the second half of the 20th century, if you had said to a boy growing up on the outskirts of an All-American, middle-class / working-class town in Connecticut - New Britain, Conn. to be exact - a town that was as ethnically, occupationally and culturally diverse as the United States itself - that he would have a chance to experience all that he has, in less than half a lifetime, and then write a book about much of it (but certainly not all of it), he probably would have looked at you with skepticism, or at least doubted you. But the childhood and teen years in that typical American town provided thousands of examples of the United States Government at work for everyone: it gave that youngster an accurate impression of the good the federal government does in all of our lives, each day, everyday. He saw first-hand the benefits – whether it be clean water, clean air, safe food, support of both secondary and higher education, safer worker conditions and better recreation opportunities. In short, he saw the humanity of the U.S. Government – how it made lives better, safer, healthier. Needless to say, when the Tea Party faction started deploying its rhetoric in 2010 – a philosophy that was negative, destructive, counter-productive, non-sensible and ill-informed from the get-go – he scarcely recognized the government the Tea Party was describing. Almost nothing the Tea Party said corresponded with reality – and it most certainly did not present the U.S. Government accurately or fairly. Even worse, its philosophy was heartless – a sad political expression of its inhumanity to humanity. Clearly then, the childhood years growing up in New Britain, Conn. with an activist federal government making life better – and the contrast of that everyday reality with the Tea Party's distortions and outright lies – was one factor that made this book possible. The metastasizing of that faction into the vile Trumpism, was another.

The graduate school years at the University of Connecticut in Storrs represented another factor or "helping hand" that made this book possible. There, the author received advanced training in political science, which contained considerable material in economics – and it was that exposure that sparked his interest in the U.S. economy, the global economy, as well as in money, sectors, markets, investment and business trends. How does it fit in? It became clear to yours truly that Keynesian economics worked: that by increasing consumer demand, and via other stimuli, one could substantially increase GDP, employment, and corporate earnings. Or, at minimum, make a recession less-severe and hasten its recovery. The significance of this epiphany is obvious enough: Keynesian economics was the correct response to the United States' economic ills in 2009 and it is today, in the nation's struggle to pull out of a deep recession caused by the 2020 coronavirus pandemic. And it's exactly the opposite of conservatives' / Republican Party's failed, flawed, supply-side economics, which simply features more tax cuts for millionaires and billionaires, the weaking of public assets and public goods, followed by still more tax cuts for upper-income groups. The graduate school years also provided the theoretical, macroeconomic, public policy and methodological training necessary to systematically and rigorously analyze the economy, public policies, capitalism, industrialization, and commerce. Or, in other words, in case you have not noticed it, this book and yours truly views the economic world and business through a Keynesian, macroeconomic lens. I'm an editor / journalist "with a public policy overlay," as my colleagues in Washington call it, and that overlay is largely Keynesian, (but not only Keynesian as I'll discuss in Book 2), and it has proved to be an accurate and valuable skill – a very good way to organize and analyze the economic and political universe.

The Washington, D.C. years, beginning in 1997 immediately post-graduate school, represent a third factor that contributed to this book. There, yours truly received the opportunity to see the center of U.S. Government operations – an invaluable experience. The Washington years provided first-hand experience regarding how Washington works – the players, institutions, norms, protocols, levers of power, and culture. Again – it was experience that is hard to replicate. The years lived on Capitol Hill in Washington were memorable, event-focused and an educational experience. It's not an overstatement to note that the ability to see the institutions of government implement policy first-hand deepened and broadened my knowledge of the federal government and the unique Washington community, and at the same time, was enjoyable for yours truly, to say the least.

The return to New York - my home since 1999 - is a fourth factor that contributed to the creation of this book. Three, memorable, rough-and-tumble years in Washington gave way to the move to New York and the "Roaring 90s" economy. It also marked my return to news/business news as an editor. And what a time to return to New York! The U.S. economy, led by the tech sector, was booming, along with the stock market. Job creation was so strong, companies had to offer bonuses to attract many, if not most employees. The unemployment rate was under 4 percent. Innovation and start-up businesses, propelled by the still very-young internet, were driving revenue growth and earnings growth at a healthy pace. Needless to say, employees, shareholders and employers were all happy. However, it was during the period when the economy slowed in late 2001, and later, at the onset of the Great Recession in December 2007, that yours truly's tenet that Keynesian economics and an activist, involved U.S. Government produces very good things was strengthened. During both periods, fiscal stimulus substantially improved economic and social conditions - as they have during the 2020 coronavirus pandemic-triggered recession - as well as markedly reduced unemployment, dislocation and human suffering. Nearly everything that increased demand helped. Conversely, nearly everything advocated by supply-side proponents / Republicans hurt the economy and/or was counter-productive. Moreover, when the latter supply siders and conservatives/Republicans started to advocate for austerity in 2011 - something that only weakened the U.S. economy - on top of their distortion of the track record of the federal government - yours truly decided to set the record straight. This book, Book 1, is the first step in that process.

I owe an enormous debt of gratitude to many people, as they contributed to the maturation of one U.S. citizen. With that in mind, yours truly would like to thank Lorna Lazzaro, Nicholas Kruczek, Frederick Barney, Rev. Augustine Giusani, Rev. Stanley MacNevin, Arshag Tarvaian, Berjouhi Tarvaian, Joseph S. Lazzaro, Sr., Concetta Lazzaro, John Borzansky, Joseph Tino, Ronald Tino, Olga Matyczyk, Walter "Big Walter" Matyczyk, Sr., Virginia "Ginny" Friedle, George Friedle, Peter 'Cousin Pete' Molchan, Elizabeth Garieri, Robert Holland, John Breen, Evan Hill, Jon Sandberg, Bill Hathaway, Bob Shaw, Jim Doody, Sarah Morehouse, David RePass, Wayne Shannon, John Garry, Henry Krisch, Jeffrey Cohen, Paul Vignati, Ira Sutton, James Rogers, Boris Kaplun, Matt Losak, Glenn Langan, Matt Walters, Lawrence Schmitt, Louis Jacobs, David Felsen, Frances Isaac, Carl Bauer, Jr., Paul Dietz, Luca Ciarrocca, Umberto Torresan, Luca Nari, David Magee, and Jeff Rothfeder.

Also, I'd like to thank author Stephen King, whose 20 writing tips answered many questions. After incorporating the tips, you realize there are very good and substantive reasons why King has sold more than 350 million books. (And counting!) His laser-insights speak truth to every writer - non-fiction and fiction. Thank you, Mr. King. And I'd like to thank the late, great author Truman Capote: he mapped out his classic "In Cold Blood" entirely, before writing it. Deploying Capote's technique, I discovered that by mapping out my book ahead of time, those gigantic subject hurdles became normal tasks, to be completed at the appropriate time. Thank you, Mr. Capote, and God rest your soul.

And, of course, this book would not have been possible without the love, care and training provided by my late parents, Joseph S. and Gloria T. Lazzaro, to whom this book is dedicated. God rest their souls: Dad and Mom left this life far too soon. Their virtue, kindness, decency, fairness, civility, conscientiousness and charity are an example of all that is good about these United States.

Finally, any success the book has, and if it contributes to learning, furthers the conversation on the best public policies and/or helps citizens in any way, is almost entirely due to the contributions of the aforementioned people. Any errors and faults are entirely my own.

Joseph Lazzaro

(Above: Joseph S. Lazzaro, "Dad" – father of the author, doing what he always did, attentively – providing for and watching over his children. The author is at the left, with his sister on the right, in Walnut Hill Park, New Britain, Connecticut, 1965. Credit: Gloria T. Lazzaro.)

Afterword

"When I was 18 years old, I could not believe how ignorant my father was. Then, when I was age 21, I was amazed at how much my father had learned in three years." -Mark Twain

As mentioned, this book is dedicated to my parents, Joseph S. and Gloria T. Lazzaro, two souls whose virtue, kindness, decency, civility, conscientiousness, sense of fairness, and charity exemplify all that is good about these United States.

However, although the book is dedicated to both, and my Mom's impact on my life path is enormous – a decade before it occurred, she predicted my ultimate return to New York, (her hometown and site of her rearing), after years in Washington – the book is also dedicated to my Dad in a special way.

My Dad and Mom were mirror images of virtue – one male, one female – only I did not see all of my Dad's virtue, early on. I do now. Young, arrogant and lacking experience and wisdom, it took me 25 years to learn that my Dad was just as strong an example of virtue as my Mom. Yours truly had to attend graduate school, then course through the corridors of power at the U.S. Capitol in Washington, and work for years high up in the steel and glass skyscrapers of Manhattan, to learn only a portion of the wisdom my Dad had known, decades before. For this reason – this book is especially dedicated to him: the book seeks to achieve the United States of America that he sought, fought for and nearly died for, as a member of the U.S. Army during the Korean War (1950-1953) – a United States where public policies enable all to prosper and flourish – everyone: factory workers, service sector employees, gig workers, artists, scientists, white collar workers, professionals, merchants, warehouse employees, delivery workers, custodians, and executives.

As noted in the Profile on the Korean War, ***"U.S. Veterans Of The Korean War - Forgotten, No More,"*** early in my life, my Dad rarely discussed his Korean War service while I and my sister were growing up – and if it had not been for the CBS t.v. show M*A*S*H (1972-1983), he probably would have discussed very little of his service; he rarely mentioned it before the show was created. But M*A*S*H prompted him to point out what actually happened in South Korea and North Korea during the war, and what Hollywood directors / writers had adapted to attract U.S. viewers, or at least took some artistic liberties with. Dad opened up, tactfully, and in terms I could understand as a young teenager, regarding what the Korean War was about, specifically, and equally significant, regarding what war is like, in general. Don't misunderstand: Dad thoroughly enjoyed the M*A*S*H t.v. show, and watched it regularly, often commenting on its engaging stories and developed, relatable characters. Still, he said he felt "a responsibility to set the record straight," and answer questions I had.

Again, Dad did not describe 1/1,000th of what happened there, but from his few testimonies - and my later research on the Korean War in graduate school at the University of Connecticut and in Washington, D.C. - I was able to piece together a semblance of his service there. He and other Korean War veterans fought up and down the Korean Peninsula - enduring the horrors of war I won't mention here. Again, Dad told me about a few incidents I will not get into detail about – perhaps I will in Book 2 – horrific things that no person should ever have to endure. But he endured them. Just one or two incidents would unsettle you, if not shock you. Trust me. But know this: Dad never complained. Ever. Dad always said it matter-of-factly, with gratitude, and in a tone that keenly knew about the alternative: *"I was one of the fortunate ones: I came home."* Moreover, Dad was always so modest about what he endured in the Korean War, always making clear to me that *"U.S. / Allied soldiers in World War II at Normandy had it worse, much worse."* Normandy was the Allies' invasion at France in May 1944 to begin to push Nazi Germany back from Western Europe, and eventually, along with the Soviet Union, defeat Hitler and Nazi Germany. Normandy, as my Dad would often note, had a horrific death rate, the Korean War's was not as high, so he felt fortunate. In terms of the number of dead / injured, he is correct, of course, but according to my analysis, that in no way diminishes what he and other Korean War veterans endured. But Dad never took credit for that. Ever. Again, he never complained. *"The Korea War was no picnic, but it was not Normandy. We were fortunate."* For that reason and for other reasons, Joseph S. Lazzaro remains the most virtuous, strongest, hardest-working, and calmest man I ever met. Nothing phased Joseph S. Lazzaro. He never panicked. He never became flustered. He was always prepared, informed, attentive and focused. He was prudent, was always aware of his surroundings, and the larger world around him, and he had no fear: none. None! Why? Because he knew the difference between a problem (someone from the communist North Korean Army, or from its supporter country Communist China, approaching you and trying to kill you) and an inconvenience (pick any, typical problem/frustration from daily life).

This is the point at which Dad, I can hear him and sense him above me now saying, *"Joe, you're making me out to be perfect, a saint. I wasn't."* (No, he wasn't perfect, but according to my analysis, he was a saint, like my Mom.) One fault he had: Dad smoked – back when many young adult Americans smoked, but that wasn't even his fault. He said he started smoking when he was on the front line for the U.S. Army during the Korean War. You're on the line, waiting, waiting, waiting, sometimes for hours, sometimes for days. The enemy, the North Korean Army, backed by Communist China, may attack. Or they may not. Some days nothing happened. You have little idea how large the attack will be. Or, your units in the U.S. Army may be called to advance, or undertake some other risky action. Or, they may not. In-between you waited. Dad waited. After Dad told me about this the first time, I thought, how does a person maintain composure? Function? Smoking cigarettes helped pass the time, Dad said. Can one imagine being in a situation like that, day after day? Month after month? The bravery he and other U.S. Armed Forces have displayed inspires and astonishes me to this day. Further, I don't want to recommend that anyone smoke, due to its scientifically-documented health risks, but under the circumstances my Dad and other U.S. Armed Forces encountered in the Korean War, developing the fault of smoking was totally understandable and justified. A second fault: Dad also had little patience for businesses, large or small, who did not treat their employees fairly or pay a living wage. A union member, and a strong supporter of unions and collective bargaining, Dad believed all citizens should be paid a living wage, with full benefits and more. And as this book has made abundantly clear, so do I. So there: two 'faults' for Joseph S. Lazzaro. He's happy I mentioned them; but know this – he's still a saint, and an American hero.

Further, Dad treated everyone the same: with respect. He lived by the golden rule. There are many who advocate living by the golden rule, or state it, but Dad lived it. Underscoring, he was the most virtuous, fairest, hard-working and egalitarian man I've ever known. I've said it many times - I'll never be three-fourths the man my Dad was, but if I mature and ascend close to that, I will have been a man of good will and will have achieved much. Moreover, as further evidence of his virtue, Dad would defend the right of today's deeply irresponsible far-right conservatives to state their views - as protected under the U.S. Constitution's First Amendment - whereas I wouldn't, (particularly those who falsely asserted that widespread election irregularities occurred during the 2020 U.S. presidential election: the 2020 election was one of the most secure, accurate, and honest elections in U.S. history, according to U.S. CISA Director Christopher Krebs). THAT's the level of virtue Dad had: he fought and nearly died for the rights of ALL Americans, *a United States of America where all can achieve the American dream and flourish.* Joseph S. Lazzaro, God rest his soul - "Kid Lightning" as he was called by his golf friends at his Stanley Municipal Golf Course club in New Britain, Connecticut - who left this life far too soon, remains the standard, the model U.S. citizen who fought for and sought to achieve the common good for all Americans, that more-perfect union. Dad did not fight for an America where only the wealthy can flourish, Dad did not fight for an America where only business owners, professionals or white-collar employees can flourish, Dad fought and nearly died for an America *where everyone can flourish* – the common good, for and *to the republic, for which it stands, one nation, under God, indivisible, with liberty and justice for all.* For that reason, this book, which seeks to achieve exactly that, the common good, that more-perfect union, is in tribute to him.

J.L.

Notes

Chapter 1:

Worldometers.org - coronavirus statistics

Cuomo press conference - https://www.governor.ny.gov/

Chapter 2:

U.S. Medicare web site - www.medicare.gov

Caro, Robert. *The Years of Lyndon Johnson - The Passage of Power.* New York: Knopf Doubleday Publishing Group, 2013.

Chapter 3:

U.S. Bureau of Labor Statistics

Minimum wage purchasing power reduction: 2020 from 2009:

https://www.bls.gov/data/inflation_calculator.htm

windpowerenergy.com

Chapter 4:

OSADI / Social Security trust fund depletion dates:

https://www.ssa.gov/OACT/presentations/scgoss_20190509.pdf

Chapter 5:

Bernie Sanders for President 2020 campaign site - https://berniesanders.com/

American Society of Civil Engineers 2017 Report Card - U.S. Infrastructure - https://www.infrastructurereportcard.org/wp-content/uploads/2016/10/2017-Infrastructure-Report-Card.pdf

Marketwatch.com bond rates page - marketwatch.com click on Rates

Chapter 6:

Wikipedia - US GI Bill - https://en.wikipedia.org/wiki/G.I._Bill

Chapter 7:

Gates, Bill. *Business at the Speed of Thought.* New York: Warner Books, 1999.

Chapter 8:

Bernie Sanders for President 2020 campaign site - https://berniesanders.com/

Bankrate.com - https://www.bankrate.com/ - mortgage rate page and FICO score page -

Chapter 9:

Forbes – Solar employees:

https://www.forbes.com/sites/joshuarhodes/2020/02/03/the-us-solar-industry-in-2020/#431e4d9e5ed3

US DOE – Solar expected to be fastest growing renewable to 2050

https://www.eia.gov/todayinenergy/detail.php?id=38112

Wind power:

https://www.windpowerengineering.com/wind-power-was-the-largest-u-s-renewable-energy-provider/

National Renewable Energy Laboratory, division of US DOE: 400,000 TWh/year – US solar energy potential

US DOE - wind power page - https://www.energy.gov/science-innovation/energy-sources/renewable-energy/wind

Chapter 10:

US manufacturing jobs: St. Louis Fed

https://fred.stlouisfed.org/series/MANEMP

Federal Reserve industrial production web site

https://www.nrel.gov/gis/re-potential.html

Chapter 11:

Paid parental leave, by nation:

https://www.pewresearch.org/fact-tank/2019/12/16/u-s-lacks-mandated-paid-parental-leave/

Meat processing plants – COVID19 coronavirus:

https://www.bbc.com/news/53137613

Chapter 12:

U.S. e-commerce sales as a percentage of total U.S. sales:

https://www.census.gov/retail/mrts/www/data/pdf/ec_current.pdf

Pope Francis's Encyclical on the Environment:

https://earthministry.org/wp-content/uploads/2015/05/Laudato-Si.pdf

Environment site notes, excerpts from the encyclical:

https://earthministry.org/advocacy/pope-francis-encyclical-on-the-environment/

Encyclical quotes:

https://earthministry.org/wp-content/uploads/2015/05/Catholic-Climate-Covenant-encyclical-excerpts.pdf

Plant more trees – don't listen to scientists who say tree planting does not cool the climate:

https://news.mongabay.com/2014/09/scientists-rebut-nytimes-op-ed-to-save-the-planet-dont-plant-trees/

Chapter 13:

Oceans can recover, and we can restock them:

https://www.marketwatch.com/story/we-can-restock-the-oceans-by-2050-netting-10-for-every-1-spent-on-conservation-heres-how-2020-04-22

2020 Great American Outdoors Act:

https://www.usatoday.com/story/news/politics/2020/06/17/national-parks-bill-addresses-long-deferred-maintenance-projects/3205195001/

Pope Francis's Encyclical on the Environment:

https://earthministry.org/wp-content/uploads/2015/05/Laudato-Si.pdf

Chapter 14:

Heritage Index of Military Strength:

https://www.heritage.org/military-strength

U.S. Department of Defense Budget pages

https://www.defense.gov/Newsroom/Releases/Release/Article/2079489/dod-releases-fiscal-year-2021-budget-proposal/

Chapter 15:

McKinsey Global Institute Study - Automation could eliminate 73 million jobs by 2030

https://www.usatoday.com/story/money/2017/11/29/automation-could-kill-73-million-u-s-jobs-2030/899878001/

United States Intelligence Community Assessment, 2016 election:

https://www.dni.gov/files/documents/ICA_2017_01.pdf

https://www.intelligence.senate.gov/publications/committee-findings-2017-intelligence-community-assessment

Chapter 16:

Andrew Yang for president 2020 - https://www.yang2020.com/

Chapter 17:

U.S. Peace Corps web site - https://www.peacecorps.gov/

Chapter 18:

Rousseau, Jean-Jacques. *The Social Contract.* London: Oxford University Press, 1962. Originally published in 1762.

Dallek, Robert. *Franklin D. Roosevelt - a political life.* New York: Penguin Publishing Group, 2018.

Keynes, John Maynard. *The General Theory of Employment, Interest and Money.* Boston: HMH Books, 2016. Originally published in 1936.

Chapter 19:

CIA.gov web site - *World Factbook*

Church Committee public records - U.S. National Archives. https://www.archives.gov/

Chapter 20:

Washington, D.C. statehood coalition:

http://www.dcstatehoodcoalition.org/why-and-how-of-the-51st-state/

2020 Puerto Rico statehood referendum:

https://ballotpedia.org/Puerto_Rico_Statehood_Referendum_(2020)

Chapter 21:

NASA - Deep Space Transport to Mars:

https://en.wikipedia.org/wiki/Human_mission_to_Mars#Deep_Space_Transport_(2017)

US Postal Service: $78 billion in operational losses in the past 13 years https://federalnewsnetwork.com/agency-oversight/2020/02/house-passes-smaller-usps-reform-bill-to-eliminate-pre-funding-benefits/

Amtrak, cuts, and post-containment outlook:

http://cs.trains.com/trn/b/observation-tower/archive/2020/07/07/amtrak-is-not-out-to-kill-the-long-distance-train.aspx

Public Broadcasting Service - https://www.pbs.org/

National Public Radio - https://www.npr.org/

Chapter 22:

King, Jr., Rev. Martin Luther. *I Have A Dream / Letter From A Birmingham Jail.* Logan, Iowa: Perfect Learning Corporation / Trail Blazers: Essays/Speech, 1990. Originally published in August 1963 and April 1963, respectively.

George Floyd - https://en.wikipedia.org/wiki/George_Floyd

Chapter 23:

U.S. Centers for Disease Control and Prevention web site - https://www.cdc.gov/

Vaccine volunteers:

https://www.newyorker.com/podcast/political-scene/to-test-a-vaccine-for-covid-19-should-volunteers-risk-their-lives

Vaccine volunteers: who can volunteer?

https://www.med.uvm.edu/vaccinetestingcenter/volunteer/volunteer-faq

Coronaviruspreventionnetwork.org

https://www.cnn.com/2020/07/08/health/coronavirus-vaccine-trial-volunteer/index.html

Bloomberg – Oxford vaccine, Gilbert interview

https://www.bloomberg.com/news/features/2020-07-15/oxford-s-covid-19-vaccine-is-the-coronavirus-front-runner

Germany's vaccine – BioNTech

https://www.wsj.com/articles/german-biotech-sees-its-coronavirus-vaccine-ready-for-approval-by-december-11594373400

Moderna vaccine:

https://www.bloomberg.com/news/features/2020-07-15/oxford-s-covid-19-vaccine-is-the-coronavirus-front-runner

Six types of COVID-19 with increasing severity levels:

https://news.yahoo.com/scientists-identify-six-different-types-185531392.html

Chapter 24:

Herbert Hoover - https://en.wikipedia.org/wiki/Herbert_Hoover

Calvin Coolidge - https://en.wikipedia.org/wiki/Calvin_Coolidge

Gore, Vidal. *Lincoln - a novel.* New York: Knopf Doubleday Publishing Group, 2000.

Pope Francis Warns Against The 'Virus' Of Radical Individualism

https://www.thetablet.co.uk/news/13698/pope-warns-against-virus-of-radical-individualism-

Chapter 25:

U.S. Immigration:

Arizona Senate Bill 1070

https://en.wikipedia.org/wiki/Arizona_SB_1070

https://www.aclu.org/issues/immigrants-rights#current

https://en.wikipedia.org/wiki/Immigration_to_the_United_States#President_Trump_policies

https://en.wikipedia.org/wiki/Deferred_Action_for_Childhood_Arrivals

https://apnews.com/4901a69e2fb198705ab4f5370b28810a

Conclusion:

Pope Francis, *"On Care for Our Common Home." Laudato Si. Huntington, Indiana:* Our Sunday Visitor, 2015.

Pope Francis Warns Against The 'Virus' Of Radical Individualism

https://www.thetablet.co.uk/news/13698/pope-warns-against-virus-of-radical-individualism-

Reiter, Howard L., *Parties and Elections in Corporate America,* 2nd Edition. New York: Longman, 1993.

Epilogue:

WhiteHouse.gov

Instrumental Works / Selected Bibliography

American Society of Civil Engineers. *U.S. Infrastructure Report Card, 2017.*

Aquinas, St. Thomas. *Summa Theologica.* Claremont, Calif.: Coyote Canyon Press, 2018. Originally published 1265-1273.

Barber, James David. *The Presidential Character.* Saddle River, New Jersey: Prentice Hall, 1992. Originally published in 1972.

Bradley, Ben. *A Good Life – Newspapering and Other Adventures.* New York: Simon & Schuster, 1995.

Campbell, Angus, Philip E. Converse, Warren E. Miller, and Donald E. Stokes. *The American Voter.* New York: John Wiley & Sons, Inc., 1960.

Capote, Truman. *In Cold Blood.* New York: Knopf Doubleday Publishing Group, 1994. Originally published in 1966.

Caro, Robert. *The Years of Lyndon Johnson - The Passage of Power.* New York: Knopf Doubleday Publishing Group, 2013.

Charles, Roger. *Social Teaching of Vatican II.* San Francisco: Ignatius Press, 1982.

Chisholm, Shirley. *Unbought And Unbossed.* Charlotte, North Carolina: Take Root Media, 2010. Originally published in 1970.

Church, Frank, chairman. *Church Committee: Foreign and Military Intelligence, the Final Report of Select Committee to Study Government Operations with respect to Intelligence Activities.* United States Senate. Washington, D.C.: U.S. Government Printing Office, 1976.

Dallek, Robert. *Franklin D. Roosevelt - a political life.* New York: Penguin Publishing Group, 2018.

Dickens, Charles. *A Tale of Two Cities.* New York: W.W. Norton & Company, Inc. 2019. Originally published in 1859.

De Montesquieu, Charles. *The Spirt of the Laws.* Cambridge, United Kingdom: Cambridge University Press, 1989. Originally published in 1748.

Dougherty, James and Robert L. Pfaltzgraff, Jr. *Contending Theories of International Relations,* 2nd Edition. New York: Harper & Row Publishers, Inc. 1981.

Dworkin, Ronald. *Taking Rights Seriously.* London: Bloomsbury. 2013. First published in 1977.

Feinberg, Kenneth. *What Is Life Worth?* New York: PublicAffairs, an imprint of Preseus Books Group, 2006.

Fonzi, Gaeton. *The Last Investigation.* New York: Skyhorse Publishing, 2018. Originally published in 1993.

Friedan, Betty. *The Feminine Mystique.* New York: W.W. Norton & Company, 1963.

Gates, Bill. *Business at the Speed of Thought.* New York: Warner Books, 1999.

Halberstam, David. *The Best and the Brightest.* New York: Random House, 1993. Originally published in 1972.

Hamilton, Alexander, James Madison and John Jay. *The Federalist Papers.* New York: Penguin Publishing Group, 2003. Originally published in 178788.

Hardway, Dan and Edwin Lopez. Oswald, *The CIA and Mexico City. U.S. House Select Committee on Assassinations.* "The Lopez Report." Washington, D.C.: U.S. Government Printing Office, 1979.

Heclo, Hugh. *A Government of Strangers.* Washington, D.C.: Brookings Institution Press, 1977.

Helderman, Rosalind S. and Matt Zapotosky. *The Mueller Report.* New York: Scribner, an Imprint of Simon & Schuster, Inc., 2019.

Kuhn, Thomas. *The Structure of Scientific Revolutions.* Chicago: University of Chicago Press, 1962.

Keohane, Robert and Joseph Nye, *Transnational Relations and World Politics.* Cambridge, Mass.: Harvard University Press, 1972.

Keynes, John Maynard. *The General Theory of Employment, Interest and Money.* Boston: HMH Books, 2016. Originally published in 1936.

King, Jr., Rev. Martin Luther. *I Have A Dream / Letter From A Birmingham Jail.* Logan, Iowa: Perfect Learning Corporation: Trail Blazers: Essays/Speech, 1990. Originally published in in August 1963 and April 1963, respectively.

Lewis, John. *Across That Bridge.* New York: Hatchette Books. 2017.

Locke, John. *Two Treatises of Government.* Cambridge, United Kingdom: Cambridge University Press, 1988. Originally published in 1689.

Marchetti, Victor. *The CIA & The Cult of Intelligence.* New York: Alfred A. Knopf, 1974.

Morehouse, Sarah. *State Politics, Parties & Policy,* 2nd Edition. New York: Holt Rinehart & Winston, 1981.

Obama, President Barack. *The Audacity of Hope.* New York: Crown Publishing Group, 2007.

Osanic, Len, producer. Black Op Radio – *"50 Reasons for 50 Years"* series.

Phillips, David Atlee. *The Night Watch: 25 Years of Peculiar Service.* New York: Atheneum, 1977.

Pope Francis, *"On Care for Our Common Home." Laudato Si. Huntington, Indiana:* Our Sunday Visitor, 2015.

Reiter, Howard L., *Parties and Elections in Corporate America,* 2nd Edition. New York: Longman, 1993.

RePass, David E., *Listening to the American Voter.* New York: Routledge, 2020.

Repass, David E., "Issue Salience and Party Choice." *American Political Science Review,* June 1971. Volume 65, Issue 2.

Rosenau, James. *Thinking Theory Thoroughly*, 2nd Edition. New York: Taylor & Francis Group, 2018.

Rossiter, Clinton. *The American Presidency.* New York: Harcourt Press, 1956.

Rousseau, Jean-Jacques. *The Social Contract.* London: Oxford University Press, 1962. Originally published in 1762.

Russett, Bruce and Harvey Starr. *World Politics - The Menu for Choice,* 3rd Edition. New York: W.W. Freeman and Company, 1989.

Schlesinger, Arthur M. *The Imperial Presidency.* New York: Houghton Mifflin, 1973.

Steinem, Gloria. *Revolution From Within.* New York: Open Road Media, 2012.

Thoreau, Henry David. *Walden.* Scotts Valley, Calif.: CreateSpace Publishing, 2012. Originally published in 1854.

United States Congress, *House Select Committee on Assassinations.* Washington, D.C.: U.S. National Archives, 1976-1978.

United States Congress, *Senate Select Committee to Study Governmental Operations with Respect to Intelligence Activities, the "Church Committee."* Washington, D.C. U.S. National Archives, 1975.

Vidal, Gore. *Lincoln - a novel.* New York: Knopf Doubleday Publishing Group, 2000.

Viotti, Paul and Mark Kaupp. *International Relations Theory.* New York; Pearson Education, 2011. Originally published in 1987.

Vonnegut, Kurt. *Slaughterhouse-Five.* New York: Dellacorte, 1969.

Warren Commission. *The Warren Report.* Washington, D.C.: U.S. National Archives, 1964.

Weisberg, Harold. *Whitewash: The Report on the Warren Report.* New York: Skyhorse Publishing, 2013. Originally published in 1965.

Wildavsky, Aaron. *Budgeting and Governing.* New York: Routledge, an imprint of Taylor & Francis Group, 2017. First published by Transaction Publishers, 2001.

Wilhelm Anthony, *Christ Among Us*, 6th Revised Edition. New York: HarperCollins. Original published in 1967.

Worldometers.info - Coronavirus updates, as of November 2020.

(Above: President Joe Biden and Vice President Kamala Harris. Credit: Official portraits, U.S. National Archives.)

Appendix

<u>Trivia Test Answers:</u>

(One point for each correct answer.)

I U.S. Presidency

1)D 2)C 3)D 4)D 5)A 6)D 7)C 8)D 9)C 10)A

II U.S. Political Culture

1)A 2)D 3)D 4)D 5)D 6)A 7)C 8)D 9)B 10)D

III U.S. Government and the economy

1)A 2)A 3)B 4)B 5)C 6)C 7)D 8)B 9)A 10)C

IV U.S. Congress

1)A 2)B 3)C 4)D 5)D 6)C 7)C 8)A 9)B 10)C

V U.S. History

1)B 2)A 3)D 4)C 5)B 6)A 7)D 8)B 9)C 10)D

VI U.S. History, Part 2

1)D 2)A 3)D 4)D 5)C 6)D 7)C 8)D 9)C 10)C

VII U.S. - 1776-Present

1)D 2)C 3)A 4)A 5)A 6)A 7)D 8)A 9)A 10)D

VIII U.S. – 1900-Present

1)A 2)A 3)D 4)D 5)D 6)A 7)D 8)D 9)D 10)A

IX U.S. Politics, Public Policy, Economy

1)D 2)D 3)D 4)A 5)D 6)B 7)C 8)A 9)D 10)B

X U.S. All-Encompassing

1)A 2)D 3)D 4)D 5)C 6)A 7)B 8)C 9)A 10)D

BONUS Question Answers:

(Two points for each correct answer.)

Bonus Question 1: C

Bonus Question 2: C

Bonus Question 3: A

Bonus Question 4: D

Trivia Test Grades:

(Based on total correct answers.)

85-100+ expert = A

75-84 very good = B

65-74 good = C

55-64 average = C-

45-54 sub-par = D

Below 45 poor = D-

Below 40 = See me after class……

List of New Programs / Services Proposed:

(Annual Cost in parentheses.)

United States Health Care Service (USHCS)

($75 billion - $100 billion.)

Medicare expansion to age 55

($100 billion.)

First-home buyer $5,000 grant

($10 billion.)

Starter Home Program

($15 billion.)

Public Housing Maintenance / Improvements

($50 billion.)

Rental Assistance (including Section 8)

($20 billion.)

Housing For The Homeless

($10 billion.)

United States Renewable Energy Authority

($10 billion.)

Higher Education / Vocational Retraining Centers

($1.6 trillion.)

U.S. Job Bank

($50 billion.)

Improved Social Security / Super Pension

($75 billion to $125 billion / $20 billion to $20 billion.)

Rebuild U.S. Infrastructure

($100 to $150 billion.)

United States Broadband Agency

($20 billion.)

Ch. 8: US housing: saving match program, starter home, expanding home loan eligibility, revitalize public housing, rental assistance, housing for the homeless

($150 billion to $200 billion.)

United States Renewable Energy Authority

($50 billion.)

Workers Injury Fund

($25 billion.)

Benefits Bank

($1 billion.)

U.S. Cyber Warfare Force

($50 billion.)

Social Media: monitoring committees in companies, with possible quarterly reporting to federal gov, later

($10 billion.)

GMI

(Undetermined.)

Paid Homemakers

($75 billion to $100 billion.)

U.S. National Service Program

($5 billion.)

NASA missions (Moon, Mars)

($30 billion.)

USPS email service

($2 billion.)

USPS display advertising

($500 million.)

U.S. Department of Minority Affairs and Diversity

($30 billion.)

Uniform Law Enforcement Psychological and Personality Test

($2 billion.)

Reparations Czar

($100 million.)

Total: Approximately $2,685 billion or $2.685 trillion

About the Author

Joseph Lazzaro is a business news editor based in New York. Lazzaro has served as a news reporter and copy editor for The Hartford (Connecticut) Courant, as a front page editor / U.S. editor for IBT Media/Newsweek, and as a news editor for ALM Media and IHS Markit in New York. In between Connecticut journalism work and New York, Lazzaro earned a Master's Degree in political science, with a concentration in U.S. Government from the University of Connecticut at Storrs, and has taught U.S. Government courses in political science at the college level for many years.

Lazzaro's next book - Book 2 in this series - will be, *"The United States Government - transforming the liberal-conservative consensus"* - expected to be published in 2022.

Made in the USA
Monee, IL
08 November 2026

67968592R00201